DON ROBERTO

The Adventure of being
Cunninghame Graham

by

James Jauncey

Published in 2023 by
Scotland Street Press
Edinburgh

A CIP record for this book is available from the British Library.

ISBN: 978-1-910895-764

Printed on responsibly sourced paper.
Cover design by Emeline Beroud and Mirrin Hutchison

"I valued Cunninghame Graham like rubies. We'll never see his like again."

~ Hugh MacDiarmid

"When I think of you, I feel as though I have lived all my life in a dark hole without seeing or knowing anything."

~ Joseph Conrad

"He achieved the adventure of being Cunninghame Graham . . ."

~ GK Chesterton

". . . an achievement so fantastic that it would never be believed in a romance."

~ George Bernard Shaw

In memory of my mother
née Jean Cunninghame Graham
1928 – 2018

CONTENTS

LIST OF ILLUSTRATIONS

Cover Image
Portrait of Robert, oil on canvas, 1884. Artist unknown. Privately owned. Photographed by Simon Jauncey.

Frontispiece
Full length portrait of Robert by John Lavery, oil on canvas, 1893. Image courtesy of CSG CIC Glasgow Museums Collection.

Images
1. Portrait of Cornet William Bontine, Scots Greys by Michael Angelo Hayes, oil on canvas, circa 1846. Image courtesy of the National Library of Scotland.
2. Robert aged six with his mother, possibly taken by his mother's older sister, the Victorian photographer Clementina, Lady Hawarden, 1858. Image courtesy of the National Library of Scotland.
3. The south-east facing aspect of Gartmore, 1898. Image courtesy of the National Library of Scotland.
4. The entrance hall at Gartmore, 1898. Image courtesy of the National Library of Scotland.
5. Robert at Harrow School, circa 1866. Image courtesy of the National Library of Scotland.
6. Sketch by Admiral Katon of Robert 'ready for the road', pen and ink, 1870. Image courtesy of the National Library of Scotland.

7. Robert photographed in gaucho costume, London, circa 1872. Image courtesy of the National Library of Scotland.

8. 'Mate', casein paint, gouache and Palladium leaf on Saunders Waterford paper, 2013. Artist Susie Leiper, writer Jamie Jauncey. Image courtesy of Susie Leiper.

9. Gabriela ('Carrie') around the time of their marriage, circa 1878. Image courtesy of the National Library of Scotland.

10. The wagon train in which Robert and Gabriela travelled from San Antonio to Mexico, 1880. Image courtesy of the National Library of Scotland.

11. Robert's younger brother Charles in naval uniform, mid-1880s. Image courtesy of the National Library of Scotland.

12. Robert's youngest brother Malise, mid-1880s. Image courtesy of the National Library of Scotland.

13. Portrait of Gabriela by Percy Jacomb-Hood, oil on canvas, circa 1887. Privately owned. Photographed by Simon Jauncey.

14. Robert caricatured by 'Spy' for *Vanity Fair*, watercolour, 1888. Privately owned. Photographed by Simon Jauncey.

15. The trial of Robert and John Burns following 'Bloody Sunday', *Pall Mall Gazette*, 1888. Image courtesy of the National Library of Scotland.

16. Robert in prison garb following his conviction for rioting, by 'Tom Merry', lithograph, 1887. Image courtesy of the National Library of Scotland.

17. Sketch of Robert, head only, by John Lavery, oil on canvas, circa 1890. Privately owned. Photographed by Simon Jauncey.

18. Gabriela photographed by Frederick Hollyer, London, circa 1890. Image courtesy of Victoria and Albert Museum, London

19. Robert and Gabriela at Gartmore, circa 1890. Image courtesy of the National Library of Scotland.

20. 'Sheikh Mohammed el Fasi' alias Robert, Morocco, 1897. Image courtesy of the National Library of Scotland.

21. Portrait of Robert by John da Costa, oil on canvas, 1901. Privately owned. Photographed by Jean-Baptiste Hugo.

22. Ardoch, Cardross, c 1904. Image courtesy of the National Library of Scotland.

FOREWORD

At the start of this book is an appreciative comment from the poet Hugh MacDiarmid: 'I valued Cunninghame Graham like rubies. We'll never see his like again.' In 1952, a hundred years after Don Roberto's birth, MacDiarmid enlarged on this assessment in a forty-page essay entitled *Cunninghame Graham: A Centenary Study*. While this cannot be claimed as one of MacDiarmid's greatest works, it has some fine moments, including the stirring closing sentences:

> He was indeed a prince and paladin of our people and will, at all events, never lack his share among readers of rare discernment. There is no finer figure in all the millenary pageant of Scotland's writers. Nor any who, in all he did and was and wrote (and most conspicuously in his Scottish Nationalism), was more scrupulously faithful to the family motto – 'For Right and Reason'.

Of the numerous qualities that the working-class, communist poet saw in the aristocrat, who was exactly forty years his senior, I think it was Cunninghame Graham's maverick spirit that he most admired, because he recognised and understood it. Their backgrounds and lives were very different but they shared an intense dislike of the mediocre, the conforming, the faint-hearted, the mealy-mouthed and the hypocritical. Both were averse to being told what to do and neither was much of a 'team player'. Each was at the birth of various political parties and organisations and each walked away from what he had helped to create when group discipline was called for. Neither of them, when it came to a choice, could sacrifice his own individualism for any cause – which is not to say that they did not genuinely believe in the causes they espoused, only that they had little capacity for compromise and preferred isolation to the dilution of principles. 'Wrang-heidit? Mm. *But heidit! That's the thing,'* MacDiarmid declared in one of his poems. 'I cannot apologise,' 'I never withdraw,' said Don Roberto.

In this welcome new study, Jamie Jauncey wonders if his great-great-uncle's life was 'too rich, too multifarious to be grasped in the round by a 21st-century society focused on careerism and narrow specialisms'. It was a life of almost continuous adventure, much of it on horseback, from the Pampas of Argentina to the deserts of Morocco. He was a rancher, a horse-dealer and an accomplished swordsman; had his head broken by a police truncheon during a demonstration against unemployment and was imprisoned for his trouble; was a gifted orator, a Liberal MP, a co-founder of the Scottish Labour Party, first president of the Scottish National Party, and a fervent advocate for his country's independence. He wrote short stories, sketches, local history, biography and accounts of the astonishing and dangerous journeys he himself made. The tale of his marriage to Gabriela (or Gabrielle Marie de la Balmondière, according to the marriage certificate) is so romantic that it would hardly stand scrutiny as a novel, and indeed it turns out that much of the 'official' version of their relationship was a fiction. George Bernard Shaw was so struck by the variety and incredibility of Cunninghame Graham's career that he wrote: 'There are moments when I do not myself believe in his existence. And yet he must be real; for I have seen him with these eyes; and I am one of the few men living who can decipher the curious alphabet in which he writes his private letters.' One senses that, far from condemning Don Roberto's scrawl, Shaw thought it an honour to be on the receiving end of it.

Hugh MacDiarmid wrote that Cunninghame Graham, whilst there was nothing defeatist about him, found failure interesting. Jamie Jauncey makes the same point but elaborates upon it: Don Roberto was intrigued by failure because it revealed the flawed nature of humans as individuals and as a species. This was true of his own life: failure could be at once a glorious escapade and an education, and there was always the possibility of it being the prelude to success.

In his story 'A Survival', contained in the collection *The Ipané* (1899), Cunninghame Graham derided the Kailyard school of Scottish writing of the late 19th century, blaming its writers for presenting a false image of 'the Scottish type' to the world:

> Today a Scotchman stands confessed a sentimental fool, a canting cheat, a grave, sententious man, dressed in a 'stan o' black', oppressed with the tremendous difficulties of the jargon he is bound to speak, and above all being weighed down with the responsibility of being Scotch. I know he prays to Gladstone and to Jehovah turn about, finds his amusement in comparing preachers, can read and write and cypher, buys newspapers, tells stories about ministers, fornicates gravely, but without conviction, and generally disports himself after a fashion which would land a more imaginative and less practically constituted man within the precincts of a lunatic asylum before a week was out.

That is a marvellous passage, bitingly perceptive and all the more so for its comedy and irreverence. One thing is certain – its author was not and could never have been that kind of Scot. All his books have great writing in them, but it varies immensely in tone and mood. I have a particular regard for his three articles in the *Daily Graphic* in 1890–1 on the plight of the ghost-dancing Sioux, and also for his story 'A Hegira' (1900) about the tragic last journey of a group of Apaches on the run from captivity in Mexico. These pieces have a common theme – the destruction of a way of life – but are quite different in temper. In them, and in many other places, Cunninghame Graham expressed his loathing of racism, imperialism and colonialism, and his sympathy for people who resist not progress so much as its lies, its insatiability, its brutality, its materialism and its (usually white, often European) sense of superiority. He would, were he alive today, have plenty to say about the current state of the world.

Seventy years have passed since his death, and well over a hundred since he was in his prime, and he speaks to us with the voice of a distant era, yet his concerns are, or should be, our concerns. The wholesale wrecking of the planet in the name of progress or growth or just plain greed, the continuing sad tale of humankind's inhumanity to itself and other species and their habitats, the gross inequalities between rich and poor, great and small – he was acutely aware of all these matters. He is somebody to whom we should be paying attention, even this late in the day.

I cannot think of anybody more suited to retelling the life of Robert Bontine Cunninghame than Jamie Jauncey, whom I have counted as a friend for many years. When he was a boy, Jamie was intimidated by Robert's reputation – as impressed upon him by his mother, who had known him when she was a child – and was determined not to live in his ancestor's shadow. Decades would pass, and Jamie would travel far and have adventures of his own, before he set out to discover who this extraordinary man really was and why he still matters. And this was not some process of dry academic research; this was personal. Yet he found connections with Robert that were not just ties of blood or inheritance:

> The one thing of which I grew increasingly certain was that I admired him. Not so much for his flamboyance and adventurous spirit, his many gifts as a politician and orator, writer and horseman, but for his magnanimity and compassion, his humanity, his sense of social justice, his affinity with the oppressed of all nations, his essential kindness.

Essential kindness seems in short supply these days. That's as good a reason as any to read this book, but there's another: it's a great and, as George Bernard Shaw indicated, at times almost unbelievable story. So nothing more is needed now than that you turn the page and begin reading it.

James Robertson
(Newtyle, January 2023)

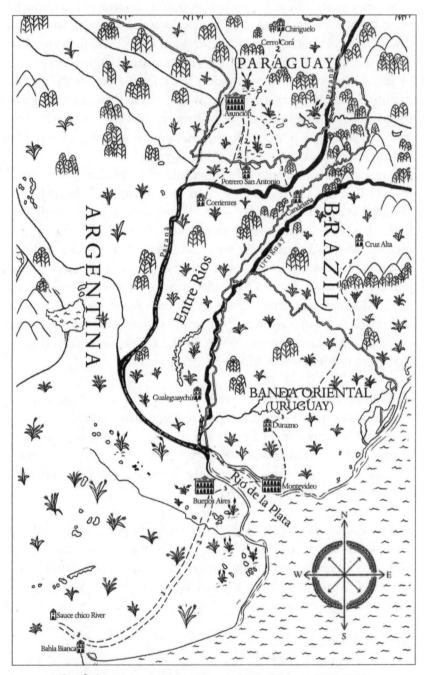

Chiriguelo

Cerro Corá
2

PARAGUAY

Paraná

Asunción
2

2
2
2

Potrero San Antonio

Corrientes

Candelaria

BRAZIL

Cruz Alta
3

Paraná

Entre Ríos

Uruguay

ARGENTINA

Gualeguaychú

BANDA ORIENTAL
(URUGUAY)

Durazno

Buenos Aires

Río de la Plata

Montevideo

N

W   E

S

Sauce chico River

Bahía Bianca

South America   1. 1870–1872   2. 1872–1874   3. 1876–1877

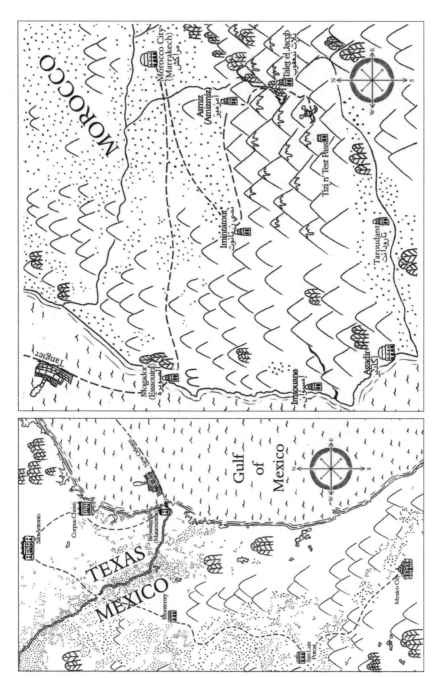

Texas and Mexico 1879–1881   Morocco 1897

Prologue

ARDOCH

Passing the baton

Summer 1935. At the top of a sloping lawn, two children look on as an elderly man makes a noose in a length of rope. Beyond, sunlight glints on the broad reaches of the Clyde. It's a hot afternoon. The briny, metallic tang of tidewrack drifts up from the shore.

Once deft, now he fumbles, mutters in a language the children don't understand. There, at last he has it. He straightens. Gives the rope a couple of practice flicks. And then . . . the children's eyes widen as it sails through his fingers, goes dancing and skittering across the grass, then looping and curling into the air, a living thing.

He smiles now and tilts his chin to the sun. He's handsome still, though the mane of white hair show signs of thinning, the white beard is no longer quite so trim. For all the cowboy showmanship, there's no mistaking the natural authority, the nobility of bearing. He continues to spin the rope. Oblivious to the children now, he is lost in the moment – or is it memory?

The rope falters and falls at his feet. He turns to them, a boy and a girl, and bows.

The girl, a curly-headed seven-year-old in a summer dress, looks away. But the boy, three years her senior, can't conceal his excitement. He steps forward as the old man nods and holds out the rope.

Later, as the children and their parents prepare to leave, he shakes the boy's hand and presses something into it as he does so. Then, to the girl's astonishment, he turns to her with a smile and does likewise. Her small fist closes around the coin and clenches it tight.

Once in the car she dares to peep. Half-a-crown. Boys receive tips. Girls never do.

She curls up on the back seat, still clutching the coin, and closes her eyes. Although it will be many years before she can voice the thought, she senses that some kind of connection has taken place. Something powerful and enduring.

Jean Cunninghame Graham, my mother, died aged ninety in August 2018, taking the memory of that summer afternoon with her. Robert Bontine Cunninghame Graham, her great uncle, died aged eighty-three in March 1936, a few months after that afternoon of confounded expectations.

Some years earlier his great friend, Joseph Conrad, had written to him: 'When I think of you, I feel as though I have lived all my life in a dark hole without seeing or knowing anything.' It was a rare compliment from a man whose own life had not lacked adventure, and it was paid with just cause. One of the most prominent and paradoxical figures of late nineteenth and early twentieth century Scottish public life, Robert Cunninghame Graham today is best known as the co-founder, with Keir Hardie, of the Scottish Labour Party, forerunner of the modern Labour Party, and later as the founding president of the Scottish National Party. But in a long and extraordinary – there is no other word for it – life he was many other things besides. As a young man in Argentina, where he acquired the nickname Don Roberto, he became an expert horseman and rode with gauchos. The instinct for travel and adventure never left him – in middle age he went searching for Roman gold in northern Spain and was held to ransom in the Atlas Mountains. At Westminster he advocated abolition of the House of Lords, declared himself the first ever socialist member of parliament, and was convicted of rioting. A radical laird and proto-environmentalist, he argued for land reform and the establishment of national parks. He was a champion of the oppressed, a crusader for social justice and freedom of speech. Fêted by his literary peers as the Scottish Maupassant, he was friends with Wells, Wilde, Shaw, Chesterton and many others. Painted by Lavery and sculpted by Epstein he was descended from King Robert II of Scotland.

He was, above all, a passionate humanitarian whose many endeavours in politics, literature and life ring more loudly today than ever. Yet though he was frequently ahead of his time, though his legacy is there to be seen in the creation of a party of labour, an eight-hour working day, the safety of miners and other workers, the vote for women, the rights of crofters, the welfare of animals, the eventual establishment of a Scottish Parliament, he remains today curiously overlooked. Perhaps, with the coming so soon after his death of the second world war and the austerity that ensued, there was no place in the national consciousness for the memory of such a flamboyant figure. Perhaps today his life is too rich, too multifarious to be grasped in the round by a twenty-first century society focussed on careerism and narrow specialisms, whether in politics, travel, horsemanship, penmanship or any of the other fields of human endeavour in which he made his mark.

At the time of his death in 1936, however, Robert was still regarded by many as the figure who most embodied the future hopes of a proud and ancient nation. 'Scotland and the world of letters is infinitely poorer by the passing of Mr R.B. Cunninghame . . .' So intones the narrator in archive footage of his funeral which shows a huge crowd of mourners proceeding to the jetty at Port of Menteith, where his coffin was borne across the Lake of Menteith to the island of Inchmahome, for interment in the ruins of its thirteenth century Augustinian priory. 'He was a Master of Life, a King among Men,' reads the memorial stone in the nearby village of Gartmore, his ancestral home.

A few weeks prior to his funeral, Robert's body had lain in state in the Casa del Teatro in Buenos Aires, as it awaited repatriation on the *Almeda Star*, the ship on which he had booked his passage home following this final visit to his beloved Argentina. Mourners included the president and ministers of the republic. They had come to pay their respects to the man who, among many other remarkable achievements, had done more than anyone else to celebrate and bring to the attention of the wider world the way of life of the Argentine horseman, the gaucho.

Don Roberto. He had been anointed thus within months of his first arrival in that great land-ocean of grass and cattle and horses, some six-and-a-half decades earlier. With his grandmother's hispanic blood roused in the southern hemisphere sun, he had looked like a 'Don', after all. A hidalgo. A someone.

Don Roberto. He had liked it and it had stuck.

For my mother, those two words were to become a kind of mantra, the invocation of a spirit that would always, to her, be something heroic, something a little more than mortal.

Within a few months of his death, her father Angus, his nephew and heir, had moved the family from the south of England to the house by the Clyde. That house, Ardoch, would have been full of him. Not only the possessions, the furniture, paintings and books, the riding paraphernalia and accumulated treasure from his travels, but the sense of him, the scent of him, the traces of a life lived with almost implausible energy, purpose and passion.

Ardoch, on the north shore of the Clyde, between Dumbarton and Cardross, was my mother's permanent home from the age of ten. She grew up to the ring of riveters' hammers from the ship-yards across the river, the constant chug of the dredgers that worked to keep the deep-water channel open for Atlantic-bound ships, and the steam whistles of the trains that rattled along the embankment separating the foot of the house's large, sloping lawn from the fore-shore. She also heard the crump of explosions, watched the noctur-nal inferno take hold across the water, as Greenock endured the blitz of May 1941; and experienced the terror of a near direct hit on the house as a returning German bomber jettisoned its remaining payload to land in the garden and bring down her bedroom ceiling. That night she happened to be sleeping in her mother's room.

A counterpoint to that contemporary soundtrack were the tales of her Graham ancestors, whose portraits hung in the dining and drawing rooms, the latter an oval-shaped room reputedly designed by William Adam. She knew that past Grahams had been enterpris-ing and adventurous and had tended to political radicalism. As Liberal MP for Stirlingshire, her eighteenth-century forebear, Robert Graham of Gartmore, had introduced a Bill of Rights which foreshadowed the Great Reform Bill of 1832. Known as Doughty

Deeds, from the opening line of a poem he had written, later set to music by Sir Arthur Sullivan, this was the Graham who had made his fortune in the West Indies and had set the benchmark for achievement – until his namesake and great-great-grandson came along.

Don Roberto was the crucible into which this heritage had been poured, the ensuing alchemy resulting in a rare and precious form of gold. Robert was handsome and fearless, a gifted orator and celebrated writer, a laird of noble lineage, a socialist politician and champion of the oppressed, a horseman and adventurer, lauded by his peers, admired wherever he went, widely painted, sculpted and photographed. Furthermore, he could throw a lasso and he tipped little girls as generously as he tipped their brothers.

With a father largely absent on naval service throughout her formative years, how could my mother not have worshipped him? That early encounter with her great-uncle rang deeply. And the more she learned about him, the more she felt its reverberations. Don Roberto furnished her with a vivid and powerful link with her past, a conduit to her heritage that mattered greatly to her throughout her life. He offered her a model of moral courage and conviction, alongside a vision of a family which, for all his peregrinations, was perhaps closer-knit than her own. He modelled a reluctance to reveal much of himself, which she readily followed, for all the personal warmth and magnetism that drew other people to her as they did to him also.

It was perhaps inevitable that she would one day write about him. On her father's death in 1981 she became Robert's literary executor, and for the next twenty-five years, until his copyright expired, she dealt with a regular stream of enquiries from academics, publishers and aficionados from around the world. At the same time she painstakingly read and re-read the many of his papers and letters she held in preparation for her book, *Gaucho Laird*, which she published in 2004.

But long before that, even when she was a young woman with children, his presence, on and off the stage of her life, transmitted itself to us, and as we grew old enough to listen, it seemed to my younger brother Simon and me that the name Don Roberto was forever on her lips. Indeed, it would be fair to say that copious servings of him were a constant and increasingly indigestible feature of our childhood. It was an object lesson in how not to interest the next generation in an illustrious forebear. But her enthusiasm for her great-uncle Robert was inexhaustible, and on she went.

I soon learned that Don Roberto had written many books, though my mother wisely did not suggest I try to read them. I knew he was a great horseman and had led an adventurous life in Argentina as a young man; he had even been caught up in a revolution and, so the story went, had been forced to ride with the revolutionaries until he had been able to make a daring escape. I knew he had been a politician and had helped to found things, though exactly what, I was unclear. I knew he had been hit on the head and arrested during a famous riot in Trafalgar Square. I knew that somehow he was descended from Robert the Bruce and there was a family joke about him being the real King of Scotland. I also knew that according to my mother he was very vain and liked to be asked to be the president of things; while according to my father he was simply 'an old fraud'. For all that, there was a certain gravity to these tales and anecdotes, a weight of history and heritage that I knew, even at a young age, attached to them and bore down through them.

We visited Ardoch regularly during my early childhood. By then my grandparents had been there for close on twenty years and their presence had erased much of Robert's. I remember the house smelling of damp dogs, potpourri and lapsang-souchong. But enter the small bookroom, the study in which he had done much of his later writing, and there he was at once. I remember the crammed and, to a small boy, towering shelves. I remember the books, many of them inscribed to him by their authors, the desk in the window where he had written, the bronze bust of him by Felix Weiss on a side table. Like cigar smoke, his presence still lingered, even then. Outside, by a rockery garden there was a small heavily verdigris-ed bronze statue of him on horseback, the centaur beside which I was photographed as a toddler. And sloping down from the house towards the railway embankment and foreshore beyond, the lawn where he had spun a lasso for the amusement of my seven-year-old mother and her brother.

Robert's nephew, my grandfather, Admiral Sir Angus Cunninghame Graham, was an establishment figure from the cut of his tweed waistcoat, pronounced 'weskit', to the brass ship's bell that hung in the porch, a memento of one of his commands, *HMS Tarantula*. Dispatched to the royal naval training ship *Osborne* at the age of thirteen, he served as a young lieutenant at the Battle of Jutland, and progressed through his naval career to become a full admiral and Flag Officer Scotland, the most senior naval officer in the country, with an official residence at Rosyth where he was stationed at the time of my birth in 1949. A keen gardener he was closely involved with the National Trust for Scotland. As Lord Lieutenant of Dunbartonshire, he held the keys to Dumbarton Castle, its official keeper. He was also a senior officer in the Royal Company of Archers, the Queen's bodyguard in Scotland, although by his own admission a very poor shot. Yet for all his obedience and devotion to crown and country, his natural conservatism, he adored the maverick uncle who all his life had questioned that very devotion. I have my grandfather's copy of Cedric Watts' and Laurence Davies's *Cunninghame Graham: a critical biography*, published just a couple of years before he died. It is heavily annotated by him in his by then slightly shaky hand. Factual corrections and the word 'No', followed by exclamation marks, pepper the margins. For all his rank and decorations, it was the playful side of Grandfa, as we called him, that I best remember. He had a booming laugh, smoked oval Turkish cigarettes, played the fiddle not very well, found the children's TV programme *Basil Brush* hilarious, and could recite *The Hunting of The Snark*. But when it came to his uncle he wanted the record straight.

Apart from Ardoch, where Robert had spent much of his final thirty years, the other constant reference point for my mother was Gartmore, even though she had never lived there; Gartmore, a place almost as mythical as the man himself. This large and imposing mansion at the west end of the Carse of Stirling, overlooking the Flanders Moss and Lake of Menteith, was where the Grahams had lived for 300 years until forced finally to sell in 1900. Most of the furniture, books and paintings at Ardoch had come from Gartmore, and some had made their way into our homes, first in Edinburgh, later in Perthshire. My mother was a Graham of Gartmore, after all, and it was Gartmore much more than Ardoch that was the family seat, the place of real substance and history: the Adam house with many rooms and much land and farms and a couple of islands in the Lake of Menteith. Here lay the weight of ancestry and the illustri-ousness of lineage that was so important to my mother; which is not to say she considered herself superior – far from it – she was by nature generous to everyone she encountered, but she felt herself very much the product of what had gone before, and believed that it behoved her to know about her ancestry and approach it with respect. Here also, at Gartmore, Robert had spent some of the happiest moments of his childhood along with some of the worst; likewise some of the happiest of his adult married life along with some of the worst. It was no longer in the family, but that didn't mean that Gartmore didn't loom large in my mother's imagination and so, inevitably, in ours.

Outside the family circle, the chances of my coming across Don Roberto were close to zero. A radical politician who had fought landlordism both in Ireland and the Highlands, an anti-imperial journalist who had described Queen Victoria as the 'Empress of Famine', an hispanophile who had written biographies of obscure Conquistadors and, most heinously, a passionate advocate of Scottish independence, he would not have been welcomed in the circles in which I moved as a child.

At that time we lived in the New Town of Edinburgh where our large second-floor flat at the foot of Forres Street, overlooking Moray Place, doubled as my father's chambers. Then a young advocate whose own father, like my mother's, was a naval officer, much-deco-rated, my father was the embodiment of the small-c conservatism that tended to characterise the legal fraternity in Edinburgh in the 1950s. As a moving force in the founding of both the Scottish Labour Party and later the Scottish National Party, Don Roberto was hardly a topic of New Town dinner party conversation, nor of casual chat-ter among the bewigged and begowned at Parliament House.

I was educated first by a governess in Edinburgh, along with half-a-dozen children of my parents' friends. Our school room for one year was our own drawing room, for another the house of my future stepfather, five minutes' walk away. A few weeks short of my eighth birthday, in September 1957, I was dispatched to boarding school in East Lothian, another bastion of conservatism, both small- and large-c, where Robert's name, I'm certain, was never mentioned. It would have been astonishing if it had been. There, Scottish history went little further than the story of Mary Queen of Scots and perhaps, with a raised eyebrow, the more recent theft of the Stone of Destiny from Westminster Abbey. Scottish culture meant learning to dance the Eightsome Reel and a passing reference to Burns or Scott. Scotland in the 1950s, still in the grip of postwar austerity – I remember going with my mother to collect our ration of orange juice – and deep in national self-deprecation, was a cheerless place and one in which there was scant room for a character as luminous and contrarian as Don Roberto. Which is not to say he was entirely forgotten. There were people in the worlds of literature, politics and academia who admired him. And there were those who had known him personally, especially his former tenants, employees and neighbours at Gartmore who cherished his memory. But I didn't know any of them.

In 1958, on the death of my Jauncey grandfather, we moved from Edinburgh to Perthshire. Later I went on to the school my father had attended, Radley College in Berkshire, one of a handful of pupils who took the night sleeper from Scotland to London at the start of every term. Here, Scotland was regarded mostly as a kind of Ultima Thule, a vague curiosity of the imagination – except, of course, by those whose vacations were spent with friends or relatives in the great northerly playground of salmon rivers, grouse moors and deer forests. This, the Scotland of my upbringing, was still to all intents and purposes the North Britain which my grandfather abbreviated to 'NB' in his correspondence: a region whose inhabitants were celebrated for their contribution to Empire and world-renowned advances in medicine and science, engineering and technology, but only occasionally for the fact of their being Scottish, and then with a note of mild irritation.

So there was no one, no independent source, to validate my mother's adulation of her great-uncle – not that I would have been that interested even if there had been. Thankfully my childhood offered me more than ancestor-worship, despite the best efforts not only of my mother, but also my father who cited genealogy as a hobby in his *Who's Who* entry; who, until he was divorced from my mother in 1969, was Kintyre Pursuivant at Arms in the Lord Lyon's heraldic court in Scotland; and who was fond of enumerating the various begats of our lineage over lunch.

By the time I was a teenager I was heartily sick of it all. It was not until I was in my early twenties that Don Roberto first registered without any form of parental prompting in my consciousness. I had graduated from Aberdeen University with a law degree and after a short and disagreeable spell as an articled clerk with a firm of London Scottish accountants – on the advice of both my father and my banker stepfather who, as Chancellor of Aberdeen University, had presented me with my degree in a curious and harmless act of nepotism – I followed my heart and went to work as a management trainee in Hatchard's bookshop in Piccadilly. Needless to say there were Scottish connections, a parental hand, even in this act of mutiny. Hatchard's was then owned by the Scottish publishing firm William Collins, and David Nickson, at that time managing director, was a friend of my parents.

The management training turned out to be an hour once a week after the shop closed, in the office of managing director Tommy Joy, a legendary figure in the book trade. During the hour, he reminisced and we sat and feigned attention while longing to get away to whatever the London evening held for us. Apart from a captive audience, what Tommy Joy really wanted was presentable young people to work in the front of the shop. Despite having shoulder length hair, floral shirts and a velvet jacket, I fitted the bill. For six months, from spring 1972 when I quit the City, I served the great and the good with their desired reading matter. Hatchard's was across the road from the exclusive apartments in Albany whose residents – Terence Stamp, slim and elegant, JB Priestley in fedora, pinstripes and ever-present carnation – were frequent customers. Others included Lawrence Durrell, visiting from France, small and tweedy, Richard Attenborough and his actress wife, Sheila Sim, John Mortimer, slightly rumpled, and there were many others, figures from the worlds of literature and the arts whom I admired and felt excited to serve. Meanwhile, my new girlfriend, Sarah, was the half-sister of a notorious playboy. She lived in the basement of his Belgravia town-house, where we watched and listened agog as a stream of actresses and models poured through the house of an evening, some staying longer than others, some leaving by the back door as another arrived at the front. I was twenty-two years old and although selling books at Hatchard's was never going to be my life's work, it was fun, I was in love, earning a wage and life was exciting.

It was about to become a good deal more so. In November 1972, Sarah and I left for Buenos Aires and a ten-month journey through South, Central and North America. It was an adventure that connected me personally for the first time with my great-great uncle, and one that continues to resonate to this day – of which, more later.

Once I was back from South America, Don Roberto receded into the background, although it was impossible to ignore him, or rather my mother's preoccupation with him, altogether. It takes energy and commitment to properly investigate a myth, let alone dismantle one. Neither of these, at that stage in my life, I possessed.

From time to time there would be a flurry of activity and I would briefly re-engage with the notion of him. I remember in 1981 the removal of the Cunninghame Graham Memorial, a large stone monument, from Dumbarton, where it had been frequently vandalised, to the more genteel surroundings of the Stirlingshire village of Gartmore, where stood the Graham family mansion. In 1986 there was a visit to his burial place on Inchmahome to mark the fiftieth anniversary of his death. That same year my mother went as guest of honour to Buenos Aires, where the anniversary was being commemorated with a series of lectures and events.

In the late 1980s my grandmother moved to stay with my mother in the Borders and from there to a home in Melrose. Alone at Ardoch since her husband's death, she had twice been woken by intruders from nearby Dumbarton, once to find a man wielding an axe at the end of her bed. She managed to ring a bell and the man and his accomplice, not realising she was alone in the house, ran off.

But it was time for Ardoch to be sold, the last of the properties to bear Robert's imprint directly.

In the mid-1990s the filmmaker Murray Grigor wrote the screenplay for a feature-length film about Robert's life, naming the production company Trapalanda after the equine heaven of gaucho folklore. But there was insufficient interest at the time and the money failed to materialise. In 1997 my mother took part in the ceremony to repatriate the remains of Long Wolf, an Oglala Sioux about whom Robert had written an essay, from Brompton Cemetery in London to his ancestral burial ground at Wounded Knee in South Dakota. Two years later I recall bumping into the Nobel Prize-winning Peruvian novelist, Mario Vargas Llosa, in the washroom at Edinburgh University where he was delivering and I was attending the annual Cunninghame Graham Lecture. That year also, the broadcaster Billy Kay aired his four-part documentary about Don Roberto's life on BBC Radio Scotland.

In 2002 a dinner was held at Gartmore to mark the 150th anniversary of his birth. And in 2004 my mother finally published her book. *Gaucho Laird* was more a semi-fictionalised account of his life than a formal biography. Working mostly from his letters, she reconstructed scenes from his life, complete with imagined dialogue. She paints a rich, intimate and highly subjective picture, her authorial presence such that sometimes it's unclear where she ends and her subject begins. But the frequent excerpts from his correspondence allow the reader to hear the ring of his voice, while her own interventions exude the sense of family warmth that was always so important to them both. By the time, four years later, that the writer Chris Dolan came to present his STV documentary about Don Roberto, my mother had let go of him, her lifelong project complete.

I should explain here that she had always hoped that I would carry forward the Don Roberto torch, without perhaps realising that she had put paid to that possibility early on in my life. Around the turn of the millennium, when I was fifty-one and she was seventy-two, she proposed that I take over the literary executorship. Having reached that age myself now, I understand well why she might have wanted to divest herself of that responsibility, and I regret that I declined; not that I would have made anything of it, I had far too many other things on my plate, but because she was by then single-handedly looking after an older second husband who had suffered two strokes. I'm sorry now that I did nothing to help lighten her load.

In 2006 Robert's copyright expired and with it her formal duties as literary executor. By then my stepfather had died, she had moved house, and all that remained for her to do, now in her late seventies, was to put those of Robert's papers that had not already gone to the National Library of Scotland into some kind of order; a task that remained uncompleted – un-begun would be more accurate – at her death in 2018.

Meanwhile, in 2012 the Scottish independence referendum had begun to loom. I was by now in my early sixties and had never considered myself to be particularly political, but this was something different. Somewhat to my surprise, I found a passion stirring. The more I thought about it, the more obvious it seemed. Scotland was another country, different in almost every respect from its southern neighbour. Of course we should have control of our own destiny. It was a matter of simple common sense and self-respect. Of course we would make better decisions about our future in Edinburgh than Westminster ever could or would. And the idea that one of the most resourceful, inventive and determined small nations on earth was uniquely incapable of running its own affairs seemed preposterous. I turned to Don Roberto, not only to validate my new-found passion but also, if such a thing is possible, for his approval.

I began to read, both what he had written and what others had written about him, and quickly found myself being led from the Scottish question to his views on imperialism, the plight of indigenous peoples, the status of women, the working conditions of factory employees, and so on. The more I read the more I realised how far ahead of his time he had been on so many issues; and how little I had been paying attention to my mother for all those years, notwithstanding her singular blind spot – a refusal to acknowledge that he had advocated Scottish independence in all earnestness. I recently found a note she had written to me in 2001, praising Andro Linklater's biography of Compton Mackenzie, another leading nationalist, for having 'got Uncle Robert exactly right . . . he also realises how purely <u>idealist</u> they were about Scottish Nationalism and never thought it would <u>really</u> happen! Exactly my opinion!' Her letters were always peppered with underlinings and exclamation marks.

Like many before me, I was starting to discover for myself the life of someone whom, today, it would be impossible to invent: a fantastic combination of Indiana Jones, Don Quixote, Sir Gawain and the Lone Ranger; a character so multi-faceted, so complex that every chapter in his extraordinary life seemed to reveal some new and often contradictory aspect of his personality.

And with the gradual filling-in of this portrait began to come the resonances with my own life. It wasn't only the constitutional status of Scotland that linked us. There were many other apparent points of intersection and this book, whose main purpose is to tell Robert's story anew, is partly also an opportunity to reflect on these links. Were they mere coincidence? Was there something genetic at play? Had I drunk more deeply of those childhood tales from my mother than I realised? Or was I simply making connections in order to justify my interest in him? The one thing of which I grew increasingly certain was that I admired him. Not so much for his flamboyance and adventurous spirit, his many gifts as a politician and orator, writer and horseman, but for his magnanimity and compassion, his humanity, his sense of social justice, his affinity with the oppressed of all nations, his essential kindness.

For all his many gifts, Robert was no paragon. He could be arrogant, dismissive, cynical, secretive, intemperate, reckless and sometimes sentimental. He made many friends throughout his life, yet he made many enemies, too. But it was his belief that we all have an equal right to a decent existence, and his willingness to speak up for it whenever he could, that struck a deep chord in me. Whether it was the nail-makers of Cradley Heath, sweltering in their wretched hovels, the Oglala Sioux, ghost-dancing to their tragic, murderous end at Wounded Knee, or the Argentine horse he rescued from between the traces of a Glasgow tram, that roused his passion, his kindness, he was manifesting his deeply held and characteristically Scottish belief that in our common humanity – and there is no doubt that he held horses in equal, if not higher, regard than most humans – 'we're a' Jock Tamson's bairns'.

Frustrated and disheartened by the outcome of the 2014 referendum, I resolved to deepen my acquaintance with my great-great-uncle and draw further inspiration from him. In 2016 at the urging of Donald Smith, director of The Scottish Storytelling Centre, and himself an admirer of Don Roberto, I began to give a talk which I called *Tales of Don Roberto*. Eighteen months later, at the Edinburgh International Book Festival, I was surprised at how many people turned out on a Tuesday lunchtime to hear about him. 'When is the book coming out?' was by now a regular question. When Claire Armitstead, the *Guardian's* books editor, put it to me in Edinburgh, I felt that perhaps the time had now come, that I should no longer resist the path that appeared to everyone but me to be waiting there. And standing in the wings with a patient smile was my agent, Jenny Brown, who had first proposed the idea to me nearly twenty years before.

Overlooked though he became in the latter half of the last century, Don Roberto was a towering, I would go so far as to say iconic, figure of late nineteenth and early twentieth century Scottish political and cultural life. Today the circle seems complete. Almost everything he stood for then has a burning relevance to our lives today. So my prime, though I admit not my only, reason for writing this book is that his extraordinary story might reach a wider audience, that more people should come to know about him, to be as amazed by him as I have been, and, I hope, to be inspired by him.

One

FINLAYSTONE

Childhood

At midday on 24 May 1852, a salvo of artillery fire rang out from Hyde Park and reverberated around central London. Robert, who had uttered his first cry a few hours earlier, shared his birthday with the woman who embodied everything he came most to deprecate about Britain: Queen Victoria.

'My dear Mum,' wrote Robert's father to his mother-in-law, 'a young gentleman appeared at one o'clock this morning, Monday. Poor Missy [his wife] is doing well, but has had a dreadfully severe trial. I had to give her cloroform [sic] for nearly half an hour. The Doctor says she is very well and quite out of danger. But for some time the case appeared very serious. She has suffered a great deal, poor child. Give my love to Katon, yours affectionately, William Bontine.'

William, or Willy, was the eldest son of Robert Cunninghame Graham, eighth laird of Gartmore. As such he was obliged by an entail, a Scots law provision relating to the inheritance of land, to bear the surname Bontine until his father's death. With his new bride, Anne Elizabeth Elphinstone Fleeming, known as Missy, he had lately returned from a nine-month honeymoon in Europe. Now, a twenty-minute stroll from Buckingham Palace, they were installed at 5 Cadogan Place where the young gentleman's future on that May morning would have looked rosy indeed. Between them the Cunninghame Graham and Elphinstone Fleeming families wove a rich tapestry of land and titles, honours and appointments. On both sides there were Whig leanings and political endeavour in the grand tradition of Scots radicalism. The Cunninghame Grahams favoured military service and the gentlemanly pursuits, the Elphinstone Fleemings naval service and the arts and letters. There were fortunes gained and, in the case of the Cunninghame Grahams, lost; although the allowance the newlyweds received from Willy's father was sufficient to provide for a comfortable enough living, so long as they managed their affairs sensibly – a task for which Willy's spectacular unsuitability had yet to become fully apparent.

In short, Robert was born to a life of privilege, his destiny to become tenth laird of Gartmore and heir, additionally, to the lowland estates of Finlaystone, Ardoch and Gallingad, with all that that entailed.

A few months later, in autumn 1852, the Bontines, Willy, Missy and baby Robert, moved north to take up residence at Finlaystone, on the south bank of the Clyde. The large Renfrewshire mansion had come to an earlier Robert Graham, the wealthy eighteenth century politician previously mentioned, from his first cousin, John Cunninghame, the last Earl of Glencairn, in 1796; and with this inheritance the names Cunninghame and Graham had become conjoined. But this Robert had died shortly after and Finlaystone had then been let, or stood empty, for many years during the absence of the two subsequent generations on the Continent. His profligate son, William, had spent most of the fortune his father had amassed in the West Indies, and ended up having to flee his creditors. He had settled eventually in Florence where he became embroiled in a forgery scandal. Expelled from Florence he had returned to London where he died in disgrace a few years later. His son, Robert, Willy's father (the names alternated), had fled to the Continent to avoid his father. There he worked as a merchant in Frankfurt, only venturing back to England in middle age. Unable to afford the upkeep of his Scottish estates, he had continued to rent them out and had settled in the hunting county of Warwickshire, where Willy had latterly been raised.

Missy also had been brought up outside Scotland, on account of her father's naval service. Admiral Charles Elphinstone Fleeming was the second son of the eleventh Lord Elphinstone, an ancient

Scottish barony, and had added the second barrel, Fleeming, to his name also through inheritance. A veteran of the South American Wars of Independence, he had married his Spanish-Italian bride, Catalina Alessandro de Jiménez, in Cadiz, when he was forty-two years old and she was sixteen. Their fourth daughter, Anne Elizabeth, had been born on board her father's flagship off the coast of Venezuela in 1828. Retiring shortly from active service, the admiral had been appointed governor of Greenwich Hospital, where in 1840 he died of influenza – on the same day as his eldest daughter, Carlotta. The adolescent Missy had turned to her scholarly uncle, Mountstuart Elphinstone, former Governor of Bombay and author of a many-volumed history of the Indian sub-continent, as surrogate father. With 'Uncle Mount' living in Surrey, and her mother now remarried to a second admiral – the 'Katon' of Willy's letter – and living in Kent, Missy's teenage years had been spent in the south-east of England.

Now both Robert's parents were to live for the first time in the Scotland of their respective forebears. But Finlaystone was scarcely welcoming. It stood gloomy and damp, with overgrown shrubbery, tumbledown stables and mouldering furniture in its unloved rooms. In *Heather Jock* (*The Ipané*, 1899), Robert would later write:

I remembered the old house in Scotland, perched on a rock above the Clyde, and set about with trees, the avenue winding through woods and crossing a little stream on bridges . . . I saw the yew trees under which John Knox is said to have preached and dealt with heresy and superstition . . . the tulip tree, the yellow chestnut, and the laurels tall as houses, the little garden with its curious stone vases and the tall hollyhocks. I saw the river with steamers passing between the fairway marks, saw Dumbarton Castle . . .

Robert's mother did her best to make Finlaystone habitable, furnishing the rooms, tending to the garden and grounds, and in due course ensuring that her children received a good education. His father, meanwhile, continued to occupy himself with the country pursuits to which he was accustomed, and began to engage in public affairs as expected of a young man of his standing, with appointments as Deputy Lieutenant of Renfrewshire and Justice of the Peace. He also spent time in the company of his younger brother, Bobby Cunninghame Graham, and his brother-in-law, William Hope, holder of the Victoria Cross for valour in the Crimean War. This was a matter of some concern to his wife.

'Unsteady' was a word which had often been used to characterise Missy's husband in his youth. Uncle Mount had quizzed her about his steadiness when she had announced their betrothal. As a school-boy, Willy had been moody and given to outbursts of rage, even writing home of the difficulties his temper was causing him. Impetuous and reckless, yet generous to the point of extravagance, he had defied his father's wish that he attend university and instead had travelled to Weimar where the family had grand connections, intent on enjoying himself. There he is said to have met Franz Liszt, fallen in love with Goethe's grand-daughter, played blind-man's-buff with the young Tsar Alexander II and his bride, and almost certainly played at the card tables for which he was developing a predilection. Eventually good sense, or family pressure, had prevailed and in his early twenties he had bought himself a commis-sion in the 15th Foot. Chafing at life as an infantryman, he had shortly transferred to a cavalry regiment, the Scots Greys, and was posted to Ireland where disturbance was rife as the Great Famine ran its course.

Here, in 1846, an accident had befallen him which was to have severe and long-lasting consequences. Intervening in a riot in the town of Waterford, so it was said, he had been struck on the head with an iron-shod stick. Now, six years later, Willy had become iras-cible and had begun to complain of headaches. Furthermore, both his new companions, his brother and brother-in-law, had reputa-tions as speculators and Missy feared that he might fall under their influence.

Her children were untroubled by such concerns. For the next ten years Robert and his younger brother Charlie, born in Edinburgh in 1854, were free to enjoy the spacious grounds and forgotten corners of the large house overlooking the Clyde. The first signs of the Spanish blood which later would have Robert likened to a sitter for Velasquez, were making themselves apparent. He was becoming slim and wiry, his forehead broad, his brown eyes deep and intelligent, his curls starting to lose the flaming red of infancy and settling to a darker auburn. His physical energy was inexhaustible. He was learning to ride and discovering gymnastics: a favourite indoor trick was to leapfrog clean over a seated and often unsuspecting adult. He was also beginning to show an interest in history, while his mother encouraged him to engage with the natural world, botanical specimens being in plentiful supply in the gardens and grounds. 'What an immense amount of information his small head has collected,' wrote a visitor of the seven-year-old Robert. The habit of observation, and a retentive memory, were to furnish him with invaluable assets in his later career as a writer.

After an interval of six years, during which Missy gave birth to a stillborn daughter, the family was completed when Robert's youngest brother was born in 1860 and named Malise after an early Graham, the first Earl of Menteith, and the ancestor through whom the line of descent from Robert II could be traced. Malise derives from the Gaelic Maol Iosa, meaning servant of Jesus. It is one of my given names, and I have always felt the affinity that a shared name affords with the quiet, thoughtful and musical person my sadly short-lived great-great-uncle would turn out to be.

The Finlaystone idyll came to an end in January 1863 when Robert was dispatched to boarding school at Hill House, near Leamington Spa. There he could be under the eye of his Cunninghame Graham grandparents, Robert and Laura, who lived nearby. But within a few weeks of the start of term Robert senior, who had been ill for some time, died. On the night of his death, 400 miles away at Gartmore all the lights in the empty house came ablaze – a phenomenon said regularly to attend the death of the laird.

Towards the end of the previous year it had been decided that Finlaystone should be sold. It was too much of a drain on the family resources. As ninth laird, Willy now set about moving the family to Gartmore. During the early months of 1863 the Bontines shuttled between a rented house in London, at 13 Chesham Place, and Finlaystone where they were packing up in preparation for the move. In the midst of all this – perhaps on account of it – Willy's headaches worsened and with them his temper. He was becoming prone to uncontrollable rages, most often directed at those dearest to him. Sending the two younger children to stay with a cousin in Dumfriesshire, Missy fled for a while to London.

In later life, Robert steadfastly attributed Willy's misfortunes to the blow said to have been received in Waterford, but the truth may have been somewhat different. The head injury is not disputed. There is an account of an examination by an army doctor who discharged his patient with the cheery admonition that it would be many years before he would experience any ill effects. There is, however, no official record of how the injury was sustained. It might have been during military service in Waterford, when struck during a town riot or it might have been in the hunting field there. Robert preferred the former explanation. Whichever it was, with all the evidence of Willy's youthful 'unsteadiness', it seems reasonable to wonder if there was not, in fact, some underlying mental illness, exacerbated by the blow, that was now making itself apparent.

At school, meanwhile, young Robert was enjoying all the diversions such an establishment could offer. He wrote home enthusiastically of football, skating, visits to Leamington baths, 'panorarmas' (sic) – one of the American Civil War was specially good, he said – and opportunities for riding and gymnastics. But he was also sensitive to events at home. 'My dear Mamma,' he wrote in February 1863, anxiously and without punctuation, 'I hope you are quite well how is Charlie why did you go to London? I have bought a frame for Papa's picture how is Papa give my love to Grandmama.'

A few months short of his eleventh birthday, he was doing his best to respond to his new circumstances as would have been expected of him: manfully. Private preparatory schools such as the one Robert now attended were junior training academies for servants and soldiers of Empire, now, in the 1860s, at its height, the globe at its pinkest. From here they would progress to secondary education at 'public' school, from which they would step into adulthood either as young officers or as members of a highly self-reliant, confident, altogether superior class of manager for the Imperial project: men who could be dropped into an African province the size of Wales, the only white men for hundreds of miles, and run it to the complete satisfaction of their masters in Whitehall. These schools were not places that fostered what today would be described as emotional intelligence. They sent a man into the world with Latin and Greek, some ability at rugby or cricket, and an overriding sense of both duty and entitlement. Robert, with his mother's intellectual curiosity and his father's physical energy, benefited from certain aspects of the regime, though much of what he later became was despite, or in reaction against, it.

There is no record of whether his grandfather's death prompted the same injunction from his headmaster, Dr Bickmore, as my Jauncey grandfather's death in my first year at boarding school did from my headmaster – to write a letter of condolence to my father. Aged just nine, I had not the slightest idea what to do. But it would not be surprising had history repeated itself. At Hill House, Robert was being exposed for the first time to Victorian Middle England and the attitudes and beliefs of the bourgeois ruling class – attitudes for which he would come to hold an abiding contempt. 'When respectability shut the door of its snug villa it showed humanity out,' he would later write.

By Easter 1863 Willy had recovered his equilibrium and the move to Gartmore was complete. Robert's return for the school holidays signalled the start of a period of immersion in the one place that would mark him more deeply than any other. With its foundations leading back into the deep past of Graham history, Gartmore would become an anchor point, a mooring to which he would return constantly for the next forty years.

Perched on its southeast-facing eminence, Gartmore had been built in the 1660s and enlarged in 1740 by Doughty Deeds' father, Nicol Graham, with the help of a Kirkcaldy builder, one William Adam. Forty years later, Doughty Deeds had added columns, porticoes and Italian plasterwork. Now, for all Missy's efforts at making the large, rambling house homely, it seemed to Robert to echo Finlaystone, another family home that had suffered many years of neglect.

'All through the house the smell of damp, of kingwood furniture, and roses dried in bowls, blended and formed a scent which I shall smell as long as life endures,' he later wrote in *A Page of Pliny* (*A Hatchment*, 1913). Furniture and paintings had gone, darker patches of wallpaper testimony to the depredations of his great-grandfather William. Known in the family as 'Bad Willy', or 'The Swindler', he had been named by the *Times* in its exposé of the Florence forgery scandal which had turned on the use of an engraving machine which he owned and alone could operate to the required standard. Over time, William had disposed of much of his father's collection of paintings, including those by Titian and Poussin, Claude and Rubens, though family portraits by Reynolds and Raeburn had been saved.

But it was the library that especially stuck in Robert's memory:

A long low Georgian room . . . with its high mantelpiece and windows looking out on the sunk garden underneath the terraces, the sides of which were honeycombed by rabbits . . . the dark and dampish chamber, with three outside walls, and deep-cut mould-ings on the window and doors . . . We called it "book-room" in the Scottish way, although the books were few and mostly had belonged to a dead uncle who had bought them all in India, and on the yellowing leaves were stains of insects from the East, and now and then a grass or flower from Hyderabad or Kolapur (as pencilled notes upon the margin said) . . .

Dim and uninviting as it was, the bookroom held plenty to fire young Robert's imagination: Macaulay's Essays, the Penny Cyclopaedia, Hume, Smollett, Captain Cook, 'enthralling' Mungo Park, books of heraldry, a set of Dickens, and a plate from one of the books depicting: 'a man upon a horse with a red fluttering cloak streaming out in the wind, galloping in the midst of buffaloes with a long knife between his teeth.' By the time he came to write this account of Gartmore, Robert had himself had occasion to embody something close to the very image which, in boyhood, had set his heart racing.

Beyond the house lay boggy farmlands, deep woods and brack-eny slopes, all frequently shrouded in the mist that seemed to rise from the River Forth and hang like an exhalation over the surrounding district of Menteith. Nevertheless, here at Gartmore was the space and freedom a spirited boy craved. He could ride out to his heart's content, through the parkland around the house to the tenanted farms beyond, down onto the Flanders Moss or to the shore of the Lake of Menteith, where rowing boats awaited for the short crossing to Inch Talla and Inchmahome. In summer the family would picnic on the islands with their ancient flowering chestnut trees, water-lilies carpeting the still, peaty waters and brown trout nosing through the sunlit shallows. The boys would crawl through creepers and brambles to explore the island of Inch Talla, whose ruined stronghold their Menteith ancestors had built in the thirteenth century, or row across to Inch Cuan where the 'earthe dogges', the terriers, had been kennelled. And in the stillness of Inchmahome's roofless priory they would listen to tales of their ancestors, while nearby lay Walter and Mary, the mid-thirteenth century Earl and Countess of Menteith, carved in stone with their arms forever around one another in loving embrace.

Robert and Charlie were close as boys and remained so throughout their lives, the younger at times a steadying influence on his more volatile older sibling, whose sharp humour and self-assurance could swiftly give way to anger when things failed to turn out as expected. Generally, though, where Robert led, Charlie followed. On one occasion they managed to portage a boat from the Lake of Menteith to the Goodie Burn and thence to the River Forth, where they were swept downstream by the current, under the bridge at Stirling and beyond, until they were able to put in to the bank where they spent the night under a tree. After frantic hours of searching, Willy was able to extract their plan from the daughters of the hotel-keeper at Port of Menteith, in whom the boys had confided. By this time the Stirling police had already located the boys, safe and sound, if hungry.

It was a happy Robert who saw his younger brother join him at Hill House at the start of the summer term. Both became immediately cricket-mad. In his letters home Robert begs for information about Willy's plans for the estate, which include the building of a new cricket pitch. He also sent home an essay for which he had been commended:

Cruelty is a very demoralising thing. It is a sure sign that a nation is getting weak, when it delights in wild beast fights and gladiatorial combats like the ancient Romans. Cruelty and cowardice often go hand-in-hand together: thus the boy who delights in tormenting animals is almost always a coward. Cruelty shows itself in all ages and is always attended with the same results. Often armies and states have mutinied through the cruelty of their leaders and kings. It would seem likely that when people see cruelty in others, they would avoid it themselves, but it often takes a directly different course and people who are accustomed to see cruelty generally practice it themselves. Nothing is so hard to eradicate as cruelty and the person who is cruel in his youth frequently in spite of all correction grows up to be very cruel and cowardly when he is a man.

Aged eleven, Robert had revealed the first glimpse of a rhetorical cast of mind. In cruelty he had also sought out the obverse of a coin that was highly valued within the Bontine family – kindness. Willy was known as a kind and affectionate man who, in his own way, cared deeply about his family; a fact which amplified the tragedy of his illness. Missy referred frequently to her husband's kindness in her correspondence with family and friends. Indeed the word became a sort of talisman against the unkindness of Willy's rages – all of which young Robert would have been aware of, and all of which served to nurture the humanitarian instinct, the lifelong loathing of injustice, that would come to define so much of his adult endeavour.

Two

HARROW

Adolescence

A year passed happily for Robert and Charlie at Hill House. 'I have begun Xenophon and Homer and Horace, and like them pretty well,' Robert wrote home. A tutor was engaged to keep them up to the mark during the holidays, which they spent at Gartmore or at Leamington with their grandmother. This was Mr Gulliver, a Cambridge undergraduate, christened Big Pudden by the boys on account of his large frame and matching appetite. For the next two years he was to be their constant and much-liked companion during the school holidays, as comfortable on fishing or boating expeditions as he was in the bookroom, where he set about preparing the boys for the next stage of their educational journey. It had now been agreed that Robert would move on to Harrow School in autumn 1865, following his thirteenth birthday.

Meanwhile Mr Gulliver's cheerful and capable supervision proved a godsend for Missy when, in June 1864, Willy took another turn and had to be put under restraint after being found wandering the house in his nightshirt, believing he was on a military manoeuvre. Painfully aware when lucid of his own incapacity, and wracked by shame and remorse, Willy wrote to his wife: 'Do not come to see me until I am well. Do not come.' He also let it be known that he wished his brother Bobby and brother-in-law William Hope, the two speculators, to become his powers of attorney. Missy was horrified. She was only too well aware that her husband had been further running down the family finances, persuaded by his relatives to invest in worthless schemes such as the reclamation of mosquito-infested marshland in Majorca. A rift was beginning to open up between Missy on one side, and the Cunninghame Grahams, including her recently widowed mother-in-law, on the other. It was soon to have unwelcome consequences for Robert.

By spring of 1865, Willy's symptoms had abated sufficiently for his doctors to recommend a spell of travel. In July the whole family set off on the first leg of an extended European tour. Their final destination was Florence, but for the rest of the summer they criss-crossed what was shortly to become unified Germany, revisiting the places and acquaintances of Willy's youth. In addition to his many Hochgeboren (high-born) connections, they also called on Dr Speiss, the former Bontine family doctor, in Frankfurt, whom they consulted about Willy's injury. The doctor advised a life of modera-tion. This, Missy knew, would be testing. Willy was still prone to mood swings which made it even harder for her to protect him from the excesses to which he was prone, in particular the gaming tables. As they dined with the Grand Duke of Nassau in Frankfurt, fished for trout with Baron von Austees in Bavaria, shot partridges with Colonel Rhein in Weimar, Robert's first experience of Europe was tinged both with anticipation at his forthcoming enrolment at Harrow, and anxiety at his father's condition, however much his mother downplayed things.

At the end of the summer the Bontines continued on their tour while Mr Gulliver met the boys in Hamburg and accompanied them back to London. A month later, Robert arrived at Harrow. Now aged thirteen, he was plunged into the unforgiving rough-and-tumble of life at one of the country's most exclusive boarding schools. He struggled during the first term, rising at 3.00 am to cram, and writing home that he found the whole thing 'dreadfully hard'. He disliked Dr Butler, the strict and donnish headmaster, in whose house he was lodged. He was also terrorised by his 'fag-master', an older boy called Marjoriebanks who inflicted the custom-ary public-school torments on his young 'fag' – a personal dogsbody, available to do whatever his master commanded. These included shutting him up in a folding bed, from which he was rescued by a friend, Reuter, son of the first foreign correspondent for the *Times*. Such were the connections to be made at a school like Harrow.

Plans to spend the Christmas holidays at Leamington with their grandmother were revised at the last minute by a summons to join Willy and Missy in Florence. Yet again, Missy had to pretend to the boys that all was well when clearly it was not. Willy seemed aimless and erratic. He rode about in a daze for hours on end. On one occasion, when Missy was dressed and ready to take part in a concert organised by the local English colony, he abruptly forbade her to leave the house. Taking his mother's upbeat cue, Robert wrote chattily to his grandmother that he liked Florence very much, and went on to list visits to the opera, ballet and galleries, skating and a hunt; though at other moments, Missy observed, he was morose and nervy. However, back at Harrow in January he reported to his parents that the detested Marjoriebanks had left and that he was doing well in class. 'I like Harrow very much now,' he wrote almost apologetically. 'I was very stupid not to like it before.' In a third letter he wrote again that he was 'doing very well in form as yet, and I have been top a great many times, and I hope I shall keep it so.' Willy replied shortly from Florence, encouraging him to take up fencing. 'It is the best exercise in the world and gives a man confidence,' he advised, while reminding his son that the eagle in the Graham family crest might hold a sword in one claw, but it had a pen in the other: keep up with your studies, the tacit injunction. Robert duly noted both and in years to come became something of an expert swordsman as well as a writer of repute.

The boys spent the Easter holidays at Leamington where Robert pined for Gartmore, while Willy and Missy, in Paris on the final leg of their European tour, attended the races at the Bois de Boulogne and visited the theatre, with seats in the Emperor's box. They returned to London in early summer 1866 and after a month there, during which Willy was examined by doctors, they went north to Gartmore.

Back at Harrow for the summer term, Robert studied diligently, falling under the spell of a young classics master called Edward Bowen. Bowen held radical views on education and required the boys in his house to wear red shirts for football as a mark of respect for Giuseppe Garibaldi, the republican hero of Italian unification, whose followers wore red. Robert also played cricket for his house and won cups for long-distance running and jumping. He was doing his best not to worry his parents.

There is no record of whether Robert was at Gartmore when the attack took place, but the month being August and the school holidays in progress, it seems likely that he was.

In a moment of rage, Willy rushed at his wife with a sword. Fortunately Missy suffered no injury, but now it was agreed that her husband was too much of a danger to his family to be allowed to remain at Gartmore. Nor was he to have anything to do with the running of it. The boys were sent to their grandmother for the remainder of the holidays while arrangements were made for Willy. Annie Speirs, a cousin in Dumfriesshire, came to the rescue with a suitable house that could be rented from the Duke of Buccleuch. This was Eccles House, an attractive shooting lodge overlooking the River Annan. Furthermore, in Dumfries there lived a Dr Sharpe, one of the few brain specialists in the country. It was his presence there that accounted for the 'several Gentlemen of good rank and position labouring under peculiar delusions' who, the Bontine family solicitor helpfully pointed out, were to be found in and around Dumfries. At Eccles House Willy was now to all intents and purposes incarcerated with Sigismondo, his loyal Italian valet, in constant attendance, and a doctor on standby. There he was to spend the rest of his life, forlornly jotting down reminiscences and maudlin poetry when his mind was clear enough to do so, visited from time to time by the family, who remained painfully fond of him, but effectively abandoned. 'How sad it must be for the poor dear boys to see their father in that state,' wrote Missy's mother, 'particularly for poor dear Robert who is now old enough to feel it much.' And there was further misfortune to come. Missy was pregnant, having conceived shortly before the attack. She gave birth in February 1867 but the child, a girl, again was stillborn.

Back at school Robert became ill and was punished for bad behaviour. Now turning fifteen, his natural adolescent turmoil was exacerbated by anxieties about home. With Willy no longer competent, and Missy and the Cunninghame Grahams at loggerheads over who should manage the family affairs, it was left to the court to appoint a *curator bonis,* in this case an Edinburgh accountant, George Auldjo Jamieson. His review of the Gartmore finances revealed the full extent of Willy's improvidence, added to which there would now be the cost of Willy's care and maintenance. There was talk that the house would have to be let, and even that the Harrow school fees – both boys were there by now – would no longer be sustainable. So it proved. At the end of the summer term 1867, when Robert had been at Harrow for a mere two years, he and Charlie were removed. Charlie, who had always been destined for the Royal Navy, was now enlisted on the training ship *HMS Britannia.* Robert was sent to a tutor, Reverend Bradley, in the London suburb of Southgate. And Gartmore, Robert's sanctuary, was let.

It is impossible to overestimate the impact of this turn of events on the Bontine family. At a single stroke Missy, now aged thirty-nine, had effectively lost her partner of sixteen years, along with her Scottish home and any financial security they might once have had. She had also lost a child. She was at war with the rest of the family, including her overbearing, acid-tongued mother-in-law whom she suspected of trying to get herself reinstalled at Gartmore. 'I wish, my dearest, that you never had anything to do with those horrid Grahams for it has been little else than misery to you,' Catalina wrote to her daughter. And now she had to make do with the meagre £500 a year allowed by the *curator.* The one consolation was that she was back in London where she felt most stimulated, away from the Scottish winters she loathed, and among the friends and acquaintances of her youth. She settled with young Malise, now aged seven, in a small rented house at Wilton Place in Belgravia.

For Robert, soon to turn sixteen, it is hard to see that there was any consolation. His father had been declared insane. The family were manifestly broke. He was denied access to the one place where he felt he could be himself. And he had begun to grow used to Harrow, even to like it – though later he would write disparagingly about the place and all it stood for. Now he travelled daily from Belgravia to his tutor in Southgate, dreaming of Gartmore as the train trundled through the dreary suburbs of north London. He had witnessed and was sensitive enough to have felt his mother's distress in recent months. He had also entertained the thought that, blow on the head or not, his father's condition might be hereditary. Meanwhile the Cunninghame Grahams, having noted Robert's mood swings and entertained the same thought, began nonetheless to make proposals for a future career in the cavalry – the Hussars or Dragoons, or an irregular regiment such as Skinner's Horse. These appealed to Robert not one jot.

There was one place where he was able to find solace – the Isle of Wight. Known in the family as Cat and Kat, his grandmother Catalina and her second husband, Admiral James Katon, had made their home in Ryde. It was the elderly sea-dog who had answered Missy's distress call the previous year and rushed to Gartmore following Willy's attack. Now he was there to offer his gruff comfort to the troubled teenager. Sailing expeditions in the Solent, in all weathers, Robert found a torment, though they put the colour in his cheeks. But striding out along the esplanade, he was enthralled as Kat reminisced about his long years in the Royal Navy – he had been at sea since the age of twelve – and spun tales of daring exploits and exotic ports. The admiral was a kindly and practical man; one, furthermore, who had made a commitment to a career in the Royal Navy during which he had acquired professional experience and expertise in seamanship. This contrasted sharply with the amateur approach to life pursued by most of the other adults in Robert's immediate orbit. More importantly still, Kat represented that inner kernel of integrity and personal authenticity that Robert would later come to admire so much in others he met, whether the gauchos of the Pampa, the workers of industrial Britain, or the artists and writers who were to become his friends. The experience set him up to detest and constantly to rail against its opposite, the fakery and humbug encountered in all walks of life.

After only a few months, the *curator* determined that they could no longer even afford Reverend Bradley's fees. In Spring 1868 Robert was shipped off again, this time to Brussels, where Willy also had concluded his education, and where less costly tuition was available to the sons of indigent gentlefolk at the British Consular Chaplaincy.

Under the supervision of the chaplain, Reverend Jenkins, Robert continued his studies, received extra tuition in Spanish and fencing, and wrote home of the miseries of the Channel crossing.

An idea was beginning to form in his mind. As the oldest competent man in the family, he must do something to restore the family fortune. He had no interest in the military career proposed by the family, still less in the kind of people it would oblige him to consort with. He would go instead to Argentina, where fortunes were being made by hardy ranchers, many of them Scots. There were family links with the New World, after all. His grandmother, Catalina, hailed from Cadiz, one of the Conquistadors' principal points of departure; while his grandfather, Admiral Elphinstone Fleeming, had been present at the siege of Maracaibo, the final act in the Spanish occupation of South America, and had mediated between the two great liberators, Páez and Bolívar.

In Brussels, Robert worked hard at his Spanish and read everything about South America that he could lay his hands on, immersing himself in the subject to such an extent that Missy and his brothers began referring to him as 'the gaucho'. But there was a major obstacle to his plans: money. The principal duty of the *curator* was to the welfare and security of his ward, Willy Bontine, until such time as he should be restored to health. Jamieson's priority therefore was to try and get the Gartmore finances back on an even keel. Progress had to be reported to the Court of Session in Edinburgh in minute detail, with even the smallest expense accounted for – three pounds for Robert's fare to the Isle of Wight in July 1868, for example. Any significant change in expenditure required a special application to the court accountant, which took time. Robert was hamstrung. Now the *de facto* tenth laird, yet viewed by the court almost as if he were his father's rival, he could neither claim his inheritance, nor make alternative plans for his future without Jamieson's assent. And Willy was still only forty-three.

Throughout the following year, 1869, Robert's determination to get to Argentina, to make his own way in the world and be free of the constraints imposed on him by dry, if well-intentioned, lawyers and accountants, grew stronger. Everyone, even his mother, seemed ranged against him. He resisted but grew moodier, more despondent, even morose as pressure from the family mounted. Meanwhile, another rite of passage awaited: he fell in love.

Countess Harley Teleki was a young English woman, born Harley Langdale, daughter of the formidable Lady Langdale who in turn was the only daughter and heir of the Earl of Oxford and his wife, Jane Harley, a former lover of Lord Byron's. The young Harley had married a Hungarian count, Alexander Teleki, but had left him and returned to England. She and Missy had become friends and Robert was invited a number of times in 1869 to hunt at the Langdale country estate in Herefordshire. Here, although more than fifteen years her junior, he fell head over heels for the sophisticated young countess. His feelings were not reciprocated. She found him tiresome and wrote to Missy that 'the spoony gaucho' bored her unutterably and that she had 'no patience with such a maundering donkey.' Nevertheless, she sympathised with him for his longing to get away and the obstructions placed in his way by the rest of the family.

In the end, Missy put aside her misgivings and convinced her in-laws to agree to Robert's plan. Years later he told his biographer, Aimé Tschiffely, that she had given in because she had grown so alarmed at how depressed he had become. Now she contacted her friend, Blanche, Countess of Airlie, whom she knew had South American connections. These included two young relatives, James and Edward Ogilvy, who were managing an estancia, several hundred miles north of Buenos Aires. Here was an opportunity for Robert to learn something practical that might also bring him some income. Jamieson was approached and wrote to the court that despite the best efforts of all concerned, including his own, Robert, although willing to listen, could not be dissuaded. Now, it seemed, the young man would be unable to settle until he had had the opportunity to visit Argentina and see whether he liked it or not – the fervent but unspoken hope being that he would not. The court deliberated and in March 1870 awarded a grant not exceeding £300 for Robert's outfitting and fare.

Meanwhile, Harley had left with her mother for a Nile cruise. She wrote to Robert from Cairo, describing how she had climbed a pyramid. From Luxor she wrote to Missy expressing her pleasure at the news that the Cunninghame Grahams had relented. 'I am so glad the Gaucho should go and see South America . . . it will keep him out of mischief, ie the neighbourhood of Bobby Graham and Mr Hope for a time.' What neither Robert nor Missy knew was that despite feeling unwell, Harley had been persuaded by her mother to continue with her from Egypt to Syria. There, in Damascus, at the beginning of May, the young countess had contracted 'an illness of the country' and died.

Robert by now had toured the London outfitters for the necessary clothing and equipment: a gun, a saddle, waterproofs, boots, hat and so on. At his grandmother's house in Leamington he had practised cooking, baking and darning. At Ryde, Kat had made a sketch of 'Bob as he will appear when ready for the road,' with spurs, gaucho knife, broad-brimmed hat and two pistols stuck through his belt.

Preparations complete, Robert was ready for adventure.

Three

BUENOS AIRES

Coming of age

In November 1972 I stood in the Casa Rosada, the presidential palace, in Buenos Aires, looking at a large portrait of a dashing, bearded man on a fine black horse. I was twenty-three years old, and I was about to embark on a journey that bore echoes, albeit faint ones, of the travels the rider in the portrait had undertaken a century previously.

This portrait of Don Roberto was by his friend, the 'Glasgow boy', John Lavery. It hung then in the ante-room to the president's office, where its presence signified the reverence in which Robert is still held as the man who had put the pre-industrial gaucho way of life on the international literary map. The portrait has since been moved to the neighbouring Museo de Bellas Artes, where Robert is celebrated as an iconic figure in Argentine national history and culture, more widely known about in Argentina than in his native Scotland. I was reminded of this in 2019 when I interviewed the then recently-retired director of the National Library of Argentina, Alberto Manguel, at the Edinburgh International Book Festival. I mentioned Don Roberto in our pre-festival correspondence. 'Cunninghame Graham!' he replied. 'Say no more! I'd love to talk with you about his importance, and perhaps about how Borges read him. I would very much like to ask *you* questions about him!' My knowledge of Borges, and more particularly of how he read my great-great-uncle, was then non-existent. In the event, I was able to keep the conversation to the more fruitful topic of my interviewee's own life and work.

That portrait, of course, was of an older, mature Robert. The eighteen-year-old who had stepped for the first time onto South American soil in May 1870, was an as-yet untempered model, still caught in the formative cross-currents and eddies of his upbringing and circumstances. Until Willy's illness had crashed in on them, correspondence, and there was a great deal of it, reveals life in the Bontine family as a warm, affectionate, humorous, irreverent, easy-going affair. The formalities of the age are present, but none of its stiffness. 'There are such pet little ponies here,' Robert writes to his grandmother, Catalina, from Florence in early 1866; 'pet' being a family term of approval or endearment. 'Mama calls them 'Smouches'! They go at a tremendous pace. Mummie and Puppie [his father] and Charlie send their love. Please give my love to dear Kat. I remain, your affectionate gd'son, R.C.Graham.' He is not quite fourteen. 'I actually heard from Charlie the other day, but he said nothing but "scuppers, booms and halliards",' he writes in gentle mockery, a year or so later, shortly after Charlie has enlisted on *HMS Britannia*, aged thirteen. He likes to play with names, his own included. He has by now become Bob to the whole family, on one occasion signing himself 'Old Bob Ridley' in reference to a popular folk song. Charlie is sometimes 'Tarlee', his baby name for himself, Malise 'Mal' or 'Mallie'; and there are 'the two Cats' – Catalina and Katon, or 'Khāt' as Catalina with her heavy Spanish accent would forever pronounce her husband's pet name.

Correspondence was central to Robert's life. The bond he formed with his mother in their exchange of letters endured until she died. Underlying his vivid, chatty and sometimes mischievous descriptions of people, places and events is a deep and abiding affection. In reply Missy signed off with a nod to her Spanish heritage, 'Your most aff. Madre A. E. Bontine'. Maintaining the family tradition, my mother also wrote copious letters through her life, replete with underlinings, exclamation marks and postscripts curling around the edges of the pages, until Alzheimer's began to rob her of her reason. Her letters, however, were always legible, unlike those of her great-uncle, whose notorious handwriting he himself referred to as 'hieroglyphics'. My mother had cemented her epistolary bond with me by placing a letter in the breast pocket of my pyjamas, to be found and read on my first night at boarding school, a few weeks short of my eighth birthday. It was a habit she maintained at least throughout my first couple of years there. It still touches me to think of it, not only for the personal emotions it stirs, but for the agony, usually unspoken, felt by so many mothers of that era, and doubtless earlier ones, on despatching their seven-year-olds to boarding school. By the time Robert went to Hill House, however, he was nearly eleven; and Missy anyway may have been glad to have him out of the house, given the advance of Willy's illness. She also had three-year-old Malise to console her.

Beyond the immediate family, Robert found warmth at Gartmore, too. Riding out to one of the farms as a boy, to be invited in for a bannock by the farmer's wife, or blethering with a forester about the laird's plans to cut down a wood, he would have experienced the mutual respect and sense of shared responsibility, the lack of deference, that passed between laird and tenant or employee. This easy connection with estate folk was a natural consequence of the tradition of liberal thought that framed his upbringing; so different from the feudal relationships he would have encountered in the hunting counties of England, and in such marked contrast to the entitled and superior attitudes of his fellows at both Hill House and Harrow – where a contemporary remembered him as being quiet, reserved and 'rather exclusive'. In some senses Robert was already an outsider and was to remain one for the rest of his life. A tendency to keep his feelings private and play the observer, his sense of a certain weight of heritage, the recent revelation of his parents' grand European connections, anxiety about his father's illness and the family's financial straits, might all have conspired to make him seem aloof in the rowdy corridors of an English public school. He was profoundly shocked at the discovery that his father had the capacity for violence and was someone not to be trusted, either with money or the safety of those dearest to him; that his legacy might even be madness. He had witnessed the adults in his family falling out over matters directly concerning his future, and he had begun to face the prospect of the seemingly endless financial constraint imposed on him by the *curator*, Jamieson. Naturally witty, he had begun to cultivate a sharp, sometimes caustic humour to defend against his own feelings. He was high-spirited, bold and energetic, yet he had shown himself prone to sharp mood swings and could become morose. Was he completely 'steady' wondered the Cunninghame Grahams? Steady enough, as it transpired, to resist their attempts to deflect him from South America. No mean feat for any seventeen-year-old, let alone one of that era.

Standing there in the Casa Rosada, in 1972, I could admire the image of the upright, handsome man, clearly at one with his steed, the proud tilt of his bearded chin, the hand light on the rein, at ease and confident in the great emptiness of the Pampas surrounding him. But of the mind that turned beneath the broad-brimmed hat, the heart that beat within the caped breast, I then knew nothing at all. I had other more pressing things on my mind, and this viewing of the portrait was partly obligation – it had been arranged on my behalf by a contact of my mother's – and partly a way of killing time while I waited for my own adventure to begin.

I had travelled to Buenos Aires with Sarah, my girlfriend, to join a group organised by Encounter Overland, a travel company which since the late 1960s had been taking enterprising travellers by road from London to Kabul. Now they were making a trial five-month journey through South and Central America, and we were among their thirty-odd guinea pigs, appropriately since we would be passing through the home of the creature, the Andes.

What was I doing going travelling again? It was a question Robert might well have asked himself on a number of occasions up until he was in his late twenties. I was only twenty-three, but it was still a question my father struggled to make sense of and one which exercised him greatly. I had already travelled widely and enthusiastically in the years since leaving school. Was it not time I now settled? My father and mother were recently divorced and it was my mother who, subversively in his eyes, had sent me the advertisement for the trip from the *Times* and encouraged me to join. 'You'll be following in Don Roberto's footsteps,' she may have said, though her motivation was more to do with the fact that I had not yet found my niche. She herself had a lifelong love of travel, formed in childhood as the daughter of a naval officer. She knew well that I was also bitten by the travel bug. She may have thought, wrongly as it transpired, that I would discover my direction and purpose while away. For my part, the fact that there was a family precedent for taking off to Argentina as a young man may have had some small influence, but I was clear that this was to be my adventure, not some kind of ancestral pilgrimage or journey of literary research.

The itinerary was ambitious, Buenos Aires to Los Angeles in five months. We drove most days and camped at night, the camping equipment contained in trailers towed behind the two bright orange, three-ton former British Army Bedford trucks. Our route took us from Buenos Aires through Uruguay and into Brazil, as far as Rio de Janeiro. From there we turned south-west, leaving Brazil and crossing into Paraguay by the Iguazu Falls. Through Paraguay we re-entered Argentina and continued south-west to Bariloche in the Andes, where we crossed into Chile. We then drove north through Chile, into Bolivia and on into Peru.

Reaching Lima, Sarah and I left the group. The deadline of the ferry crossing from Barranquilla in northern Colombia, to Panama, meant that the trucks would be travelling for more than twelve hours a day; and at a similar pace through Central America and Mexico in order to meet the planned end date in Los Angeles. For our part we sauntered on from Lima, hitching lifts or taking public transport, and eventually flew home from Toronto seven months later, in September 1973.

Robert has been described more than once as being mythogenic. That is to say he was someone around whom myths naturally grew up. But while they help to keep him alive in the popular imagination, they tend to stand in the way of anyone who wishes to get to the man behind them. Robert knew this in his lifetime and did nothing to prevent the myths accruing, perhaps for the very good reason that they preserved the inner man from the public scrutiny he deplored. All one needed to know about him was there in his writing, he would aver later in life. When first starting to research this book, I complained to an acquaintance of the difficulty of disentangling the man from the myth. Write about both, he wisely replied.

One of the most enduring of the Don Roberto myths is that having travelled to South America as a young man he became a gaucho. The gauchos of Argentina, Uruguay, Paraguay and Southern Brazil in the late nineteenth century were the last of a line of mixed-race horsemen, part Guarani Indian, part European who lived wherever their work took them and were frequently outlawed for their wild and often brutal ways. Distinguished by culture and ethnicity, they were more than merely the cowboys that their name has come to signify in more recent times.

Robert did not become a gaucho. In the literal, ethnic sense of the word he could not have done. In the practical sense he would not have, for there was no money in being a gaucho and Robert's mission in South America was to make his fortune. He did however spend time with them, ride with them often, and come to know them and their ways as few Europeans ever had.

The gaucho way of life was just one aspect of an eight-year South American odyssey that shaped him utterly for the rest of his life. Over the years he spent, on and off, in Argentina, Uruguay, Brazil and Paraguay, between the ages of eighteen and twenty-six, he ripened as the full-grained barley that catches the distiller's eye. For all his curiosity, sharp intellect and physical energy, the shock of arrival was nevertheless immense. Difficult as things had become at home, his life to date had been one of privilege and shelter. In South America, aged eighteen by only a few weeks, he would find himself exposed immediately to a frontier life of knives and guns, alcohol and ruinous mismanagement, physical hardship, drought and civil war. Gualeguaychú, the nearest town to the estancia where he would be working, sat like a chessboard on the open plain, its flat-topped, white-painted houses laid out in a rectangular grid of sandy, unpaved streets. It had many pulperías (drinking shops-cum-stores), where the locals hung out, and a couple of hotels where the foreigners gathered. It also boasted a plaza, a police station, a number of hovels in which 'china' girls entertained their clients, and a cock-fighting ring. There were horses everywhere as befitted a gaucho town in which all men went armed, their knives and pistols sticking out below their coats, and where, if one was so inclined, on any pretext one might fight with anyone else, no questions asked, and if one killed one's man, get on one's horse and ride into the 'camp' (the open country) sure of never being caught.

Of necessity, Robert quickly perfected the Spanish he had studied in Brussels, and of which he had already had a smattering from his mother and grandmother; though there is no evidence that he had visited his grandmother's family in Cadiz during childhood, as has been suggested. Again of necessity, since the horse was the only means of conveyance and to be horseless in that part of the world was considered to be worse than destitute, he also mastered his horsemanship in short order. With the horsemanship came physical courage. He wrote later of the terror he felt on riding out to round up cattle or hunt ostriches with *las tres marias*, the bolas – three lead weights attached to linked strips of rawhide which, when accurately thrown, could bring down a running bird, a galloping steer or, for that matter, a fleeing man. The cattle which roamed the unfenced expanses of the Pampas in huge herds of several thousand beasts were half wild, while the terrain was so vast and empty that an injury to horse or rider could easily mean death. Robert was frequently injured, either by falls or kicks from horses, suffering life-long pain as a result. He witnessed violent death by shooting, stabbing and throat-cutting with the facón, the long-bladed gaucho knife. He himself may even have killed, according to one story, in a desperate bid to escape captivity.

The powers of observation he had cultivated as a boy were at play all the time, consciously or unconsciously. They are evident in the letters he wrote home, with their chatty but vivid descriptions of people, places and events. And though he may not have realised it, all the while he was storing up memories for the time, a quarter of a century in the future, when he would start to draw on them for his stories and sketches.

For young Robert the experience of that extraordinary part of the world was infinitely more prolonged and intense than my own, but I understand the compulsion to write about it only too well. I kept a detailed journal during my own South American trip and have twice since drawn on it to set novels partly in South America, partly in Scotland. It has been a way of mediating my experience from all those years ago, for me also one of the most formative periods of my life; though what I learned from it still feels elusive. Perhaps that is because the process of growing up, cutting loose one's ties and throwing oneself wholeheartedly into an unknown adult world, is a slow tempering. There are no flashes of insight or illumination, but rather a thorough steadying and settling into some new form or shape. Neither of those novels have found publishers, one because it was simply not very good, the other because there no longer seemed to be a market for the kind of story I had to tell. And so I come five decades after the event to be writing about it almost vicariously, through the medium of my great-great-uncle's life.

The South America I experienced in 1973 was one of rattletrap buses chugging over mountain passes; plunging out of the Andes into Amazonia at the start of the rainy season, a terrifying three-day journey down precipitous mountain roads under the constant threat of landslides; sleeping in hammocks on the deck of a local ferryboat plying its way 600 miles down the Ucayali River to Iquitos and the Amazon; travelling hammock class again on a small cargo boat making its two-week trip around the Galapagos Islands where, once ashore, one could go on foot wherever one wanted; crossing the vast high altitude salt lake, the Salar de Uyuni, twenty miles of featureless, ankle-deep saltwater which much of the time was indistinguishable from the sky, with only a Russian map and a local on a bicycle to tell us where the Bolivian border post was; changing dollars down dark alleys in Santiago, six months before the military coup of September 1973; being chased through the ruins of a near-deserted Machu Picchu by a bad-tempered llama. These memories have scarcely dimmed in half a century.

Today air-conditioned buses with reclining seats cruise the vast distances between major cities on well tarmacked roads. Along with Machu Picchu, the Salar de Uyuni is now a major tourist destination with four-by-fours criss-crossing its great milky-white emptiness, where tourists stand ankle deep in salt water to take perspective-defying selfies. Access to the Galapagos Islands is, quite properly, heavily restricted. Twenty-first century Chile is one of the most prosperous democracies in South America.

This is the progress against which Robert so often railed, hankering instead for a slower, simpler, nobler past. He had arrived in

Argentina at a turning point in its history. The gaucho way of life he revered for its untamed purity would within a few years face the onslaught of mechanisation and enclosure. The railways were coming, iron roads to swallow up the vast expanses of open grassland. Land-ownership and large-scale cattle-ranching meant fences criss-crossing the same grass oceans, obstructing the passage of free-roaming horsemen. Cheap imported goods flooded the country stores and put paid to local craftsmanship. Telegraph enabled the hand of government to reach into regions previously untroubled by bureaucracy. Robert's recollections of a previous era would draw the attention not only of literary figures such as Jorge Luis Borges, but also the national authorities who renamed streets and schools after him and, years after his death, invited both my mother and my first cousin, the present day Robert (Robin) Cunninghame Graham, on separate occasions, to attend commemorative events in Buenos Aires.

But for seventeen-year-old Robert, about to set forth, Argentina was *terra incognita* in which would shortly play out the greatest adventure of his life.

Four

ENTRE RÍOS

Winning spurs

On 13 May 1870, eleven days before his eighteenth birthday, Robert sailed from Liverpool on the *SS Patagonia*, bound for Rio de Janeiro and Montevideo. His mother travelled with him to Liverpool, accompanied by Homer, her German maid, to see him off.

The first of his hieroglyphics reached Missy the following month, June 1870, from Montevideo. No sooner had he disembarked than he wrote, with an eighteen-year-old's disregard for the impact his news might have:

> There is a revolution here and one in Entre Rios, so we are rather uncertain of our movements . . . I am afraid that Entre Rios will be in a very bad condition after Urquiza's death as they say he was the only man who could rule the gauchos. The rebels have been driving off all the cattle from the Estancias and behaving generally in a cussed way.

Entre Ríos, with Urquiza its late governor, was the north-eastern province that lay between the great rivers Paraná and Uruguay, an Argentine mesopotamia, flat and humid and criss-crossed by rivers. It was there that Robert would be working on the estancia of Santa Anita, run by Edward and James Ogilvy, whose business at that moment was to rear cattle for leather. The small, wiry beasts brought with them by the Spaniards three centuries previously had not yet been widely crossed with more modern breeds for beef,

and the Argentine tanneries of the day shipped their products to
the world.

Some sources, including my mother, have it that Robert's travelling companion on the SS *Patagonia* was James Ogilvy, who had
been home visiting his family, and that on this voyage the whiff of
caña, cane rum, was already in the air, presaging the ruin that was
eventually to befall the estancia. It makes for a good story, but others
suggest that Robert made the voyage alone. In any event, from
Montevideo, the onward journey to the estancia required an overnight passage up the River Uruguay to Gualeguaychú on a stern-
wheeled paddle steamer, followed by a ride on horseback of several
leagues through rough country. Many years later, Robert described
that memorable first South American river journey in the sketch
Gualeguaychú (*His People*, 1906).

The steamer glided from the yellow waters of the River Plate into
a narrow channel over-arched with trees, which almost swept the
deck. A thick white mist rose from the stream, which shrouded
both banks and rose half up the mast and funnel, leaving the tops
of trees hanging like islands in the air. Upon their highest branches
cormorants and vultures sat asleep, which at the passing of the
boat woke and screamed, then dropped into the mist.

The channel narrowed, or appeared to do so, in the gloom
which brooded on the river and its banks, although the moon
shone brightly and the Southern Cross was hung above our
heads, the black Magellan clouds looking like the mouths of
funnels in the sky, deep and mysterious. Capella was just rising,
and the stars, though not so bright as in the northern hemisphere,
seemed far more luminous and gleamed more yellow and more
phosphorescent, than do their sisters of the North. Carpinchos,
starting from their sleep, plunged with a splash into the stream
and swam for refuge to the reedy banks, backs awash, and their
flat heads stretched out upon the water, looking like giant predi-
luvian rats.

Moths, large as hummingbirds, hung around the binnacle,
making the helmsman curse, although his compass was a sine-
cure, as from the bow, the pilot, sounding with a cane, guided the

vessel up the stream. From both the banks and from the islands with their feathery canes, the shrill mosquitoes' oboe piped its unpleasing tune. Nothing was heard but now and then the pilot's nasal cry as the stream shoaled, or the faint distant neigh of some wild stallion gathering up his mares.

Hours, which seemed long as days, went past, and still the steamer struggling with the current pressed into the night. At times she ran her nose against the bank, and from the trees the mist, congealed upon the leaves, poured down like rain upon the awnings and the shrouds. At times she grounded on a sandbank, backed, and was helped by all the crew, pushing her off with poles, then, shivering, swung into the stream, strove for a minute with the hurrying water, and once more glided through the mist.

Great rafts of canaloté floated past her sides, and now and then she swerved to let a tree come swirling lazily along. At last the mist grew lighter, and the moon, sinking below the trees, showed that the morning was at hand. The stars waxed paler and the air more chilly, and men, sleeping upon the deck beneath the awning, their heads upon their saddles, with the long silver-handled knives close to their hands, stirred and drew close their ponchos in their sleep. Others sat up and lighted cigarettes, smoked silently and then lay down again, the white dew glistening on their blankets and their hair.

Robert quickly discovered that normal life on the estancia Santa Anita was at a virtual standstill, reined in by a civil war in which bystanders were often more at risk than the combatants themselves. Opportunities for learning about the business of cattle ranching were minimal, and his letters home showed little interest in the subject. For the first few months he spent his time perfecting his Spanish, reading the books that arrived regularly from home, and riding out with the gauchos, whose entire way of life derived from the animals they herded: from the beef they ate monotonously, day after day, in the absence of any cultivated vegetables or fruit, to the dung and bones they burned for heat, the hides they used for furnishings and the skulls on which they sat.

There are photographs of Robert on his return to London, striking a variety of poses in full gaucho costume of *chiripá*, a length of cloth folded to form loose riding trousers, riding boots and spurs, a rakishly angled beret, poncho flung over one shoulder, and a *facón*, the long-bladed knife, thrust through his belt. These portraits offer early evidence of what was to become a lifelong preoccupation with the way he presented himself to the world.

'For months the revolution had been going on,' he later wrote in *A Silhouette (Faith, 1909),*

> the rival bands roaming about and stealing horses, slaughtering the cattle and now and then if they could catch a man or two alone, cutting their throats just as they cut a sheep's, driving the knife in at the point with the edge outwards, and bending back the head.

This had all the trappings of the chaotic and bloody revolutions for which South America had long been famous. On one side of the conflict were the followers of Lopez Jordán, a gaucho leader who had recently assassinated the governor of the province, the self-styled Napoleon del Sur, Don Justo Urquiza, also of gaucho origin. On the other side were government forces directed from Buenos Aires by Urquiza's successor. For combatants on both sides the whole business was largely an excuse to plunder the countryside and settle old scores, while avoiding one another as far as they could.

Robert was later taken to see the site of Urquiza's assassination, a mirror-walled, gold-ceilinged ballroom, adorned with statuettes of Napoleon Bonaparte, in the gubernatorial palace at nearby San José. Urquiza had previously ruled Argentina for a number of years as dictator. Deposed by a rival, he had been handed the governorship of the province and left to run it as he pleased, so long as he caused no further trouble. Robert was greatly taken by his guard, who appeared wilder even than the horses they rode. Yet they remained respectful of the penalties that awaited them for disobeying Urquiza's decrees, one of which had been to ban all hunting to the benefit of the throng of ostriches, deer and warthogs that wandered freely around his vast estate. 'The first offence a fine,' Robert noted of these penalties, the next to be stretched out between four posts with fresh hide ropes which the hot sun contracted; the third deprived of horses and obliged to march among the infantry (to go on foot was shame and disgrace to a gaucho), the fourth and last, death by the knife, for cartridges were dear and knives and cutting throats a subject for a jest amongst the population to whom the sight of blood was constant from its youth.

Just one of the many snapshots that correspondence and later writings (*San José, Progress*, 1911) would offer of the chaotic and often alarming but seductive world into which the privileged young Scotsman had tumbled. At this time his peers would have been preparing to join the army or navy, continue their studies at Oxford or Cambridge, enter the clergy, or travel east with one of the great trading enterprises of the day. Robert's choice of South America had already set him apart. Now that he was here, the spirit of adventure would set him apart still further.

In September 1870, three months after arriving, he wrote home that he intended to set off into the Banda Oriental, the territories east of the River Uruguay and north of the River Plate, as modern Uruguay was then known. Any such journey at this time would have been perilous in the extreme. Not only was there danger from revolutionaries and bandits, often indistinguishable from one another, but also from the neglect which led to huge herds of tame mares running wild and a proliferation of feral cattle, aggressive and unpredictable. Robert offered his mother no forwarding address, and several months of anxious silence ensued. Then, in February 1871, he wrote again to say that he had had to abandon his plans owing to the disturbances, and that to compound the problems of the revolution the southern summer had become blighted by a severe drought.

'I have been unable to get up country at all on account of the revolution,' he wrote,

and I think the best thing I can do is to come home as I think I see my way to a good thing now. Ogilvy and another Escoces having had all their cattle killed, horses destroyed, and lost everything by the war are going about the country buying hides and wool and making immense profits by it. They have proposed to take me into partnership which might be thought of when I come home and can explain everything properly . . . For the last three months there has been not a drop of rain so that the camps (pastures) are in a very bad state. At this place there is the only water for leagues and it is a very curious sight to watch the wild horses and cattle and deer come down to drink in thousands. They come with clouds of dust and a noise like thunder with the galloping on the hard ground and then they all bathe and jump about. I caught a fine horse one evening there, a tame horse that had got away and had been running wild a long time. I could do nothing with him, however, owing to a trick he had of throwing himself over backwards and refusing to get up again.

Concluding with the details of a narrowly avoided fall from another horse, Robert conveyed his affections and asked his mother to request the money for his passage home from the *curator*. The sum of eighty pounds was duly forwarded by banker's draft and was met by another, even longer silence. By June 1871, when the money had still not been collected, Missy was at her wits' end. A request for help to the British Consulate in Buenos Aires elicited little more than the disquieting information that the capital was in the grip of a virulent outbreak of yellow fever. Then came the news that Robert was gravely ill with typhus.

The overseer of a nearby ranch had fallen sick with the disease. Robert had ridden to Gualeguaychú to fetch provisions for him. On the way to deliver them he had had to cross a swollen river and was soaked through when he arrived, then spent the night at the man's bedside without a change of clothes. He paid dearly for this act of kindness. He collapsed and lay seriously ill for several weeks. During this time he was attended by the manager, who had recovered, and his Indian wife, along with a Scots doctor, Forbes, who was summoned from the up-river town of Concepcíon del Uruguay. Doctor Forbes stayed on at the ranch for a fortnight, until Robert was out of danger. For this service he later submitted a bill for £100.

Late in August, James Ogilvy wrote to Missy to say that Robert was on the mend and now convalescing at the house of Doctor Forbes, though 'he has been very seriously ill'. Ogilvy went on, 'I have advised him to go home as soon as he is strong enough to bear the journey, which I expect he will soon be now, as after such a severe illness it would scarcely be prudent for him to knock about any more in the country.'

But Robert was not done knocking about. Nothing more seemed to have come of the hide- and wool-buying venture with the Ogilvies. The calamitous effects of the civil war on their business had driven Edward Ogilvy to the caña and now he was suffering from *delirium tremens*. There was talk that Robert should accompany him back to Scotland. First, though, Robert intended to travel to the provincial capital of Córdoba, some 450 miles northwest of Gualeguaychú.

Horses were in great demand in Córdoba, he wrote to Missy in October 1871. Not only were the local Indians in the habit of making off with them, but now there was an influx of foreigners who had come to see an exhibition celebrating the recent arrival of the railway line from Buenos Aires. He had bought thirty or forty horses and hoped to sell them at a large profit. He was getting stronger, he reassured her, though he was still 'a fearfull (sic) object without any hair', much of it having fallen out during the fever. He had also had 'a very bad fall the other day from a wild horse . . . The brute fell on top of me and squashed me a good deal' – news his long-suffering mother would doubtless have preferred not to hear.

Córdoba was one of the earliest colonial capitals, a place of cultural interest, home to an ancient university, and a centre for the Jesuits in whose earlier sway over this part of South America Robert was to become fascinated. But since there is nothing about the place in either his correspondence or later writing, it's reasonable to assume he never got there. Perhaps, after the illness, he found the journey too arduous. Perhaps his way was blocked.

If indeed he did set out for Córdoba and made it beyond the River Paraná and into Santa Fé province, he would there have had his first glimpse of the Pampa:

All grass and sky, and sky and grass, and still more sky and grass . . . well did the ancient Quichuas name the plains with the word signifying 'space', for all was spacious – earth, sky, the waving continent of grass; the enormous herds of cattle and of horses; the strange effects of light; the fierce and blinding storms and, above all, the feeling in men's minds of freedom and of being face to face with nature, under those southern skies.

No matter when he first made their acquaintance, in the Pampa Robert found his spiritual home, a place where he could throw off the shackles of his upbringing and set his face to a future of boundless possibility; a place to which he would return whenever he could in life, and again and again in his imagination. The Pampa were where he observed a beguiling, if frequently brutal, simplicity and purity in both nature and humanity; an inclination towards truth and honour, natural justice, individual freedom that chimed with what he considered to be the best of Scotland and the Scots, and which endured until his death.

Nothing could be more typical of the wild life of forty years ago upon the plains than was the figure of a Gaucho dressed in his poncho and his chiripa, his naked toes clutching the stirrups, his long iron spurs kept in position by a thong of hide, dangling below his heels, his hair bound back by a red silk handkerchief, his eyes ablaze, his silver knife passed through his sash and tirador (belt), and sticking out just under his right elbow, his pingo (horse) with its mane cut into castles, and its long tail floating out in the breeze, as, twisting Las Tres Marias around his head, he flew like lightning down the slope, which the mere European horseman would have looked on as certain death, intent to 'ball' one of a band of fleet ñandus (ostriches) all sailing down the wind.

The Pampa were a place whose landscape and customs, whose people and creatures, brought inspiration to some of his most vivid and wistful writing – witness the two preceding passages, both from his sketch *La Pampa* which first appeared in *Charity* (1912), later in the collection *Rodeo*, published in the year of his death, 1936.

Meanwhile, the trip to Córdoba is never referred to after that first letter home, and Robert was back in London three months later, his ship having docked in Liverpool on 12 January 1872.

I consider my own early adult years to have been reasonably adventurous. Four months after my eighteenth birthday, in February 1968, I also had found myself on a steamer, sailing from Southampton to South Africa to visit a godmother in Cape Town, then to work on a winery in Stellenbosch and travel round that beautiful, but then still divided, country in an unreliable second-hand car.

Unlike the *SS Patagonia*, the *SA Vaal* was fully stabilised and I did not have to endure the seasickness that afflicted Robert every time he made the long Atlantic crossing, usually on a cheap fare in small cargo boats, where the conditions were cramped and he spent much of the time incapacitated in his cabin. 'We arrived this afternoon in tremendous joy as I was sick up to the time we entered the River Plate,' was the opening sentence of his first letter home from South America. I could empathise, having been horribly seasick as a twelve-year-old on a National Trust voyage to St Kilda on board the *Dunera*, a former troop ship converted to run educational cruises. Today I remember little about the voyage to South Africa except a riotous crossing-the-line ceremony, the endlessly entertaining spectacle of flying fish, and sailing into Table Bay at dawn. The culmination of that African gap year journey was a close encounter with an elephant at Treetops Lodge, in Kenya, on my way home. It was the only time in the history of the place that an elephant had had to be shot to protect the visitors. It left us all, including the ranger who had had to fire the shot, very shaken; although with the benefit of hindsight one might wonder why he had not avoided exposing us to that danger in the first place.

A year later, in the summer of 1969, I had driven with three friends from London to Tehran to visit an Iranian university friend. Highlights of that trip included being almost driven off the road by a column of Turkish army trucks in the shadow of Mount Ararat; being entertained by the children of the Shah's sister, Princess Shams Pahlavi, in her astonishing desert residence, the Pearl Palace (one of my travelling companions had connections); and watching the moon landing, in Tehran, with commentary in Farsi. I had also driven to Greece, hitchhiked there, even sailed third class on a ferry-boat from Marseille to Piraeus. My South American trip, the biggest adventure of all, was still to come.

Yet my own hippyish wanderings of the late 1960s and early 1970s were tame by comparison with what Robert had experienced a century previously. Not yet twenty years old, he had already seen life in ways that would shape him and set him apart not just from his family and peers but from most Europeans, forever. There is a story told by two of his biographers, and given some credence by a third, that on his way back from visiting Urquiza's palace, he was swept up by a passing band of Lopez Jordan's revolutionary supporters and forced to ride with them for several weeks as they plundered and pillaged. In one version of that story he is driven finally to kill a guard in order to make his escape. The story also contains a tragic sub-plot concerning a fellow captive, a young man of German extraction named Vogel, nicknamed by his captors Pajarito (German and Spanish respectively for 'bird' and 'little bird'), who one night finds himself forced to take part in a raid on his own farmstead, and in the darkness and chaos accidentally kills his brother.

The capture and dramatic escape is possible, although Robert never refers to it directly in his own letters or later writing. He certainly witnessed brawls, possibly even fatal ones – gauchos were quick with their knives – and most likely knew people who had been 'conscripted' by one or other side in the revolution, even if he himself hadn't. One such character was a *payador*, a gaucho minstrel, called Angel Cabrera, who was to feature often in Robert's later writing, and with whom Robert formed a bond that was to endure throughout his life.

He had ridden with, and seemingly earned the respect of, these men who were dismissed by a contemporary British consular report as being

illiterate, rude, greedy of money, addicted to gambling, implaca-ble and vengeful, distrusting the foreigner as much as the towns-man and more openly displaying his hostility . . . they are the originators of all the disturbances that afflict the country and at times little better than paid assassin.

Yet Robert had found in them – these hard-riding, fast-talking, knife-wielding 'punks of the Conquest', as the writer Chris Dolan has christened them – qualities that resonated with him strongly: courage, loyalty, a quick sense of justice and extraordinary horsemanship. And they, in turn, had found qualities to admire in the young Scotsman upon whom they had bestowed two singular honours: the title of 'Don Roberto', and the brand mark of the late President Urquiza, the 'gaucho's president', which Robert had 'differenced' with the addition of a circle around the upper stem. He would be distinguished by both for the rest of his life.

There in Entre Rios, seven thousand miles from home, Robert had won his spurs.

Five

ASUNCION

In search of green tea

Over the next five years, Robert made two more trips to South America. Twice during his first trip he had written to his mother of 'seeing his way to a good thing'. Amid all the activity and excitement, it's easy to overlook the fact that money and the notion, however naïve, of restoring the family fortune, were at the back of his mind all the time. Things were not right at home and he earnestly wanted to put them right. But he had also tasted adventure, he was still only twenty years old, and he wanted more.

He had left Scotland in 1870 a boy and returned eighteen months later a man. He had experienced fear and physical hardship, life-threatening illness, boredom, disappointment and the company of hard men and wild horses. He had witnessed political chaos and violence at first hand and in a way that had shaken him, for all his youthful sense of invincibility. His Spanish blood had been roused by the language, culture and climate. He had immersed himself in a world where the British pre-occupation with class counted for nothing, in welcome contrast to his recent experiences of Harrow School.

He had arrived back in Britain in January 1872. Cattle ranching had failed. Now it was time to look for alternative money-making opportunities. He spent most of that year in London, staying with his mother and using family connections to explore openings. One of these was with the trading firm of Holland Jacques whose directors had been offered a share in a concession from the Paraguayan government to grow *yerba mate (ilex paraguariensis)* from which mate, the popular green tea of the region, is made. During Paraguay's recent, disastrous war with her neighbours, the plantations, *yerbales*, had fallen into a ruinous state of neglect. The commercial potential of reviving cultivation and production of this staple of daily life was thought to be worth consideration. With the help of a distant relative, Robert convinced Holland Jacques that he was the man they needed to go to Paraguay and investigate; although the terms of engagement, and particularly the financial arrangements, were more than a little vague. Once again the *curator* was approached. In the previous year the Bontine estate had shown a surplus of one pound, ten shillings and one penny. Encouraged by this turn of fortune, the *curator* agreed to advance Robert £150.

Before leaving, Robert made another brief transatlantic voyage to visit his brother Charlie, now a junior naval officer, whose ship was stationed at Halifax, Nova Scotia. Returning to Glasgow via New York, he endured an appalling crossing in the steamer *SS Alps*, later recalled in one of the first stories he published. In *SS Atlas* (*The Ipané*, 1899), with the name of the ship altered, he describes how for most of the twelve-day voyage he was confined to his bunk in a stifling, waterlogged and rat-infested cabin, reduced to drinking arrowroot tea laced with whisky, the only thing he could hold down, and reading the only book he had with him, Spencer's *Faerie Queen*. Yet for all the misery, he seems to have enjoyed this and the other similar voyages he was to make throughout his life.

Sailing finally into calmer waters and up the Clyde, he would have looked out on Finlaystone, where he had spent his early years, on the south shore, and Ardoch, where he would spend his later ones, almost directly opposite on the north. He disembarked in Glasgow, and travelled to London for a week of socialising and theatre-going, before picking up the *SS Alps* once more for the voyage to Montevideo.

They sailed in early December 1872. First port of call was Pauillac, on the Gironde, where a party of Basque emigrants were taken on board. These wretched people, driven by poverty and hardship to seek a better life in the New World, were crammed into dormitories below decks with all their worldly possessions. These included great wicker birdcages, one for each family; although, as Robert wrote in

SS Atlas, 'they were going to a land of parrots, macaws, toucans, hummingbirds, cardinals, and flying spots of jewelled rainbow, compared to which the birds of Europe all seem made of sackcloth or mackintosh'. More emigrants came aboard in Lisbon, 'chiefly peasants from the Galician hills, who emigrate en masse, leaving the villages deserted and their houses closed, for wolves to scamper through the deserted streets on winter nights.'

Huddled on deck whenever the weather allowed it, the emigrants fared even worse during the voyage than Robert. As the sole Spanish speaker aboard he spent much of the time interpreting for them, despite being crippled by seasickness. It is clear that he sympathised with them and was struck by this first-hand experience of mass migration forced on an underclass by poverty and neglect. The thought of the empty Galician villages summoned echoes of the Highland Clearances, even helped fuel the indignation roused in him later, at the start of his political career, by the plight of the Highland crofters. There was, after all, plenty to remind him of home on that voyage, at least according to the account in his story, *SS Alps*. The crew were all Scots. Come Hogmanay, off the coast of Brazil, they somehow managed to get hold of liquor and proceeded to celebrate with such zeal that the mates, migrants and other passengers were obliged to help the captain man the ship for the next twenty-four hours while the crew recovered under lock and key.

Arriving in Montevideo, Robert spent three months waiting on further instructions from Holland Jacques. He killed time by riding which proved as risky as ever. In the early months of 1873 he wrote to his mother of two bad accidents, one involving a kick to the leg, just above his ankle, so painful that he passed out and spent a week in bed; the other involving a fall with one foot caught in the stirrup, which resulted in him being dragged.

Instructions arrived in late April. He was to assess both the prospects for the cultivation of *yerba mate* and the current political situation in Paraguay. So Robert set off upriver again, this time on the thousand-mile journey to the capital, Asunción. Paraguay at this time was barely recovering in the aftermath of a suicidal war with its three neighbours, Brazil, Argentina and Uruguay. In pursuit of this five-year-long conflict, known as the War of the Triple Alliance, the legendarily brutal and intransigent Paraguayan dictator, Francisco Solano López, had brought his country to ruin. Defeated by conventional warfare, López resorted for the final eighteen months of hostilities to a guerrilla campaign, in the dying stages of which he fled up country, executing those of his followers who wouldn't follow him, and driving a large number of prisoners of war with him. He was eventually cornered by Brazilian troops at Cerro Corá, on the northeastern border with Brazil, and killed. It was March 1870, only weeks before Robert first set foot in South America.

Casualties in the war, the bloodiest in South American history and possibly the most destructive, proportionally, of any modern state ever, were astronomical. Modern estimates put deaths from fighting, hunger, disease and physical exhaustion at two-thirds of a population of about 450,000 people. A census conducted shortly after the end of the war suggested that fewer than thirty thousand adult males had survived, leaving the country with a ratio of four women to every man. Large territories were ceded to the victors and the country's agricultural economy decimated, with livestock driven off or left to starve, and plantations abandoned and overgrown.

Robert later wrote a biography of López, *Portrait of a Dictator*, published in 1933. When turning to my copy to check details of the story, I found it was a first edition, inscribed by Robert for his nephew, my grandfather, Angus. Glued to the inside cover was a small envelope containing a photograph of a benign-looking, round-faced, full-bearded López. Today he is regarded as a hero of Paraguay's struggle against its larger neighbouring oppressors.

Robert's long journey by steamer to Asunción took him first up the Paraná and then the Paraguay rivers. His introduction to Paraguay, as they passed the border, was the sight of Curupaity, a ruined town on a bluff above the water where Paraguayan forces had held out doggedly against Brazilian invaders. It had been entirely destroyed by shellfire.

Further on, the river formed the eastern boundary of the Chaco, Paraguay's great primeval wilderness of palms and swamps, backwaters and lakes, infested with alligators, eels and stingrays. The humidity was intense and the air alive with stinging and biting insects. It was a place as alien and menacing as any Robert could imagine.

Situated around a lagoon on a bend in the river, Asunción was the oldest city east of the Andes. Founded in 1535, it had been the seat of government from Spain for the whole cis-Andean region, and the stronghold of the Jesuits, whose college still stood from that time and now housed the present, pro-Brazilian government. Amid the colonial-era buildings rose an extravagant but roofless theatre and a vast half-finished palace, while a rusting tramway connected the docks with the railway station; symbols of López's dream that Asunción should stand with the great capitals of Europe. Meanwhile, a mile across the water rose the stubby palm trees of the Chaco, a reminder if any were needed of the implacable forces of nature and civilisation's tenuous grip on them in this part of the world. In the city, barefoot Brazilian soldiers, the occupying troops, lounged in the stifling sub-tropical heat.

The history of Robert's time in South America was one of long periods of enforced idleness, punctuated by furious bursts of activity. This was no exception. He spent several months in Asunción staying with Doctor William Stewart, a Scot from Galashiels, who had been surgeon-general of the Paraguayan army and personal physician to López and his family. Stewart had recently applied for and been denied the British consulship by a British government unready to overlook his service to the dictator. Nevertheless, married to a wealthy Paraguayan, he was still a person of some influence. Armed with Stewart's introductions, Robert visited government ministries daily. He also communicated fruitlessly with Holland Jacques, and began to investigate the possibility of yet another 'good thing', his own *yerbales* concession – all of which he reported in letters home.

He was managing well with Portuguese, he said, but finding the indigenous language, Guarani, very difficult. He had also acquired a very nice horse, a tordillo (grey). I paid 40 dollars for him which is very dear further south, but considered quite cheap here! He says his name is "pingo' [a gaucho term for a horse] and I think he is the tamest horse I ever saw in South America. I call him 'Bunny' and the Brazilian sentries (who have got to know me and him pretty well as I am almost all day trying to see someone or other – who, of course, is always 'infermo' or 'siestando'!) call out 'Ola, Jose Maria, acquit ven Dom Roberto com o Bonee!' and some fellow always answers 'Si, Jose Antonio, cabalo mexito bein!' Although not near such a pretty or lively horse as my entrepelado I had in the Banda, he should be, I think, a very good journey horse as he is rather lazy, which is always considered good sign of a horse's endurance in these parts. He follows me about and comes when he is called.

Bunny was to become the first of the three great equine companions in Robert's life. His task now was to carry his new master 250 miles south to the Argentine town of Corrientes, where Robert was to collect a troop of mules for Dr Stewart; a commission perhaps kindly intended to keep the young man busy and provide him with a little income while he waited on instructions from London.

Returning safely with the mules, Robert finally set off to inspect the potential Holland Jacques concession in July 1873. The appointed sixty square miles of *yerbales*, formerly belonging to the López family, lay in the south-eastern department of Alto Paraná, towards the Brazilian border. For a solitary twenty-one-year-old – unarmed, since he had left in a hurry and forgotten to take his rifle – the journey was rash to the point of foolhardiness.

The countryside was almost empty of people. Those few Robert encountered went on foot, all the horses having been killed in the war, and greeted him warily. Villages were deserted, farms abandoned and overgrown. There was practically no food to be had apart from small, hard oranges and manioca. The way lay across swamps and through great tracts of forest, so dense that the sun never penetrated. Wild animals proliferated since there was no one left to hunt them. Robert slept out, with Bunny tethered close by, devoured by mosquitoes and soaked by rain, the latter leading later to bouts of rheumatism, sometimes so severe that he had to be lifted onto his horse.

From time to time he would meet processions of Guarani women, whom he described later in the story *A Meeting* (*Charity*, 1912):

> . . . dressed in their low cut sackcloth garment, embroidered round the neck with black embroidery. Their hair, cut square across the forehead and hanging down their backs, gave them a mediaeval air. All were barefooted and all smoked thick cigars, which they kept lighted at the torch their leader carried in her hand to scare the jaguars. Upon their heads they carried baskets full of oranges, of mandioca and of maize. Sometimes they all saluted, sometimes they only smiled and showed their teeth, and sometimes one of them would say, amidst the laughter of the rest, 'we all want husbands' and added something else in Guarani that made a laugh run rippling down the line.

As a consequence of the war, Paraguay had become in effect a gynarchy, and the young Scotsman on his horse would likely have been an object of some interest to such a procession. Robert doesn't relate whether he reciprocated that interest, although it's not unreasonable to assume that he would have done. He does relate how travellers joked about preferring to sleep in the woods than risk entering villages populated only by women. Though sleeping in the woods, as he well knew, exposed them, or at any rate their horses, to the threat not only of vampire bats but also of the jaguars that had now grown large and numerous and emboldened by the absence of hunters. Even in the daytime, Robert was on constant alert and more than once had to fire the borrowed rifle he now carried to ward off an advancing *tigre*, as jaguars were known.

> Occasionally a crashing in the bushes near the trail told of the passage of a tapir, through the underwood, and once as I came to a little clearing a tiger lay stretched flat upon a log, watching the

fish in some dark backwater, just as a cat lies on the garden wall to watch the birds. Butterflies floated lazily about, scarce moving their broad, velvet wings, reminding one somehow of owls, flitting across a grass ride in a wood, noiseless but startling by their very quietness.

The snakes, the hummingbirds, the alligators basking in the creeks, the whir of insects and the metallic croaking of the frogs, the air of being in the grip of an all-powerful vegetation, reduced a man, travelling alone through the green solitude, to nothingness. One felt as if in all that wealth of vegetation and strange birds and beasts, one's horse were the one living thing that was of the same nature as oneself.

The story *A Meeting* is a meditation on the loneliness Robert himself experienced on this trip. He relates how he comes across a solitary old man living in a clearing. As he approaches he is startled when Bunny neighs shrilly and is answered by another neigh. A fine horse canters from the trees and the two nuzzle one another. Robert is persuaded to let them play together, which they do for hours, leaping about like lambs, galloping to and fro. Later they spend the night with their heads resting upon one another's shoulders. The old man explains that his horse has not seen another for six months. He adds that he himself was imprisoned in Asunción for two years, held in solitary confinement. On his release he accosted the first man he met in the street and embraced him.

There is a photograph of an older Robert, leaning casually against the upright of a verandah, legs crossed at the ankle. He is wearing highly polished boots, leather trousers, a shirt, waistcoat and neckerchief, and a stetson of sorts. He appears to be smoking a long-stemmed pipe. Looking directly at the camera from under the brim of his hat, he could be one of Yul Brynner's fellow gunslingers in *The Magnificent Seven*.

Closer inspection, however, reveals that he is not smoking but drinking mate, sucking the astringent green tea through a drinking straw from the small gourd he grasps in his left hand. The gourd is decorated around the rim with silver, in the traditional fashion.

Brewing the mate was an early morning ritual Robert would have observed countless times when out on the plains with the gauchos, blowing up the fire at dawn to heat the water, packing the leaves into the *mate* (as the gourd itself is also known), pouring on the water and waiting for the tea to infuse, before passing the mate round from hand to hand.

Mate made an unexpected appearance in my own life during the early stages of researching this book. I took part in a project in which writers and artists were paired, given a word chosen at random from the dictionary, and invited to respond to it. My partner was the Edinburgh artist, illustrator and calligrapher, Susie Leiper. Our word was 'mate'.

Susie and I had not met before and we agreed to go for a walk in the Edinburgh Botanical Gardens, near where she lived, to discuss what we might do. As we strolled among the shrubs and plants I found myself thinking not of 'mate', in the sense of friend or partner, but of mate. I voiced the thought to Susie, explaining that I had a forebear who had spent time in South America as a young man, and that the mate ritual had featured prominently in his experiences of daily life there.

'Not old whatsisname . . . Cunninghame Graham?' Susie asked.

Surprised, I replied that it was, and asked how she knew of him.

'My family are the Stewarts who bought Inchmahome in the early 1900s,' she replied.

Small place though Scotland undoubtedly is, this seemed well beyond the bounds of probability.

With Robert encouraging us from the wings, I wrote a short poem, using the 62-word constraint dictated by the project, and Susie set the poem within a montage of objects: pale, elongated hands, taken from paintings of medieval Spanish bishops, to signify the passing round of the gourd; a variety of silver-trimmed gourds and silver drinking straws; a pair of spurs; and discreetly placed in one corner, the famous brand mark. The whole work was enclosed by a decorative border comprising the green leaves and red berries of *ilex paraguariensis*.

No es un micrófono
They say in Buenos Aires
As the *mate*
(Pronounced *maté*
Though the accent
Would make it
'I killed' in Spanish)
Makes its ritual round
Don't Bogart that gourd
Another way of putting it
Mate, the drink of gauchos
Those galloping plainsmen
Who brew in the chill of dawn
To infuse the new day
With the warmth
Of comradeship

Mate, on this occasion at least, was not to be Robert's salvation. His long and arduous journey to the site of the concession, on the banks of the Paraná, proved fruitless. Based at Potrero San Antonio, a property owned by Dr Stewart (no relation to the artist), he spent several months, first recovering from yet another riding injury, then exploring the region. But his investigations revealed no *yerbales* waiting to be brought back under cultivation, as his letters to Holland Jacques – 'of extreme length, dullness and promptitude' – reported.

In a small jungle town he did, however, come across the overgrown ruins of a large Jesuit community – three churches, a college and a complex of administrative buildings. Here, by moonlight, he watched a jaguar steal out of one of the abandoned churches and across a deserted square to vanish into the forest.

Robert was becoming interested in the Jesuits. In the early 1600s they had gained a foothold in the remote interior of Paraguay, and had championed the cause of the Guarani Indians, who were otherwise maltreated by the European settlers. Under Jesuit protection, the indigenous people were able to live in semi-autonomous 'reductions', or Christian missions, free from interference by Spanish colonists and Spanish rule. The Jesuits had created a kind of benign colonialism which appealed to Robert. The historian in him aroused, he had already spent time with the early books and papers to be found in Asunción's crumbling libraries. Now, in outlying mission posts such as this one, he was able to see at first hand traces of the Jesuit 'state-within-a-state'. A story that especially caught his imagination was that of Father Ruiz de Montoya. Faced with attack by the piratical Mamelucos from Sao Paolo, who regularly captured Guarani people and carried them back to slavery in Brazil, the Jesuit led a party of several thousand Indians to safety on a dramatic journey down the River Paraná.

The fruit of this research, some twenty years later, was his book *A Vanished Arcadia* (1901), in which he recounted the history of the Jesuits in Paraguay from their arrival in 1607 to their expulsion in 1767. This book was later to form part of the research for the 1984 film *The Mission*, written by Robert Bolt and starring Robert de Niro and Jeremy Irons. In a curious twist, following my separation from my first wife, I happened to be lodging in the London house of a friend, the actress Cherie Lunghi. At that time she was about to play Carlotta, the female lead in the film, and her then partner was its director, Roland Joffé. But I was ignorant of Robert's book, it was never mentioned, and no one knew of my connection to him anyway. It was only many years later that I found out about the link between Robert's book and the film.

For all the hardships and disappointments he endured within its borders, Robert was captivated by Paraguay. With its sleepy little towns, gentle people and majority of women, its dense forests, sluggish rivers and swamps, birds and butterflies, and abundance of wild animals, it had a dreamlike, other-worldly quality which lodged deeply in his imagination and later gave rise to some of his most vivid writing.

In *The Station Master's Horse* (*Writ In Sand*, 1932) he describes a dash on a borrowed horse to catch up with the local train, the only way to guarantee prompt delivery of an important letter.

It . . . ran, or rather staggered, along on a rough track, almost unballasted. Sleepers had been taken out for firewood, by the country people here and there, or had decayed and never been replaced. The line was quite unfenced, and now and then a bullock strayed upon it and was run down or sometimes was found sleeping on the track. Then the train stopped, if the engine driver saw the animal in time. He blew his whistle loudly, the passengers all started, and if the bullock refused to move, got down and stoned it off the line . . . The bridges luckily were few, and constructed of the hard imperishable woods so plentiful in Paraguay. They had no railings, and when, after the downpours of the tropics, the streams they crossed were flooded, the water lapped up and covered them to a depth of several inches, so that the train appeared to roll upon the waters, and gave the passengers an experience they were not likely to forget.

The wood-burning engines moved at no more than ten miles an hour, but the local people, who were used to bullock carts, were delighted by this turn of speed. After several miles of hard riding, Robert came abreast of the engine and passed his letter up to the engine driver 'who put it carefully into the pocket of his belt, crumpling it up so that it looked like a dead locust.' Then he headed back to return the horse to the station master and join his friends who were playing billiards in the station café.

Robert had arrived in Asunción in March or April 1873. I arrived there a couple of months short of a century later, in January 1973, crossing into Paraguay from Brazil at the Iguazu Falls. Paraguay then was known largely to the outside world as a dictatorship where human rights abuses were rife and fugitive Nazis were welcomed. Alfredo Stroessner, the president, had come to power in 1954 and would not relinquish it for another sixteen years. Until the early 1970s, the Paraguayan economy had been largely based on agriculture and the export of tropical hardwoods. But now, with construction just starting on the world's second-largest hydro-electric dam, a joint venture with Brazil, Paraguay was on the threshold of a decade as one of the fastest developing countries in Latin America.

Like Robert, I caught Paraguay on the cusp, and like Robert I found it entrancing. But I had yet to read anything he had written on the subject when I recorded in my journal the scene that greeted us as we made our way through the countryside towards Asunción:

Our trucks slithered and bumped along muddy roads at a top speed of fifteen miles an hour. In places lay deep floods which we took turns volunteering to walk through, to look out for potholes or streams, expecting to sink up to our necks at any moment. At the roadside were little mud and thatch houses with very dark, raggedy or naked children playing outside. Frangipani, poinciana, mango, lime and orange trees flowered in profusion. There were little fields full of pigs and hump-backed cows. Ox-drawn carts trundled down the road. Further on, the country opened out into great expanses of grass bordered by eucalyptus woods, the sky huge and spacious. At one point we had to cross a wooden bridge. We disembarked and watched our truck teetering along with an inch of wheel protruding either side.

After an hour or so we came across a small town with a river flowing through it which had flooded badly. This happens every year and they are prepared for it, with houses built on stilts, and bridges – two lengths of steel girder, one for each wheel –spanning the worst parts. Cowboys splashed down the street, up to their horses' bellies in water, hairy brown pigs paddled about at the edges and families sat on their verandahs watching, washing clothes from the front door, or chasing pigs from the living room into the water.

Robert would doubtless have been pleased to know that so little had changed. In his story, the railway engine symbolised the progress which he so deprecated, its dilapidated state a way of underlining his negative feelings about what it represented. This was a theme to which he would return time and again in his writing, one of the many paradoxes that characterised him, an ever-present tension in his world view. He was in so many ways a progressive, ahead of his time in so much of his social and political thought; yet in his writing about Paraguay, as with other parts of

South America, also Scotland and later North Africa, he found himself constantly lamenting vanished Arcadias and all they stood for.

With hopes for the Alto Paraná *yerbales* now extinguished, Robert made one final journey to investigate a further concession which had become available through Dr Stewart. This lay in the far north of the country, another hard trek, but one which gave him the opportunity to visit Cerro Corá and the natural amphitheatre in which López had finally been corralled and killed, three years previously.

The land here, at a place called Chiriguelo, seemed a good deal more promising. Since he had by now run out of money, Robert decided it was time to go home and submit his report to Holland Jacques in person. By early 1874 he was back in London.

Six

CRUZ ALTA

To the back of beyond

Financial salvation for the Graham family was not to be found in the *yerbales* of Paraguay. Robert's hopes for the Chiriguelo concession were dashed when Holland Jacques turned him down. The practical difficulties of cultivating and processing the mate in this ruined country were too great, Paraguayan politics were still deemed too unpredictable, and caution prevailed. Through the early months of 1874 Robert maintained contact with Dr Stewart in Asunción and pursued openings with other importers in London, but all to no avail.

Now what was he to do? He was only twenty-two. His life over the last three years had set him utterly apart from his contemporaries, even from his nearest and dearest, despite the intermittent flow of hieroglyphs to be deciphered by his mother. South America had lodged in his soul. Yet, for all the hard miles behind him, the maturity beyond his years, who was he? A trust-fund adventurer with a string of half-baked business ventures to his name? A serious, sensitive and physically courageous young man with a burgeoning sense of social justice? A high-spirited, curious, upper crust wanderer, happy to be blown around the world on the winds of fortune?

Something of all of these, no doubt. But more than anything he was still in the grip of that quest for identity that brings turbulence to the lives of so many in their twenties. Returning from my own South American trip, I well remember the sense that I had been to places and witnessed things for which no one else had any references. It was an intensely alienating feeling. Aged twenty-four, uncertain about my direction and purpose in life, torn between the pull of my conventional upbringing and the dreams of a creative career I had little idea of how to pursue, I was derailed for a time by anxiety and depression. A recurring concern was that I might have inherited whatever the destabilising condition was that afflicted my mother's brother, Robert Cunninghame Graham, later diagnosed as a form of bipolar disorder. Whether I was aware of Willy's affliction at that time, I'm not sure; but the mere suggestion of mental illness in the family seemed, in those moments of personal uncertainty, a potentially troubling legacy.

A couple of years younger, Robert was ahead of me. In some respects, he had already made the break. His family had by now almost given up trying to steer him into a more conventional career. But while the money was just about there for him to do whatever he was able to make a case for, it came with significant strings attached, and with no end to those in sight. Willy, his father, was only forty-nine and in good health, despite his mental incapacity. The estate would remain in administration and the *curator bonis* would hold the purse strings until he died. While his father remained alive, Robert would continue having to ask for every penny he needed. It was hard to thole for someone whose life experiences had already carried him well over the threshold of adulthood.

Robert's mother had made sure, while he was in South America, that he was regularly supplied with a wide range of reading matter. One figure whose ideas excited him was William Morris. With his passionate denunciation of the 'civilising' effects of industry and commerce, his rage against poverty and inequality, Morris was to become a key figure in Robert's literary and political awakening. For now, however, it was Morris's fascination with Iceland and the Norse sagas, with their themes of courage and stubborn resolve, that caught Robert's imagination. In the summer of 1874 he and Charlie made a short visit to Iceland. This trip doesn't feature in his later writing, apart from one short story, *Snaekoll's Saga* (*The Ipané*, 1899). Strange though it is, it's one of my personal favourites. It conjures Iceland's bleak, volcanic beauty as the setting for an epic journey with a darkly comic twist. It could only have been written by one who valued horses as highly as his fellow human beings.

Still at a loose end, Robert kept his mother company in London over the following months, attending plays, visiting galleries, and helping her host gatherings at her house in Ebury Street. She fretted about him, as did other members of the family. The much disliked uncle, William Hope VC, proposed sugar growing in the West Indies, or coffee planting in Ceylon. By December 1874, Robert had come close to caving in, going so far as to write to the *curator* seeking funds to travel to Ceylon. But for reasons unknown, that venture never materialised. In December 1973, following my return from South America, aimless and miserable, I was persuaded by my father to take up articles with a law firm in Edinburgh. That plan, equally, never reached fruition and I look back now with gratitude. It would not have gone well. It seems to me likely that Robert was similarly troubled in those winter months a century earlier.

The following summer, still without gainful occupation, he set off to meet Charlie in Gibraltar where he was now posted. He made his way slowly through Spain, justifying the trip to himself and perhaps to those at home, by pausing in libraries and out-of-the-way seminaries where dusty archives could be scoured for accounts of the Conquest or of the Jesuits in Paraguay. Arriving finally in Gibraltar, he spent time riding out with Charlie and his shipmates. One in particular, Robert took a liking to. George Mansel was three years older than Robert and hailed from a landed family in Dorset. Robert described him as dark and nervous, with round prominent eyes, a sparse moustache, a skin tanned by the sun to a dark brick red, and thick, brown hair cut short. Rough-tongued and irascible, he was also fearless and loyal. The attraction was mutual and immediate.

Mansel had booked passage on a trading ship sailing down the west coast of Africa, for a spell of leave. He persuaded his new friend to join him and they set off at once. The journey that followed provided Robert with the setting for his story *Bristol Fashion* (*The Ipané*, 1899), in which the *Wilberforce* plies the coast between Morocco and Angola, laden with rum and gin, gaspipe muskets long as a spear and painted red, brass dishes, musical boxes, trade powder, cheap German clocks and French indecent prints (as presents for the chiefs), beads, bells and looking glasses. These are to be traded for palm-oil, camwood, ivory, gum copal, kola nuts, bees wax, gold dust and ostrich feathers.

The story turns on the theft of a ship's boat by three native Krooboys (Pidgin English for crew) named Tom Coffee, Little Fish and Joe Brass, whom the sanctimonious and irascible English captain then pursues, tricks, and sells to a cannibal chief. Despite the irony of her name, there is no suggestion in the story that the *Wilberforce* is carrying slaves; but in choosing where to exact his revenge, the captain 'ran into a small river that he knew, from whence Brazilian slavers shipped their "rolls of tobacco".'

Robert made the journey in 1875. Although the Atlantic slave trade had been brought conclusively to an end five years previously by a combination of diplomacy and naval enforcement, he would still have been confronted in ports all down the West African coast by evidence of the trade in human life. As it is, he sets the story in the 1860s, when large numbers of Africans were still being traded illegally to Brazil, the last country to have banned the Atlantic trade, in 1831; and the last country in the Americas to ban the owing of slaves, in 1888. His sympathies, it's clear from the story, are not with the captain.

This journey also held another significant milestone for Robert. An early stop at the Moroccan port of Mogador offered him his first glimpse of North Africa, a part of the world which would come to mean almost as much to him in later life as South America had when he was a young man.

By the time they returned to Gibraltar, Robert and George Mansel had decided to go into partnership. They would try their hand at ranching in Argentina. George had been thinking of resigning his commission. Now he did so. Robert informed the family of his plans and in January 1876, two years after Robert had arrived back in Britain, they sailed from Lisbon for Buenos Aires. For once the voyage was calm and Robert was able to practise fencing on deck. For reading matter he had with him *The Rubaiyat of Omar Khayam*, also *The Canterbury Tales* which he read in its entirety while the ship lay quarantined for a week on arrival in the River Plate estuary.

To Robert's great delight, Buenos Aires was a town in which horses almost outnumbered humans; although a glimpse of things to come was there in the form of a brand new tram system, each car preceded by a mounted boy blowing a horn. Robert and George lodged near the centre of town at the Universal Hotel. Its owner, George Claraz, was a tall, scholarly Swiss who had opened his doors to guests in order to fund his research into the natural history of the region. Now Claraz's, as it was known, was the first port of call for frontiersmen, ranchers, travellers, engineers, prospectors and the like; up-country types in whose company Robert felt immediately more comfortable than that of the fashionably black-clad Porteños, the residents of this city whose steady influx of migrants from Southern Europe rendered it daily more cosmopolitan.

On arrival at Claraz's, guests would stride in with Basque porters carrying their saddles, take off their pistols and hang them on their bedposts, call loudly for drink, and stamp about in their long riding boots and spurs. All the rooms opened onto a single courtyard across which, once installed, guests conversed loudly with one another from the comfort of their beds. Sometimes, after a long evening at the bar, they would amuse themselves by shooting out the candles in the rooms opposite. The place reminded Robert of a kind of school, though one where there was much of interest to be learnt. With its rough-and-ready chaos, this eccentric establishment came to be his favourite of any hotel in the world.

Robert and George had heard of a property on the Sauce Chico river, in the vicinity of Bahia Blanca, some 500 miles south of Buenos Aires. Here they had it in mind to start their own ranch. Nearby was the embattled English colony on the Sauce Grande river, whose ranchers had been offered generous incentives to settle by the Argentine government, only to find themselves under sustained attack by dispossessed Indians, from which the government had done nothing to protect them. Claraz himself knew the region well and had led unsuccessful representations to the government on the settlers' behalf. After listening dutifully to his warning that the area was still extremely unsafe, the two young men set off in March 1876.

Islands in the ocean of grass that surrounded them, the scattered ranches they encountered were surrounded by deep ditches and sometimes armed with small brass cannons, as much for purposes of signalling to one another as for protection. The Indians mounted their malones, or raids, in daylight, Robert wrote in *José Antonio Paéz* (1929), his biography of the Venezuelan liberator.

> Once seen never forgotten. For hours before the Indians actually appeared, troops of wild horses or cattle, herds of deer and bands of ostriches preceded them, fleeing as before a prairie fire. Then in the distance arose a cloud of dust. As it came nearer, through it flashed the heads of the lances, twenty feet in length, the Indians carried. They usually rode bareback . . . yelling and striking their hands upon their mouths. This made their yells sharper and like the howling of a pack of wolves. Around their bodies smeared with ostrich grease they carried three or four pairs of bolas, known to the gauchos as Las Tres Marias. With these they hardly ever failed to entangle the hind legs of a horse or to break in a Christian's skull. They used to pass so rapidly it seemed like a dream. The looker-on who generally sheltered himself in a thicket of tall pampa grass, holding his horse whose head was muffled, hardly could believe that in a moment death had passed him by.

Robert and George met Scots cousins, Hay Edwards and John Walker, known respectively as Facón Grande and Facón Chico (the facón being the gaucho knife) on account of the weapons they carried. One long-haired and wild-looking, the other soberly dressed and meek, both were ferocious fighters and implacably committed to resisting the Indians. They were later to feature in Robert's sketch *Facón Grande* (*Mirages*, 1936). From the two Scots, Robert learned that the Indians had lately driven off vast numbers of cattle, in excess of a hundred thousand head, and had scorched the Pampa for miles around. There might be money to be made by rounding up strays for re-supply to the Sauce Grande ranchers. But Robert and George soon found themselves having to travel further and further to find any remnants of the herds, with little food and no shelter against the bitter Pampa nights of the southern winter. After two months they gave up and headed back to Buenos Aires.

Here the story surfaces again of Robert having killed a man, recounted by Aimé Tschiffely in his biography *Don Roberto*. It is connected with a version of events in which Robert and George take possession of the property at Sauce Chico, along with livestock of which they are shortly relieved in Indian raids; they themselves surviving only thanks to the stockade and ditch surrounding the house. Ruined by the raids, they abandon the property and on the way back to Buenos Aires, Robert and another man, who together have become separated from their fellow-travellers, are caught by Indians. Seeing how young their captives are, the Indians choose not to kill them or peel their feet to prevent escape, but to stake them out, spread-eagled overnight. Come dawn, with their guard asleep, Robert manages to get hold of his penknife and cut their rawhide bonds. Then, in scenes worthy of a Western, they throttle and lance the guard, untether two horses and flee, bareback, for the settlers' stockade at Mar del Plata, the war party in full pursuit.

Robert himself makes no reference in his letters or later writing to the incident, and what is recorded of this short spell in the south of the country with George Mansel mitigates against them having had time to settle at the Sauce Chico property. Tschiffely had no means, or perhaps no wish, to verify the stories told to him by a man in his eighties, and one whom he clearly held in the highest regard. But it is, at the very least, more evidence of the fact that Robert was mythogenic: a person around whom stories gathered.

A few weeks later, in June 1876, Robert wrote to his mother from Montevideo that another 'good thing' was in prospect. On the basis of past experience, this can hardly have gladdened her heart. She had other concerns, too. Her brother-in-law, the improvident Bobby Cunninghame Graham, had recently launched an action to have Jamieson removed and himself appointed as *curator bonis* of her husband's estate. Robert, as heir, had been advised to contest the action. Now he was about to vanish on yet another improbable mission.

The 'good thing' this time concerned horses. In Rio de Janeiro, where the ship had called on the voyage out, Robert had been impressed by the Brazilian cavalry and their fine mounts. Such horses were at a premium, he learned, costing up to eighty dollars apiece. He already knew that in Uruguay he could buy decent horses at a fraction of the price. Surely handsome profits awaited anyone who could drive a caballada north for sale. Had he paused to consider why no one else was doing precisely that, he might have spared himself many months of hardship. He would also have denied future readers the account of an extraordinary, if ultimately fruitless, journey.

In *Cruz Alta* (*Thirteen Stories*, 1900) Robert offers the longest and most complete account of any of his South American adventures. Although told in the first person by an anonymous narrator, this is clearly an account of actual events and the unnamed companion is clearly George Mansel.

With the 'good thing' beckoning, the two partners travelled to Durazno, a country town 120 miles north of Montevideo, where they planned to buy the horses. From there they would drive them to Rio de Janeiro, a journey of eight hundred miles. Lodging with an acquaintance, yet another of those hardy Scots who might be thought from Robert's reminiscences to have taken over the entire South American hinterland, they began to scour the locality for horses.

> Gauchos, Brazilians, negroes, troperos, cattle farmers, each man in the whole 'pago' had at least a horse to sell. Singly, driven, led, pulled unwillingly along in rawhide ropes, and sitting back like lapdogs walking in the park, the horses came. We bought them all after much bargaining, and then began to hunt about at farms, estancias, and potreros, and to enquire on every side where horses could be got.

At one point in the search they were invited to a 'ball'. For a description of life in the 'camp' (the countryside), there can be none better than what follows.

Fastening our horses to long twisted green-hide ropes we passed into the house. Carne con cuero (meat cooked with the hide) was roasting near the front door on a great fire of bones. Around it men sat drinking mate, smoking and talking, whilst tame ostriches peered into the fire and snapped up anything within their reach; dogs without hair, looking like pigs, ran to and fro, horses were tied to every post, fireflies darted about the trees; and above all, the notes, sung in a high falsetto voice of a most lamentable Paraguayan 'triste', quavered in the night air and set the dogs a-barking.

Under the straw thatched sheds whole cows and sheep were hung up, and every one, when he felt hungry, cut a collop off and cooked it in the embers, for in those days meat had no price, and if you came up hungry to a house a man would say: 'there is a lazo, and the cattle are feeding in a hollow half a league away.'

A harp, two cracked guitars, the strings repaired with strips of hide, and an accordion, comprised the band. The girls sat in rows upon rush-seated chairs, and on the walls were arranged either great bowls of grease in which wicks floated, or home-made candles fixed onto nails, which left them free to gutter on the dancers' heads. The men lounged at the door, booted and spurred, and now and then one walked up to the girls, selected one, and silently began to dance a Spanish valse, slowly and scarcely moving from the place, the hands stretched out in front, and the girl with her head upon his shoulder, eyes fast closed and looking like a person in a trance. And as they danced the musicians broke into a harsh, wild song, the dancers' spurs rattled and jingled on the floor, and through the unglazed and open windows a shrill fierce neigh floated into the room from the wild horses shut in the corral.

It may have been scenes just such as this that encouraged Robert to correspond with his mother from Durazno on the subject of writing. 'Decidedly it is reserved for me to be the Bret Harte of the South, but in Spanish or English?' he asked her. Bret Harte was an American journalist who had made his name as a writer of short stories about the miners and gamblers of the California Gold Rush of the 1850s. But it was to be many years yet before Robert would begin seriously to exploit a talent he was never, to the end, entirely confident he possessed.

Delayed by bureaucracy and bad weather, Robert and George finally left Durazno in late August with a troop of eighty horses. At once the horses proved to be jumpy and prone to taking flight at the slightest disturbance, requiring hours in the saddle, in rough country, to round them up again and corral them for the night into a bend in a river, if one happened to be nearby, with fires lit across its mouth. Many such rivers lay ahead of them and Robert soon found out that the horses were not only flighty but also reluctant swimmers.

> Rivers we passed, where the horses grouped together on a little beach of stones refused to face the stream. Then, sending out a yoke of oxen to swim first we pressed on them and made them plunge and kept dead silence, whilst a naked man on the other bank called to them and whistled in a minor key; for horses swimming, so the gauchos say, see nothing and head straight for a voice if it calls soothingly. And whilst they swam men in canoes lay down the stream to stop them drifting, and others swimming by their side, splashed water in their faces if they tried to turn. The sun beat on the water calling out the scent of flowers; kingfishers fluttered on the water's edge, herons stood motionless, great vultures circled overhead, and all went well till in the middle of the stream a favourite grey mare put up her head and snorted, beat the water with her feet and then sank slowly standing quite upright as she disappeared.

Crossing the border into Brazil, it seemed they had stepped back in time. In the Banda Oriental (Uruguay), men and women lived openly and freely, and gaucho hospitality prevailed, even among the many Brazilians who had settled there. Once in Brazil, men still wore swords, slaves trotted behind the horses of wealthy farmers, women never sat at table with the men and, when a visitor arrived, were sequestered as jealously 'as they had all been Turks'.

The weather was not kind. The drovers spent many nights taking turns to ride round the horses, muffled against the bitter cold, then sleep as best they could on damp ground until first light, when they would ride out again, praying for the warmth of the sunrise to come. Some of the hired men became mutinous and Robert was only spared the thrust of a knife by George's timely brandishing of a pistol, at which all the men departed. A number of Brazilians were hired in their stead. These men advised that food and lodging would be still harder to come by on the trail ahead. A bullock was bought and slaughtered. The meat was jerked and soaked in orange juice to make it less tough, then carried in bags made from the hide of the slaughtered beast. And the trail ran ever on.

So one day told another, and each night found us on horseback riding round the drove. Through forest, over baking plain, up mountain paths, through marshes, splashing to the saddle flaps, by lone 'fazendas' and again through herds of cattle dotting the plain for miles, we took our way. Little straw huts, each with a horse tied day and night before them, were our fairway marks . . . So on a day we crossed the hills, rode through a wood and came out on a plain, at the far end of which a little town appeared.

This was Cruz Alta. Robert made straight for the town's main store where a short conversation with the owner brought all their hopes crashing down. He learned that the country between Sao Paolo and Rio de Janeiro was dense forest which it would take a year to traverse, should the horses survive the change of climate, and any chance of profit would be lost. Further, Robert learned that between Cruz Alta and Sao Paolo, some five hundred miles distant, horses were worth little more than mules which were much in demand throughout Brazil. And finally, that once on the plains beyond Cruz Alta, what little pasture there was possessed poisonous properties that caused horses to sicken and die. The only cure was rock-salt, of which the store-owner naturally had the best and cheapest supply in the vicinity. At this fateful encounter, Robert recalls that he stood out like a blot of colour among the quietly attired Brazilians, dressed as he was for the trail in the fashion of the

Uruguayan gauchos, a hat tied under his chin with a black cord, a vicuña poncho and a pair of large resounding silver spurs.

The horses by now were thin and weak, their condition too poor either for sale or for further travelling. Robert and George found a farmer who rented them a *potrero*, a large fenced pasture where the whole caballada could be fed, watered and rested. Then they settled down to wait. Weeks went by, the daily routine enlivened by visits to the town for cakes and glasses of sweet Malaga; dances, cattle-markings and races; encounters with local characters such as the reputed Inglés who turned out to be an alcoholic Dutchman, sharing his forest dwelling with his wife and daughters, a family of pigs, a half-grown tapir and two screaming macaws; and a fast friendship with Luis, an elderly slave from Angola who, despite being sent by his master on errands into Uruguay where he could have remained, a free man, chose to return each time, a slave, to Brazil, to what was familiar and where people had been kind to him. And there was constant observation of the surrounding countryside, sights and sounds which imprinted themselves on Robert's memory.

The quiet sleepy place, the forests with their parrots and macaws, their herds of peccaries, their bands of screaming monkeys, the bright-striped tiger-cats, the armadillos, coatis, capibarás, and gorgeous flaming 'seibos', all intertwined by ropes of living cordage of lianas . . . still after twenty years is fresh, and stirs me.

By the end of January they had been three months in Cruz Alta and still had found no buyer for the horses, some of which had by now escaped while others had died of snakebite. They were on the point of abandoning the horses and leaving for Rio with only those mounts required for the journey, when a pawnbroker appeared and offered to buy the whole *caballada* for a combination of cash and silver saddlery. Flat broke and looking like Robinson Crusoe, Robert and George were nonetheless in good spirits. Keeping four of the best horses for themselves, they settled their debts, bade farewell to their new friends, including Luis who they presented with a silver-mounted whip, and saddled up.

Cruz Alta, a white patch shining against the grey-green plain encircled with its woods, was just in sight, the church tower standing like a needle in the clear air against the sky. Half a league more and it dropped out of view.

After the recent months of enforced idleness, the two companions were not ready to return directly to Buenos Aires. Instead they chose to make a five hundred mile detour via Asunción. Crossing the river Uruguay into the Argentine province of Corrientes, they rode through a great expanse of woods and grasslands and rivers, largely deserted except for scudding bands of ostriches. Ever-observant, Robert found his interest in botany excited by the profusion of flora to be found in the forest, the orchids, cacti, eucalypts and other 'flowers and plants to drive a thousand botanists to madness, that blossomed and died unnamed in the sub-topical undergrowth.'

Here among the abandoned missions of Corrientes, Robert's curiosity about the Jesuits was also re-ignited by the decaying cloisters and churches they encountered. His admiration too, as he describes how two centuries previously, this vast territory had been administered solely by a couple of hundred priests, in whose care lived peacefully a population of some two hundred thousand Indians; though only a few thousand of those now remained. Robert's ability to speak Guarani, almost unique among Europeans, gave him access to the stories handed down to these Indians through the generations; stories which told that, contrary to popular belief, their ancestors had been treated with kindness by the priests.

After a stop at the former Jesuit centre of Candelaria, now a sleepy gaucho town on the Argentine side of the Paraná, where they stayed at El Hotel Internacional, drank suspect wine, and felt themselves to be in Paris after the months on the trail, they crossed into Paraguay. Here they paused for a further day or two in the border town of Ytapua with an old acquaintance of Robert's, Enrico Clerici. An Italian who had served with Garibaldi, Clerici was a born fighter who kept a *pulperia* (a grocery store-cum-grog shop) where he dispersed rowdy customers by hurling empty bottles at them from behind the bar. Further along the way lay Dr Stewart's ranch, Potrero

San Antonio, where Robert had stayed on his mate-prospecting trip three years earlier. As he approached, memories returned of riding through the forest at night and in terror, with a pistol in his hand, heavy foliage brushing his hat, and thinking that at any moment a jaguar might leap out. Now the place was abandoned.

They moved on towards Asunción and came upon Paraguay's only railway line, which ran between a small town called Paraguari and the capital. Seven years on from the war the country was still in ruins, women still vastly outnumbered men, business was at a standstill and food scarce. Labouring and puffing through the woods, the furnace stoked by two women wearing nothing but cotton shifts, the train ran empty but for the odd bale of tobacco or sack of *yerba*; though to accommodate the country people who flocked to the capital in search of work, several extra trucks were always attached.

On them the people (mostly women) swarmed, seated like flies, upon the top and sides, dangling their legs outside like people sitting on a wharf, talking incessantly, all dressed in white, and everyone, down to the smallest children smoking large cigars. Six hours the passage took, if all went well, the distance being under 50 miles.

Arriving in Asunción they found the mail-boat delayed by low water. They passed a week at a hotel known as Casa Horrocks, 'the resort of all the waifs and strays storm-bound in Paraguay.' There in the capital they renewed the acquaintance of Dr Stewart and certain Brazilian officers Robert had come to know previously. Then they bade sad farewells to their horses and climbed aboard the steamer. They arrived in Buenos Aires in April 1877. A few weeks later, around the time of his twenty-fifth birthday, Robert was back in London.

Robert would return to South America, but not for many years. In the meantime, the echoes of these three great adventures would ring on, their impact on his life incalculable and unrepeatable. I understand. My own Latin American journey lasted nine months, a fraction of the length of his three trips combined. I undertook mine half a century ago, yet still hardly a month goes past when I don't relive some experience from it or turn to my journal.

In those short years, from the ages of eighteen to twenty-five, Robert had packed in more experience of life at the raw edge than his contemporaries would see in many lifetimes. South America had marked him indelibly, brought him to manhood, planted the seeds of political thought, opened his mind to the idea of a literary career, and above all, through his association with the gauchos, encouraged him to believe that he could live a life beholden to no other.

Furthermore, he had witnessed a society, several societies, on the cusp of modernity. He had glimpsed Arcadias that would soon be overtaken by commerce, mechanisation, enclosure and all the other manifestations of progress against which he would rail throughout his life to come.

Not that we minded that our fortunes were not made, he concluded in Cruz Alta, but vaguely felt that for the last five months we had lived a time which, in our lives, we should not see again, and fearing rather than looking forward to all the approaching change.

He had also begun to ruminate on another theme that would recur throughout his later writing:

Had but the venture turned out well, no doubt I had forgotten it, but to have worked for four long months driving the horses all the day through country quite unknown to me, sitting the most part of each night upon my horse on guard, or riding slowly round and round the herd, eating jerked beef, and sleeping, often wet, upon the ground, to lose my money, has fixed the whole adventure on my memory for life.

Failure alone is interesting.

It's certainly true that by the age of twenty-five Robert was no stranger to failure. But he was well into his forties by the time he came to write, and failure interested him then not, I believe, because he either glorified or aspired to or was ashamed by it, but because, with his endless curiosity about human nature, he found it more rewarding to write about what is flawed than what is perfect; and with his storyteller's instinct he recognised that in conflict and challenge, in the possibility that things will not end well, whether or not they actually do, lay the essence of every good tale.

He had many to tell.

Seven

PARIS

Gabrielle de la Balmondière

Robert arrived in London with every intention of returning to South America. Throughout the rest of 1877 he and George Mansel, who had remained in Argentina, corresponded enthusiastically about a plan to buy horses in the River Plate region and ship them to Europe. He had potential customers lined up, Robert told his friend, including a tram company and both the British and Turkish governments. He would sail again for Argentina in January 1878.

But it was not to be. He had come of age under Scots law on his twenty-fifth birthday, in May 1877, and now he must contest his Uncle Bobby's claim to take control of the family affairs. The continued wrangling may even have been what had brought him back from South America. In any event, no agreement was reached between the Bontines–Robert and his mother; and the Cunninghame Grahams – chiefly Bobby and the now elderly Laura, Robert's grandmother. So the *curator* kept hold of the reins. He now made the decision that Robert should be awarded an allowance of £250 per annum, later that year increased to £400. Little though it may sound, this was life-changing. For the first time Robert was independent. He no longer had to account for every penny he spent. The *curator* also approved two additional payments, one for the cost of a horse and stabling in the vicinity of Ebury Street, the other for Robert's membership of the Devonshire Club, bastion of the Liberal party. At last, it seemed, he was yielding to family pressure, not merely to settle down but to be groomed for a future in politics. At the Devonshire Club, where preferential membership was offered to sitting MPs, relatives such as the Marquis of Lansdowne would introduce him to other Liberal grandees and encourage him to follow his forebears into public life in the best Whig tradition.

That summer Robert spent first in London then in northwest Spain, joining Charlie at Vigo, in Galicia, where the Fleet was at anchor. From there he travelled inland to Simancas whose ancient castle housed the Spanish national archive with its records of the Conquest. In a letter home he noted that his time in Vigo had offered him a new perspective on the Conquistadors and their leaders, Pizarro and Cortez. It was not the hot-blooded and amusing Andalucians who had conquered and settled, he remarked, but the dour northerners from Galicia and neighbouring Extremadura who were much better suited to soldiering and colonising.

From Vigo he travelled to Paris where his mother had aristocratic connections and where, among other things, he competed in an international fencing competition at which he gained fourth place. Then came the autumn. On 24 October 1878, quite out of the blue, and without telling a soul, Robert married. On the marriage certificate, issued at the Registry Office in the Strand, London, his bride declared that she was Gabrielle Marie de la Balmondière, aged 19, the daughter of Francis de la Balmondière (deceased), merchant.

Thus began a deception that was to last the rest of their lives.

Sometime in the mid-1980s my mother called me in a state of excitement.

'I've discovered who Gabriela really was,' she told me.

Gabriela, the Hispanicised version of Gabrielle, and the name inscribed on the memorial plaque on the priory wall at Inchmahome, was the name by which we knew her in the family.

A few years earlier, on the death of my grandfather, Angus, who was Robert's nephew and heir, my mother had inherited the executorship of Robert's literary estate along with what remained of his papers – the bulk had already gone to the National Library of Scotland. Now she was under way with the research for her own book about Robert, *Gaucho Laird*, a project that would take her two decades to complete. One of the challenges facing her was how to tackle the story of Robert's wife, a woman around whom an air of mystery had always lingered, and about whom many questions had been raised but none satisfactorily answered.

Some of those who had written previously about Robert had treated the matter of Gabriela's identity with a note of genteel intrigue, one such being Alexander Maitland, whose portrait of the Cunninghame Graham's marriage, *Robert and Gabriela Cunninghame Graham*, had been published only a few years previously, in 1983. By 1987, when the film-maker Murray Grigor completed his script for a movie about Robert's life – sadly unrealised – the cat was out of the bag, but even then Murray trod delicately. The majority of biographers and other commentators, meanwhile, had appeared to accept at face value the story Gabriela herself told: that she had been born in Chile to a French father and Chilean mother; that she had become orphaned at a young age and sent to live with an aunt in Paris; that she had been educated there at a convent; and that she and Robert had met in the Bois de Boulogne – the moment at which, for most people, certainly those of her and Robert's generation, her life had to all intents and purposes begun.

At the time of my mother's call, my interest in Robert lay a couple of decades in the future. I congratulated her on her discovery and the conversation moved on. How I wish now that I had quizzed her about her investigations. By the time I had become sufficiently interested to enquire further, she had succumbed to dementia and it was too late. Nevertheless, I do know that the final clue, or perhaps the opening clue, had all along been close at hand. Angus, my grandfather, was born in 1893. Gabriela died in 1906 when he was thirteen. Given the closeness of the two brothers, Robert and Charlie, Angus would certainly have met his aunt, would have been familiar with stories about her, and would have heard his parents, Charlie and his wife Barbara, discussing her. But despite my mother's persistent questioning he steadfastly refused to reveal anything and it was my grandmother, Patricia, who relented in the end, though only after her husband's death. Even then she could not bring herself to utter the necessary words. She had written a name on a piece of paper which she now placed on my mother's dressing table.

I have since seen what I believe to be that piece of paper. In my grandmother's distinctive handwriting (she was an accomplished calligrapher), it is dated 1953 and has 'Gabriela', in capitals and underlined, at the top. Beneath is written: Dr & Mrs Horsfall of Masham, Bedale, Yorks. And below that: Mary Helen Horsfall. My mother has crossed out the 'Mary' and substituted 'Carrie', and placed a question mark over the 'Helen'.

Carrie Horsfall. So far so good.

But what was it that had caused my grandparents' lips to be sealed? What had deflected potential enquiry by previous biographers and other interested parties? Was it merely that Gabriela was not who she purported to be, or was there something else?

Until the time of my mother's discovery, few people outside the Horsfall family had shown any inclination to doubt the facts as stated on the marriage certificate, even though they were false in every particular.

Of events leading up to the wedding, the received wisdom – as recorded by both Robert's early biographers, Herbert Faulkner West and Aimé Tschiffely, and repeated with certain modifications by my mother – was that one day, aged nineteen, Gabriela had been walking in the Bois de Boulogne when a gentleman approached on horseback. Something made the animal shy, whereupon she lost her footing and fell to the ground. The gentleman, who was Robert, brought his horse under control, dismounted and went to her aid. Unaccountably, he spoke to her in Spanish. She replied in Spanish. And so the romance began.

Cut to 32 Ebury Street, where Missy now resided, a day or two after the wedding. Robert's formidable mother stands in stony silence as Robert introduces his new bride, an intense, elfin-looking young woman, her figure slight, her dark hair cut in a boyish bob, with a strangely unplaceable accent, part French, part Spanish, who resembles in no way the Scottish or English heiress Anne Elizabeth might have wished for him. With that silence settles a frost that was never completely to thaw. I sympathise with Robert. A century later, I had a not dissimilar experience with my mother and the Caroline, also known as Carrie, whom I later married, in a London flat not very far from Ebury Street.

For my mother, that name, Horsfall, most likely led her to the record of Gabriela's burial, with which she would have been familiar, and the officiating clergyman, a certain Reverend William Horsfall – Gabriela/Carrie's younger brother, as it was to transpire. From there her enquiries would have drawn her in due course to a pleasant, stone-built house in Masham, Yorkshire, and the noisy childhood of Caroline Horsfall and her twelve brothers and sisters.

Their father Henry Horsfall had studied medicine in Edinburgh and gone on to become a surgeon and the local medical officer in the Harrogate area, marrying Elizabeth Stansfield. Caroline Stansfield Horsfall, the second of their thirteen children, was born on January 22nd 1858. She was named after her Horsfall grandmother, Caroline Needham, about whom there was speculation that she may have been an illegitimate daughter of George IV. There was already one potential skeleton in the Horsfall family cupboard.

Photographs taken when she was a young woman show Carrie with cropped hair and direct gaze, a strong, straight nose and sensuous mouth. As a child she was by all accounts attractive, curious, intelligent and exceptionally high-spirited. From an early age she showed a natural flair for languages and performance, and a passion for the theatre, entertaining her siblings by putting on plays which she wrote herself; so absorbed that she was prone to forget the younger children and infants in whose charge she had been placed. For a while her adolescent passion was indulged, but once it began to show signs of becoming a professional aspiration, father Horsfall's hackles rose. The stage was an anathema and Carrie was forbidden the very thought of it, so Horsfall family history goes. But her father's prohibition merely encouraged her and aged sixteen, she ran away. It is hard to imagine what that must have required of a sheltered, provincial, teenage girl in the 1870s; the courage, the confidence, the idealism and the sheer bloody-minded determination not to be fettered. There are conflicting accounts of how long she was absent and how far she managed to get – some say all the way to London, others merely across the moors to Ripon. But her father soon caught wind of her whereabouts and hauled her home.

What happened next seems severe even by Victorian standards. For several months she was confined to her room under lock and key, forbidden to speak to her siblings, and only permitted outside to walk in the house's walled garden in the company of her mother. But towards the end of Carrie's incarceration, in March 1875, a baby was born, named Grace – which invites the question: might Carrie's confinement have been not only a literal but also a maternal one?

There is no proof of this in the Horsfall family records, but it seems not impossible that the little girl raised as Carrie's younger sister was in fact her daughter. Such a thing was not uncommon, and the hypothesis is borne out to some extent by subsequent events. It has even been suggested that the name Grace might have served as a kind of remedy for the *dis*-graceful circumstances of her birth.

Released eventually from house arrest, or perhaps having recovered from the birth, Carrie was dispatched to live with her grandmother in Ripon, who found her work as a governess: the older Caroline, with a potentially scandalous paternity, *in loco parentis* to her granddaughter, the younger Caroline, the scandalous runaway. In any event, the younger was not to be thwarted. With savings from her employment she took off to London again and theatreland where this time she is supposed to have made contact with a theatrical producer. This person, it has been suggested, was none other than the celebrated actor-manager Henry Irving.

When she then turned up on the doorstep of his private residence where he was given to holding auditions, his wife, aware of his predilection for young actresses, told Carrie in short order that the appointment had been cancelled. At this point, with the seventeen-year-old Carrie standing penniless in the street outside the producer's house, the trail goes cold. It only starts again in the Bois de Boulogne, some three years later, as she encounters Robert.

The story thus far is known and to some extent documented within the Horsfall family; though in the century between Carrie meeting Robert, and my mother making contact with the Horsfalls, they had done nothing to break the silence. Apart from Robert, and perhaps those in his immediate circle, no one else knew, or at least no one was admitting that they knew, the real story.

What was it about Carrie that was so scandalous that even my mother preferred to gloss over the details in her own book about Robert? The second time Carrie ran away, she was seventeen. When she and Robert married, in October 1878, she was a few months short of her twenty-first birthday, despite declaring on the marriage certificate that she was only nineteen. This raises two questions. Why did she run away – not once but twice? And what was she doing during the missing years between the ages of seventeen and twenty-one?

Firstly, why did she run away? Was she merely stagestruck? This has always seemed to me something of a cliché, a slim pretext for such a dramatic and courageous step, even in someone so spirited. Was there something else going on in Masham?

Both Grace and her daughter Martha would later offer possible clues. In 1919, after she had left home and married, Grace published a novel, *Benjy*, writing under the name of her Irish doctor husband, George Stevenson. The first half of the novel is the thinly disguised story of Carrie who, as the fictional heroine, Adelaide Ainsworth, makes it to London but dies tragically under the wheels of a brewer's dray before her dream of the stage can be realised. Adelaide, Grace wrote, 'had the consciousness of a gift; and with it she cherished the determination that Adelaide Ainsworth should not die unknown and unsung.' Her heroine has a 'fantastic aptitude for transferring herself into some favourite heroine of romance or history – Hélöise writing to Abelard, perhaps, or Lady Hamilton.' A fictional yet by all accounts accurate description of the imaginative powers of a woman whose identity in real life was a fiction.

The novel also portrays father Horsfall as a tyrannical figure – albeit one who mellows later in the story – and suggests that he may not only have locked Adelaide up but also beaten her after her first, failed attempt at escape. Dramatic license perhaps, but perhaps not. Martha, in a note written shortly before her death, describes her grandfather as having been particularly harsh with his older children, and suggests that, aware of the potential scandal of his own mother's paternity, he was determined that his own family should suffer no such stain. Speaking of her uncle, William, she goes so far as to say that her grandfather 'broke the boy's spirit' when he began to show leanings towards Anglo-Catholicism.

So Carrie's second escape, and perhaps even the first, may have derived as much from a desire to flee her father's tyranny as to join the stage. None of which is any less pertinent had Grace indeed been Carrie's child. Carrie would have conceived aged sixteen in late June 1874, in which case she might have had good reason to run away a couple of months later, only to be hauled home and confined for the remaining six months or so until Grace's birth; although how she might have conceived under such an authoritarian regime is hard to imagine.

None of this can be anything more than speculation. My cousin Robin points out that Grace was born at the established interval of roughly two years after her preceding sibling and two years before the succeeding one, suggesting that there was nothing out of the ordinary about the timing of her birth. But had Carrie indeed fallen pregnant, regardless of the circumstances, it would go further towards explaining the family's subsequent silence about the whole affair. Anne Taylor in *The People's Laird* suggests that in later life running away was what Carrie always did when the going got too tough, notably during their honeymoon when she would leave Robert ill and alone in San Antonio while she took off for a prolonged period to New Orleans. But with a little further guesswork as to the dynamics within the Horsfall family, one can perhaps be more forgiving of this response to difficult situations.

The second question is this: where had she been and what had she been doing during those three unaccounted-for years following the second time of absconding? How did an attractive and spirited seventeen-year-old girl make her way in the world with no support in the late 1870s?

My mother suggests that when she and Robert met she had been working as an actress with a small Parisian theatre company; Gabrielle de la Balmondière being her stage name. There is no evidence of this, although she did later, with Robert's help, stage a disastrous play in London. There is no evidence that they even met in Paris. There is, in fact, no evidence of anything. Assuming that she was in Paris, Carrie might have found employment as an English governess or tutor, or worked as a shop-girl, but from everything known about her adolescence it seems unlikely that she would have settled for anything so humdrum if there were alternatives.

Attractive, adventurous and sophisticated Carrie was in every respect a match for the charming, well-travelled, twenty-six-year-old Robert. She spoke French and Spanish fluently, albeit with an accent that confused people. She was intelligent and worldly and since fleeing Yorkshire had lived by her wits, as Robert himself had done during the South American years. For Robert, their meeting was a *coupe de foudre*. Yet while he felt strongly enough about her to want to marry her, he was worried enough by something not to tell his mother that he was going to do so. If not the theatre for survival, then had she found herself a patron? Or had she resorted to prostitution? For the great numbers of young women in this era who found themselves without support, for whatever reasons, prostitution was very often the only way to survive. Nevertheless, it seems more likely from what we know of her, her resourcefulness and sophistication, that she would have found herself a benefactor, on whatever terms. I hope for her sake that that was the case.

As Robert's writing would later reveal, he was always sympathetic to members of the oldest profession. Given that there is no reference to romance in his copious correspondence with his mother up to the time of his meeting Carrie, it is reasonable to suppose that he had acquainted himself with the brothels of South America and other places he visited, notably when ashore with Charlie in the various ports at which they had met. Frequent references in his South American stories and sketches to the *china* girls, as the country prostitutes were known, suggest that, at the very least, he observed them with interest; while his choice of certain *demi-mondaines* as the protagonists of other stories speaks for itself and perhaps reflects the fact that the prime years of Robert's life coincided directly with the *Belle Epoque*, the era of progressive social and cultural tastes, from the 1870s until the outbreak of the First World War, when among other things it was expected that men of a certain class would lead alternative lives outwith their marriages.

It is also probable that he was describing Gabriela in some of his stories, notably as Elise, the courtesan, in the companion stories, *Un Monsieur* and *Un Autre Monsieur*; also as the nameless 'cocotte' in *100 Degrees In the Shade* – an Englishwoman who likes furniture and plays the piano, dresses stylishly, speaks several languages and reads the same books as Gabriela.

So Robert meets Caroline Horsfall in Paris when his horse shies and she falls – or so he recounted in older age to both his early biographers, Herbert Faulkner West and Aimé Tschiffely. Next thing, they are married in London. She has an almost implausibly exotic name: Gabrielle, an angel, de la Balmondière, of a certain worldliness. A worldly angel. Had she, as my mother suggests, already created this identity when they met? Or did they cook it up together?

Back in Masham, things were not going well. Following Carrie's second escape, father Horsfall visited an Old Testament wrath on the entire family. The severe and protracted gloom that descended is said to have blighted the childhoods of many of Carrie's younger siblings who, according to Martha, were forbidden to mix with other young people or mention their sister's name, and only allowed out of the house to go to church. In a note dated 1954, a year before she died, another member of the family, one of Carrie's younger sisters, Madge (Margaret), wrote that mother Horsfall had taken to her bed for several months and remained an invalid for a full year following Carrie's second escape.

Following marriage to Robert, Carrie's ties with her family were not severed entirely, although her conversion to Catholicism may have placed added strain on those that remained intact. Disinherited by her father, she continued to write to her mother, to send gifts for the children, and occasionally to meet with them, presumably without the knowledge of her father. Robert was present at some of these meetings and he is reported to have been especially fond of Grace, remaining in touch with her until his death, and perhaps even providing her with details when she came to write *Benjy*. However, Grace's daughter relates that her mother visited Carrie in Hyères, in France, when she was in her early twenties, and there learned something that horrified her so much that she fled back to

Yorkshire. Was it that Carrie had shared details of the lost three years? Or was it that she had revealed to Grace that she was not her sister but her mother?

That will never be known. The one constant relationship Carrie maintained was with her younger brother William, the churchman with 'Anglo-Catholic leanings', whom Robert later summoned to Hendaye, on the French-Spanish border, where Carrie lay dying. William arrived a day too late, but accompanied her body back to Scotland and conducted the funeral service in the family mausoleum at Port of Menteith, prior to her burial on Inchmahome.

For my mother the trail in due course led to at least two members of the Horsfall family. One was Grace's only daughter, Martha Stevenson, who had written the note about her grandfather. Martha, like Carrie, converted to Catholicism. Horsfall family papers include a letter from her father, Dr Stevenson, beseeching her not to do so; an episode foreshadowed in *Benjy* where one of Adelaide's brothers also converts, to the great consternation of the rest of the family. The other Horsfall my mother contacted was Shirley Toulson, granddaughter of one of Carrie's younger sisters, Ethel – thus Carrie's great-niece. My mother and Shirley, a writer and authority on ancient drove roads, corresponded for some time.

Sadly, I have not seen this correspondence. In 2011 we moved my mother back to Scotland from Kent where she was suffering the onset of dementia. Her small Kent apartment was an Augean Stables of possessions and boxes full of papers and correspondence, some personal, some relating to Robert, and all salted through with old shopping lists, bank statements and telephone bills. My brother Simon and I flew down from Scotland on three separate weekends to meet up with our sister Arabella who lived nearby. We separated out what Cunninghame Graham material we could and later sent it to the National Library of Scotland; but perfection of the task was beyond us and for a certainty there was some material that ended up being thrown away. At that point, to my regret, I had still not fully engaged with Don Roberto. Had we tackled the clearance three or four years later I would have been a good deal more assiduous.

Nevertheless, Carrie was to come my way by other oddly seren-dipitous means. In 2018 I was contacted from Vancouver by some-one called Barbara Constantine who had come across a blog I had written about Robert and his wife. As the great-granddaughter of Carrie's younger sister Margaret or Madge, Barbara was Carrie's great-great-niece, my opposite number, she explained. As it happened I was scheduled to run a writing course in Seattle in the summer. We arranged to meet and in June of that year I spent a short time with her in Vancouver, where she shared with me her family research.

A couple of months later I chaired an event at the Edinburgh International Book Festival with two writers. One of them was Clare Clark, a London-based novelist and social historian. Her name rang a bell, although I couldn't figure out why. After the event I looked again through her back catalogue. In 2012 she had published a novel entitled *Beautiful Lies*. My conversation in Vancouver came back to me at once. Barbara Constantine had shown me a copy of the book, a fictionalised telling of the story of Gabriela and Robert and their marriage. Names and locations are changed, but certain events and details of their life together are faithfully recorded; and at the heart of the novel – as the title of the book suggests – are the mystery of Gabriela's identity, along with broader questions about the nature of truth. The fictional Gabriela is cast as an early photog-rapher. When I later met Clare in London I asked if she had known that one of Robert's Elphinstone Fleeming aunts, Clementina, later Lady Hawarden, had been a notable Victorian portrait photogra-pher. She had not.

In Vancouver, along with Clare Clark's book, Barbara Constantine had shown me a note written in the 1980s by her grandmother, Carrie's niece, Marjorie Douglas, the daughter of Madge. Marjorie was in her late eighties when she wrote this and I trust for my moth-er's sake that Martha and Shirley had a better grasp of what had gone on than Marjorie did. Nevertheless, it seems appropriate that a Horsfall voice should be heard here.

'Now we come to the lurid part of the family history,' writes Marjorie.

Carrie she wanted to be an actress! Mama must have had the vapours, even Papa who was quite broadminded put his foot down. [Marjorie is here referring to her grandparents.] While they were growing up Carrie and Willie wrote and staged plays which if Mama had understood them would've shaken her to her Victorian foundations. Tom and Willie brought home the original Gilbert and Sullivan scores which Mama thought 'a bit naughty' but tuneful. In the end Carrie ran away, aided and abetted by Willie I would imagine. Though he became a staid and highly respected clergyman Willie was a bit of a lad, but he kept in touch with Carrie for the rest of her life. How I don't know but Carrie wound up in Spain and got herself adopted by a wealthy couple who had lost their only child, a daughter, whom Carrie reminded them of, another shockwave Carrie changed her name to Maria and became a ROMAN CATHOLIC. If her name was not already erased from the family bible it would be then. Again I don't know how she met Don Roberto (Robert Bontine Cunninghame Graham umteenth earl of Menteith, a gloomy old castle in Scotland) but he too was a rebel who had fled to South America and become famous in his own right. I barely knew his name until I was married when I picked up a book in the library called Chifferley's ride . . . I still fail to see why all the cover-up . . . When mother was about 20 Carrie and Robert came to Masham, no doubt for a reconciliation, all the children which included mother hurriedly banished . . . what went on behind closed doors and drawn curtains has never been revealed but the RBCGs left and never came back, the book was closed. [After Carrie died] Robert stayed in Scotland gave up his wanderings and went into politics in a big way and became socialist member for Scotland, he was a true socialist and gave away all his money to worthy causes, he too is buried on the Isle of Menteith.

Why all the cover-up? asks Marjorie plaintively. For the Horsfall family, regardless of what Carrie had done during her lost three years, the fact of her running away to join the stage, let alone the possibility of anything else including a pregnancy, was sufficiently scandalous to merit a kind of *omertà*. In such a situation, it was easiest for a respectable middle-class Victorian family to close ranks. And as fragments of the story made their way down through the generations, they became increasingly garbled.

For Robert and Carrie, the reasons for the deception are less clear. Was it simply to render Carrie more acceptable to Missy? If so, in terms of the personal relationship that followed, this ploy was not a success. Even if the intention was to provide cover for whatever Carrie had been doing during the three lost years, the name and fictional back story were nothing if not theatrical. They could surely, had they wanted to, have come up with something more prosaic and less likely to arouse curiosity or even suspicion.

In the widely accepted version of the story, Missy is only made aware of the marriage once it is a *fait accompli*. But is it possible that she herself was in on the act? Missy was well aware of her aristocratic antecedents, which is not to say that she was a snob. Broadminded and highly cultured, the friend of writers and artists, she had a keen and wide-ranging intelligence, nurtured in adolescence by her scholarly and much-loved Uncle Mount. She would surely have weathered Robert's marriage to someone of lower social standing. But were she to have known of a darker, more shocking episode in Gabriela's past, she might, in those censorious days, and in light both of her deep affection for her son and concern for his political ambitions, have wanted to protect his reputation – and thereby her family's and her own. She would also have wanted to avoid the further complications that an unsuitable marriage would have brought to the already fierce wrangling over Robert's right to take over Gartmore during his father's lifetime.

Missy is known to have been friends with the daughter of London's then Assistant Metropolitan Police Commissioner, one Douglas Labalmondière. She might, with her considerable persuasive powers, have prevailed upon him to step in at the marriage – and to perjure himself in the process – as the guardian needed to provide consent since Gabriela, being under the age of twenty-one, was still a minor at the time; although, in fact, as a purported orphan she would have been exempted this condition. Or he might simply have lent her his name, or a version of it.

Rather a lot of *mights*. And here is another. The deduction on the marriage certificate of two years from her real age *might* have served conveniently to excise most of the missing three years from her history.

Once she has Gabriela and Robert married, my mother makes no further reference to Gabriela's past, although she does at least dispense with the horse-fall episode and simply has them catching one another's eyes in the Bois de Boulogne on successive days until at last a conversation takes place. The idea that a horseman of Robert's skill and experience might lose control of his mount is too preposterous.

Nevertheless, her contact with the Horsfall family must have left her asking many of the questions that I and others have continued to ask since she made public Gabriela's true identity – questions which will be addressed further in a later chapter.

My mother worshipped Robert and I believe it is fair to say that she viewed Gabriela through the singular perspective of that lens. Although she had every reason to be proud of her own detective work, she would never have written anything that might, in her consideration, be to Robert's detriment. And for someone as invested in a hero as she was in Robert, there is always personal risk attendant on any breaking of the spell. Thus, in my mother's story, Gabriela soon settles into the role of loving companion and dutiful wife until her early death aged only forty-eight, in 1906.

Eight

SAN ANTONIO

The Wild West

Tensions between Robert's new bride and her mother-in-law were apparent from the outset. Under Missy's haughty and disapproving gaze, Gabriela retreated into sullen silence. Replying to one of the Spanish aunts who had written from Gibraltar following a visit by the newlyweds that she found Gabriela *animada*, lively, Missy declared that that was the last quality she would have credited her with. Even Robert was forced to remonstrate: 'Do try and look Mother properly in the face.' Gabriela, for her part, would later refer in her diary to her 'dreadful' mother-in-law.

Missy was now fifty years old and a ship in full sail. It was more than a decade since Willy's removal from the scene. She had successfully fended off her in-laws' attempts to take control of the family affairs and was getting by on the £1,200 per annum allowed her by the *curator*. The Hon Mrs Bontine – she had been elevated to the rank and style of a baron's daughter when her brother became fourteenth Lord Elphinstone – now held court at 32 Ebury Street, visited by the writers, artists and musicians in whose company she felt most invigorated. A Whig to her marrow – lofty, curious, sceptical, outward-looking and humane – she kept one foot in an aristocratic past, another firmly in the here-and-now of arts, letters and politics. To her daughter-in-law she must have appeared terrifying; doubly so since the relationship was compromised by the deception – either colluded with or concealed, we will never know which – at its heart. She failed even to be charmed, as others were, by Gabriela's curious pronunciation of English: an accent that seemed to reside somewhere in the Pyrenees, neither wholly French nor wholly Spanish.

Robert responded by keeping his new wife as far from his formidable mother as possible. He had come to adulthood in South America and now his marriage could be seen as an act of defiance, a final cutting of the apron-strings. Yet it was far from the end of the relationship, and in any case he was still not free. As the *de facto* laird of Gartmore, he would ordinarily have taken his young bride back to his ancestral seat, but for legal and administrative reasons this was not permitted during his father's lifetime. Meanwhile, he remained dependent on the goodwill of the *curator* for his allowance of £400. His plans were now also subject to the scrutiny of a long-standing friend and adviser of his mother's, a London barrister named Robert Wright, whom Missy had enlisted in the oversight of Robert's future. As a newly married man aged twenty-six, Robert must have found this intolerable. Yet he and Missy continued to communicate – simply without any reference to Gabriela.

There now followed a period of what appeared to be exile. Whether Missy had a hand in it, insisting that Robert remove his unsuitable bride from general view, or whether it was the couple's choice to distance themselves from London, again – we shall never know. In any event, Robert and Gabriela began their honeymoon in Spain. Both were fluent Spanish speakers, both had an interest in the history and culture: Robert in the Conquistadors and in his personal heritage; Gabriela in Spanish literature, in which she was already well read, also in the more esoteric extremes of Catholicism. In February 1879, Robert wrote from Spain to say that Gabriela had fallen ill and he needed money to pay the doctor; early evidence of the delicate constitution which would hamper her throughout her life. Yet she could still prove herself remarkably tough when circumstances demanded it – as they shortly would.

With the encouragement of Wright and certain relatives, Robert was now busy preparing the case to the *curator* for a new enterprise. Fortunes were being won in Texas now that the railroad made it possible to transport longhorn cattle to the eastern and northern states, where they commanded good prices. And a 'good thing', yet again, was what Robert had his eye on. In April 1879, the funds granted, they sailed on an emigrant ship from Bremerhaven for New Orleans, from where Robert's first letter home arrived in May. Writing only in the first person, with no mention of Gabriela, he observed that in Louisiana 'long lank faces abound, feet are elevated (on chairs) high above the head and everyone chews. To speak to they are decidedly better than the Northern people . . .' He also noted that 'the British sabbath reigns here with all its accustomed horror and want of charity,' although for balance 'quite as much French is spoken here as English.'

From New Orleans, a stomach-churning crossing of the Gulf of Mexico in a flat-bottomed steamboat delivered them to Brownsville on the Mexican border, the most southerly town in the eastern United States. Here all seemed to go well at first. Robert wrote that he was planning to breed mules, which in these parts were still the preferred means of transport, being hardy and a good deal cheaper to feed than horses. He had found a small place with 'a good wooden house and a garden, which is a great thing' – a great thing because the unmentionable wife had green fingers and would later come to count gardening as one of her passions. But within weeks they realised that life on the frontier was too dangerous. Mexican bandits raided constantly across the Rio Grande, life was cheap and anyone who appeared to be worth anything was a target for thieves and murderers.

In June, accompanied by Jack, a stray fox terrier they had adopted and who was to become their faithful companion for many years, they left Brownsville for Corpus Christi, 160 miles up the coast. Along the trail brittle grass grew from sandy soil. Antelope and deer bounded off at their approach, quail and wild turkey whirred through the mesquite, and rattlesnakes and sidewinders were despatched by locals with the crack of a whip. As guide they had with them a *vacquero* who remarked, to Robert's delight, that he resembled a member of the Spanish royal family. When Jack and Gabriela tired, Robert flagged down the stagecoach so that they might travel in comfort while he led the horses on to the next stage.

Their plan now was to export horses back to England, but only once they had bought a hundred acres of uncleared land did they discover that the port at a drought-ridden Corpus Christi was too shallow for the embarkation of livestock. After six weeks they sold the land again, at no profit, and moved on once more, this time heading inland to San Antonio. The drought broke as they left, the rains turned the wagon trails to thick mud, and the 150-mile journey took seventeen days.

They were as relieved to have left Corpus Christi as they had been Brownsville which was later flattened by a hurricane, prompting Robert's wry observation that the pious had seen His hand in the destruction of this frontier nest of gamblers and murderers. Corpus Christi – where there were many churches 'all hating one another for the love of God, in the usual manner' – had likewise been unhealthy and dangerous to live in, he reported to his mother. The country was ugly and the people revolting and mean, the Mexicans being the only redeeming feature, and they were chiefly thieves and murderers. The heat was 'simply awful & the hardest to bear I ever experienced,' he wrote, while words were inadequate 'for the citizens about here . . . I don't believe in Italy, in the Middle Ages, there was so much assassination as there is in Texas today. Every day there is one or two; such a thing as a fair fight is unknown and if you enquire how so-'n-so was killed, "I guess, Sir, they waited for him in the chaparral and shot him in the back, Sir."' It was Robert's misfortune to have arrived on the American frontier at the height of the gunslinging era.

In San Antonio – where the Battle of the Alamo was still well within living memory, the ruined mission bearing witness in the city centre – Spanish colonial history collided with progress in the form of an express train to Houston, mule-drawn streetcars, gas lighting and gold plated spittoons at the Menger Hotel. Said to be the finest hotel west of the Mississippi, this was where Robert went in search of connections and opportunities. It was also where he encountered an Anglo-Saxon distaste for all things Hispanic, including the language and its principal class of speakers, the recently dispossessed Mexicans; who, in turn, made no effort to conceal their distaste for the local Indians. This hierarchy of contempt stirred Robert's indignation even more than the lawlessness and mindless violence of Brownsville and Corpus Christi. It would surface in his later writing.

Nevertheless, there was much in San Antonio to entertain them. The Mexican citizenry dressed flamboyantly in tight velveteen trousers decorated with rows of buttons and enormously heavy sombreros adorned with gold or silver braid. In the market bird-trappers, hay-dealers and fruit-growers cried their wares in Spanish. This was 'by far the most picturesque place in Texas, and in the time of the Mexicans must have been wonderfully quaint. It is intersected in all directions by the river, and by little irrigation canals, like in Spain.' Mindful of the authorities to whom he answered, he asked his mother to 'tell Mr Wright, who I know loves guns, that I use exclusively the 12-shooting Winchester, and find it a very good weapon: no one in Texas stirs without his rifle. I saw a Mexican Methodist preacher the other day. He was on "pingo", of course, black clothes, white tie, Mexican hat, and a bulge at his back indicated that he had either a bible or a pistol there!'

In London, Mr Wright had other things than rifles on his mind. Robert's money-making schemes seemed to be leading nowhere. He needed a career. With Texas booming, foreigners flocking to settle there, could he not be found a diplomatic post of some kind – as Vice Consul or Queen's Messenger (a diplomatic courier), perhaps? Yes, he was perfectly qualified, Robert replied mischievously. He could speak French and German (badly) and had no political or religious convictions that could not be altered promptly. But in truth he was underwhelmed by the prospect of such – or perhaps any – employment, and he was restless. It was a return to Spanish America that he really hankered after; that, and the excitement of the trail, his panacea for all difficulties and disappointments.

In January 1880 they learned of a mule-drawn wagon train carrying cotton that would shortly be leaving San Antonio on a six hundred mile journey to the central Mexican city of San Luis de Potosi. Robert jumped at the opportunity for more adventure. Gabriela appears to have shared his enthusiasm. She wrote to Malise describing their departure:

The excitement is unbounded as we leave . . . the mule boy, a sort of savage, brown and ragged, his hair coming through the crown of a silver embroidered hat, and iron spurs on his dilapidated boots, which have evidently belonged to some bigger man than himself, drives the spare mules furiously hither and thither.

Leaving San Antonio they soon emerged into flat, brush-covered plains where 'the mules, of which many are half-broken, and some in harness for the first time, now steady down into a soberer pace, although one of them kicks himself free and escapes into the chaparral.' She would keep a journal, she promised her brother-in-law. True to her word, her account of this journey was published as *The Waggon Train* (*The Christ of Toro*, 1908), two years after her death.

The journey was as arduous as anything Hollywood would later devise. Once across the Rio Grande, in the lawless and empty wastes of northern Mexico, Apaches and others of the desert tribes raided homesteads and murdered settlers, while travellers were as likely to be robbed and killed by Indians as by bandits. 'Upon arriving at Juarez,' Gabriela wrote,

we found that the savage Mescalero Apaches had on the previous night murdered a family in the neighbourhood and burnt their hut. The mother was pierced through by a lance; and a boy, a rickety-looking little fellow about two years old, was found among the bushes, where he had crept for safety. His brothers and sisters to the number of ten were all killed.

As the trail traced the long spine of the country, the landscape alternated between desert, scrub and mountain. Each night the wagons were circled and laced together with rawhide tethers. Once the mules had been fed at portable mangers, laid out around the inside of the circle, the fire would be lit and the company would dine on stewed beans, fried bacon and maize bread baked in skillets. Coffee, and a toddy if the winter wind was stiff, accompanied a last cigarette around the fire. Then all rolled themselves in blankets and slept – some by the fire, some under the wagons, some among the cotton bales. Robert and Gabriela, with Jack between them for warmth, preferred the fire; though sleep did not come easily since they believed there to be as much danger from within their company as from beyond it.

In Monterey things came to a head and they quit the caravan following an altercation with the *capataz*, the wagon-master. In one version of the story Robert discovers that the *capataz* had been planning to kill them and steal their possessions, although Gabriela makes no mention of this in her account. In another story, told many years later by Robert to his first biographer, Herbert Faulkner West, he is woken by a nocturnal disturbance and creeps naked into the scrub to investigate, rifle in hand. He sees nothing in the darkness, but next morning finds the signs of an Indian's presence a few feet from where he had lain looking. For her part, Gabriela merely refers to the incident as a false alarm. In any event, Robert wrote to his mother:

> Since leaving [San Antonio] I have not slept in a bed, nor, in fact, much at all . . . I carry a revolver, a Winchester carbine of 12 shots, a sword and a knife, and I am not safe for a minute, and have to sleep with my horse tied at my head . . .

– news she must have been less than delighted to receive.

From Monterey they continued for several weeks with another southbound convoy. Finally reaching the small town of Tula, they stabled their horses and took a train to Mexico City, fifty miles down the line. The journey of some eight hundred miles had taken them fifty-eight days and had thrown Robert and Gabriela together in ways they would never otherwise have experienced. They were entirely free of Robert's family and all the baggage of the past. On the trail no one knew them. And for all the dangers and discomforts, the exhilaration of riding together through an open and often spectacular landscape must have been immense.

In Mexico City, Robert was at once in his element. Almost the first thing he had seen on arrival was a plaque marking the place where the conquistador, Pedro de Alvaredo, had used his lance to vault a canal and escape his Aztec pursuers. Now, while Gabriela strolled the city and sketched churches and abandoned Jesuit missions, Robert visited libraries and archives to further his research into the

Conquest. He found a fashionable fencing academy where he could keep his hand in, and was awarded a master's diploma, in the name of Robert Bontini, by its director, one Louis Cavantous. He was also able to catch up with the mail from home. In his chatty replies he comments on international affairs, referring to both 'the Afghan affair' (the second Anglo-Afghan War), and 'the curious turn things seem to be taking in Egypt' (the incipient Anglo-Egyptian War). He wonders how Sarah Bernhardt will be received when she makes her American debut. To the news that Charlie has been appointed to the Royal Yacht he suggests that 'The Yacht will bring him into contact with the pestilential caste of swells again – a class decidedly below the average intellectually, and resembling waxworks corporally, and therefore damaging to the artistic sense.' Throughout his life he would tease his brother about his royal connections – Charlie had befriended Prince Louis of Battenberg when they were both midshipmen and, being a first-class shot, now received invitations to shoot at Sandringham – just as another correspondent, his mother's great friend, Blanche Fane, now teased him about his ancestry and radical views: 'I still wait for the day when you take your seat as Earl of Menteith in the House of Lords, as a prop of church and state!'

Prompted perhaps by Gabriela, he also put pen to paper, but without success. 'I have tried two or three times to make a magazine article of the Mexican journey,' he wrote to Missy, 'but find I have no talent whatever in that line . . . I think I have no literary ability whatever.' Even once he was published and critically acclaimed, Robert would continue to doubt his ability and remain evasive about his motivation for writing; though the compulsion to recapture those intense travelling experiences is one I understand well. Once in Mexico City, in yet another unwitting echo, I also took time to write up highlights of our eight-month journey from Buenos Aires. I was more confident than Robert and the months of diligent journal-keeping paid off. The *News*, Mexico City's English-language newspaper, commissioned a series of three articles, my first foray into journalism. One described our crossing of the Salar de Uyuni in Bolivia; one the journey by road out of the Andes to the Peruvian jungle town of Pucallpa; and one the six hundred mile voyage from Pucallpa, down the Ucuyali River to Iquitos on the Amazon. Later, back in Scotland, I wrote a longer piece about our voyage to the Galapagos Islands which was published in *Blackwoods Magazine*, the Edinburgh literary periodical founded in 1817, to which Robert had certainly subscribed if he did not actually contribute.

Robert may have lacked confidence as a writer, but he could no more help himself storing up experiences than he could hold them back when they later burst from him in a torrent of sketches and tales. The Mexican journey, ultimately, did not feature prominently among them, but it gave rise to two stories that offered stark reflections on fate, injustice and man's inhumanity to man.

Un Pelado (*The Ipané*, 1899) describes in matter-of-fact terms the hanging for murder of a dirt-poor Mexican in the Texan border town of Encinal (*pelado* literally meaning 'peeled'; so penniless). Based on a newspaper account of actual events, the story blends the journalist's report with Robert's description of the place and people. At the end the condemned man acknowledges his guilt and accepts his fate with courage, but a Texan onlooker observes that he was no better than an animal: 'Like killing a goat, he didn't have sense enough to be afraid.'

A Hegira (*Thirteen Stories*, 1900), tackles a similar theme but at greater length and is widely considered to be one of the most powerful and polemical stories Robert ever wrote (the title word *hegira* deriving from the Arabic for an exodus, or journey of flight). While in Mexico City, he and Gabriela visited the castle of Chapultepec where they came across

a small courtyard in which, ironed and guarded, a band of Indians of the Apache tribe were kept confined. Six warriors, a woman and a boy, captured close to Chihuahua, and sent to Mexico, the Lord knows why; for generally an Apache captured was shot at once, following the frontier rule which, without difference of race was held on both sides of the Rio Grande, that a good Indian must needs be dead. Malnourished, heavily shackled and wearing only breech-clouts, the captives stare unseeingly yet seeing everything, as fierce as the tigers in a nearby cage. I asked the nearest if he was a Mescalero and received the answer 'Mescalero-hay' and for a moment a gleam shone through their eyes, but vanished instantly as when the light dies out of the wire in an electric lamp.

A few days later, having made the decision to leave Mexico City and return to Texas, Robert and Gabriela are riding north with a mule train when they receive word that – against all the odds – the Mescalero have murdered two guards and escaped from the fortress. Robert imagines their trails running in parallel as the Indians, accompanied by a small white dog, also head north, making for their mountain territory, six or seven hundred miles distant; 'trotting like wolves all through the night . . . sleeping by day in holes, killing a sheep or a goat when chance occurred and following one another silent and stoical in their tramp towards the north.'

Approaching San Luis de Potosi, the former silver mining city with its immense plazas, churches and bells, its groves of pepper trees and gurgling water in stucco channels, they come across the Mescaleros' tracks and soon meet a band of vigilantes whose leader has the heads of two of the Indians hanging from the pommel of his saddle. Two more of los bravos have meanwhile stolen a horse and made off. The next day a second gallant band approaches. They report that they have killed another and hung his body by the feet from a tree at the next crossroads. 'We came upon him sitting on a stone, too tired to move, called on him to surrender, but Indians have no sense, so he came at us, tired as he was, and we, being valiant, fired, and he fell dead.' The dead man is half-starved and so emaciated that almost no blood has run from his bullet wounds.

As the Santa Rosa mountains come into view, signalling the start of Apache territory, they hear that a shepherd has sighted the remaining three fugitives, the man, the boy and the woman, who comes last, carrying the little dog in her arms. Robert imagines them in the mountains, finally safe in their own country. But it is not to be. They hear distant shots and a little later arrive at a smallholding whose Texan owner describes how he and his 'vaquerys' had come across the Indians and opened fire.

At the first fire [I] tumbled the buck; he fell right in his tracks and jest as I was taking off his scalp, I'm doggoned if the squaw and the young devil didn't come at us just like grizzly bars. Wal, yes, killed 'em, o' course, and anyhow the young'un would've growed up; but the squaw I'm sort of sorry about. I never could bear to kill a squaw, though I've often seen it done.

Robert and Gabriela take their leave to the howls of the small white dog, squatting dejectedly on the grave, freshly dug beneath a palm tree.

The story is sad beyond words, made more so by the unsentimental manner of the telling and by its many ironies: the terror the pathetic little band of fugitives inspire wherever they pass, the pride taken in the killing of exhausted, unarmed Indians by armed and mounted Mexicans, the scalping of an Indian by a European.

With the couple back in Texas, there are differing accounts of what happened next. Picking my way through them during the pandemic of 2020/21, without access to the papers and correspondence held in the National Library of Scotland and the Scottish Records Office, proved to be one of the major challenges in writing this book.

At one end of the spectrum sits my mother with the romantic, semi-fictionalised, family-focused, largely unreferenced version of events described in *Gaucho Laird*. At the other is the academic, Anne Taylor, with her meticulously researched and referenced *The People's Laird*. In between are the two early biographers, Herbert Faulkner West (*Cunninghame Graham: his life & work*) and Aimé Tschiffely (*Don Roberto*), whose accounts were at least partly handed down in tablets of stone by the grand old man himself; Alicia Jurado, a member of the Argentine Academy of Letters, biographer and friend of Jorge Luís Borges, who was awarded a Fulbright Scholarship to write her *El escocés errante* (The Roving Scot); and Cedric Watts and Laurence Davies, whose *Cunninghame Graham: a critical biography*, like Alexander Maitland's portrait of the marriage, *Robert and Gabriela Cunninghame Graham*, offer more critical analysis but still, through no fault of their own, predate my mother's uncovering of Gabriela's identity, albeit by only a few years.

There is general agreement that Robert and Gabriela were back in San Antonio by May 1880. On their round trip to Mexico City they had travelled one thousand five hundred miles, mostly on horseback, and spent more than a hundred days on the trail. They had so far made no money and were running up debt. Robert may then have taken some employment over the summer months, schooling horses and interpreting for European hunting parties with Mexican guides. He also continued to look for ranching opportunities and to pursue the possibility of a diplomatic post. Tschiffely claims that during this period he bought a share in a ranch owned by a Mexican-Greek, a week's hard riding from San Antonio; and that while the two partners were absent one day, an Apache raiding party burnt the place down and drove off all the livestock. But as with other anecdotes related by the septuagenarian Robert to the young Tschiffely, this features in none of the contemporary correspondence, and scarcely fits the known timescale of events.

Correspondence does confirm that the previous year, 1879, Robert had been in touch with George Mansel and had confided in him how much he disliked Texas. Mansel was in Argentina, helping run an estancia not far from Gualeguaychú. Now, in the summer of 1880, he wrote to Robert in San Antonio with the prospect of a new ranching venture. The temptation proved irresistible and by August Robert was back in Buenos Aires – alone.

In my mother's account, Robert and Gabriela had honeymooned in Dorset before leaving for Spain. Here they had stayed with Robert's old partner, George Mansel, at his ancient family home, Puncknowle Manor. They had also visited Chideock, a pretty coastal village in the lee of Golden Cap, the highest point on the South Coast of England; a visit that was sufficiently memorable – for reasons at which one can only guess – that 'Chid', short for Chideock, henceforth became Robert's pet name for Gabriela. (By mutation, hers for him became 'Lob'.) She herself adopted Chideock as a middle name, even signing her will Gabriela Chideock Cunninghame Graham.

Thus, according to my mother, when Robert, recently arrived in Buenos Aires, writes to Gabriela in San Antonio, he addresses her as My dear Chidling'. The letter goes on:

I have long promised to write to you but have been so much occupied I have never done so yet. This is a charming part of the country, splendid open plains for miles; all over long Pampa grass and absolutely covered with horses and cattle; in the distance there are a range of low hills . . . The house is built around the patio in the oval Spanish style and the courtyard is planted with orange and lemon trees . . . I wonder how you can still stay on among those odious Yankees in Texas when down here is so much nicer and we might have such horse and ostrich hunts and also deer hunts together. If you can come just drop me a line to say by what steamer you are coming and I will meet you . . . with a tropilla of horses and we will gallop out. Affec yrs Roberto el Gaucho. PS mind and bring Jack with you.

The reply came by telegram: 'Prefer stay Texas. Come back soon. Chid.'

With this terse communiqué ringing in his ears, Robert was back in San Antonio within a month. Here my mother has the couple joyfully reunited and Gabriela tending to Robert, who is in severe pain from inflammation of the kidneys, the result of a kick by a horse in Argentina. Under doctor's orders, he recuperates in San Antonio throughout the autumn. He reads Morley's life of Voltaire and T.H. Huxley's life of Hume, noting how 'so few people have been struck by the idea that Huxley sets forth in Hume's life that every argument for the immortality of the soul holds equally good for dogs and pingo souls, also shrubs . . .' He writes amusingly to Wright to thank him for copies of the *Spectator* which in the past have been regularly stolen from the Post Office, only then to be quoted in the local paper, the *San Antonio Democrat*. 'On visiting the editor, who was seated in a small bullet-proof room with a Winchester rifle and a sling-shot on the table before him, he at once owned up to the fact of them being mine – the Spectators – from which he had quoted!' Robert also writes reassuringly to his mother who has become increasingly worried about him: 'I am alright now, the visitation was partly of God and partly of pingo, owing to the former directing pingo's near hind foot on me when thrown down. It is still awfully hot here though the nights are getting cooler.'

Once Robert has recovered sufficiently to venture out, my mother continues, he takes Gabriela to a circus where they first see Colonel,

1. Robert's father, Cornet William Bontine, as a young officer in the
Scots Greys. While stationed in Ireland in the 1840s he suffered the
blow to the head that would bring years of financial anxiety and legal
wrangling to blight the life and prospects of his eldest son, Robert.

2. Robert, aged six, with his mother, born Anne Elizabeth Elphinstone Fleeming and known
as 'Missy'. She was cosmopolitan and cultivated and a powerful influence in Robert's life.
They corresponded copiously and remained close until her death in 1925, aged ninety-six.

3. Gartmore's grand south-east facing aspect. The Graham family seat for 300 years, it was to Gartmore that the Bontines moved when Robert was not yet eleven. Surrounded by boggy farmlands, deep woods and brackeny slopes, it would be an anchor point to him for the next forty years.

4. The interior of Gartmore where, amid the bustle of family life, Willy's growing mental illness remained mostly unacknowledged until in 1866 he rushed at his wife with a sword and was removed to a rented house in Dumfriesshire. There he remained until his death in 1883.

5. Robert was initially sent to Harrow School when he was thirteen, in 1865, but within two years the family finances had deteriorated and so he was removed and tutored in North London. He later wrote that he disliked the snobbery of Harrow, disparaging his fellow pupils as 'sprigs of the nobility'.

Bob as he will appear when ready for the Road

6. 'Bob as he will appear when ready for the Road.' Robert's step-grandfather, Admiral Katon, drew this sketch shortly before Robert's eighteenth birthday, as he left for Argentina. He would spend six of the next eight years in South America, pursuing an elusive fortune. The continent would mark him for life.

7. Robert reclines in full gaucho costume in this photograph taken on return from his first expedition (1870–1872): poncho, *chiripa* (a length of cloth wrapped around the waist to form baggy trousers), boots and spurs. In his left hand he holds a *rebenque,* the gaucho rawhide whip.

8. On his second trip to South America (1872–1874), Robert's plan to grow *yerba mate (ilex paraguarensis)* took him to Paraguay. From a project pairing artists and writers to interpret randomly selected words, this artwork was created by the artist Susie Leiper and the author, in response to the word 'Mate'.

9. Robert married Gabrielle de la Balmondière in 1878. Known in the family as Gabriela, she was in fact Caroline (Carrie) Horsfall, daughter of a Yorkshire medical officer. Her true identity and extraordinary story only emerged when the author's mother was researching her own book on Robert, *Gaucho Laird*.

10. The wagon train in which the newlyweds spent part of their honeymoon. The five-month, 1700-mile round-trip from San Antonio to Mexico City was extremely perilous. In *The Waggon Train*, Gabriela later described how each night they slept by the fire with weapons to hand, encircled by the wagons.

11. Robert mercilessly teased his younger brother Charlie, seen here in naval uniform, for his grand connections. As a naval cadet Charlie had befriended Prince Louis of Battenberg. Invitations to shoot at Sandringham ensued and later, Edward VII became godfather to his son Angus, the author's grandfather.

12. Malise, the youngest of the three brothers, was a gifted musician and, briefly, a much-loved curate at the church of St John the Baptist in Winchester where he had been educated. Known in the family as 'Mallie', he died of tuberculosis aged only twenty-five, in 1885.

13. Painted by Percy Jacomb-Hood in the late 1880s, Gabriela appears pale and ethereal, the crucifix a nod both to her own Roman Catholicism and to her growing interest in the Spanish mystic, Saint Teresa of Avila, whose biography she would publish in 1894, beating her husband into print by a year.

14. 'Advent of the new man . . . Outward aspect: something between Grosvenor Gallery aesthete and waiter in Swiss café. Person of 'cultchaw', evidently, from tips of taper fingers to loftiest curl of billowy hair.' Thus *Vanity Fair* described Robert in 1887. Here the new MP for North-West Lanarkshire is caricatured by Spy.

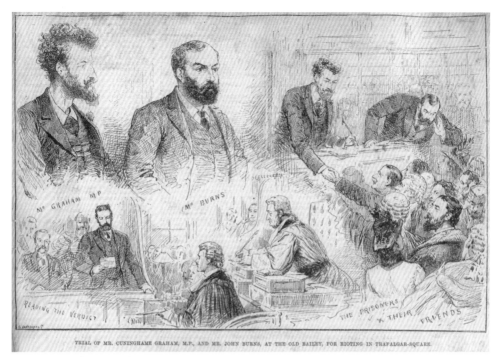

TRIAL OF MR. CUNINGHAME GRAHAM, M.P., AND MR. JOHN BURNS, AT THE OLD BAILEY, FOR RIOTING IN TRAFALGAR-SQUARE.

15. The trial of Robert and John Burns in January 1888, following their arrest in Trafalgar Square on 'Bloody Sunday' for protesting in defence of freedom of speech. Convicted of unlawful assembly, they were gaoled for six weeks which they spent picking okum in solitary confinement in Pentonville prison.

MR ROBERT BONTINE CUNNINGHAME CUNNINGHAME GRAHAM, M.P.

16. The convict. Having endured his time in Pentonville with a head injury inflicted by a police truncheon and a bladder infection resulting from a kick to the stomach, Robert was sketched by the popular satirist and caricaturist 'Tom Merry' in unruffled pose, even down to the artfully upturned cuff.

later 'Buffalo Bill', Cody. He also travels through Texas and neighbouring states in the footsteps of the conquistador Hernando de Soto, whose biography he would later write. And in a letter unusually revealing of her own vulnerability – even to the point of self-pity – Missy sends him the sad news that his grandmother Catalina has died. 'I thought my memory was full of sadness and terrible recollections, but it would seem there is always room in the human heart for another bitter drop, as long as it can feel . . . Poor old Khāt sends you his kindest love. It is very mournful to see him in so much grief.'

Robert then succumbs to a severe attack of malaria and has to be once more attended by doctors. But Gabriela is on hand to see him through the physical crisis and reassure him that they will survive the financial crisis now looming: Robert still has no job, the hoped-for diplomatic post having failed to materialise, and their debts are mounting. By December, Texas is experiencing unusually harsh winter weather, with blizzards in the Panhandle and cattle dying in scores. The couple spend a most un-Texan white Christmas with a German family named Vögel at Helotes, outside San Antonio. On their return they are overjoyed to learn that Charlie is coming out to visit them. He arrives in February and stays until April. He and Robert, once more recovered, make an expedition into the Texan back country, in the course of which they come across Cody again and fall in with his buffalo-hunting party for a few days. They also happen on a lone horseman whom Robert instantly recognises as Pancho Pajaro, the young man who had accidentally killed his own brother during a nocturnal raid with the Argentine revolutionaries, a decade before. Unable to lay the past to rest, Pajaro has wandered the length of the Americas and is now at last returning to his native Uruguay where his family, by coincidence another branch of the immigrant Vögels, have settled. Finally, in the only acknowledgment she makes that anything might have been amiss, my mother has Charlie enquire into the state of his brother's marriage. He concludes that all is well and that he will return to London to convince Missy that his brother has made a good and lasting match. Before leaving, he writes home that his visit has 'livened Bob up a good deal, as he is dead tired of the place.'

Anne Taylor has a different version of events. Firstly, she places the visit to the Mansels and the Chideock incident at a later date, once the couple have returned to England, and has Robert write to Gabriela from Buenos Aires with the more formal salutation: 'My dear Caroline'. She goes on to wonder at the general tone of the letter, at once oddly stiff yet cajoling. Had they had a row before he left; and if so, had he left because of it, or was his leaving the cause of it? Whatever the answer, according to Anne Taylor Gabriela then takes off to New Orleans, possibly even before Robert has returned from Argentina, where she stays until Charlie comes to dig her out, eight months later. Meanwhile Robert, having returned to San Antonio, remains there alone, ill and depressed, unable to find work, in a country he doesn't like, mourning his grandmother and fearful that he may have lost his wife. In January he writes to his mother that he is thinking of going to Havana to escape both the cold of the Texan winter and the malaria from which he has been suffering; then shortly writes to Wright saying he has abandoned the Cuban plan on account of the expense. Missy now grasps the gravity of the situation and sends Charlie out on a rescue mission.

New Orleans doesn't figure in my mother's account, other than as their final port of embarkation for France; though Tschiffely sends Gabriela there, without explanation, teaching French, Italian, music and painting, while Robert rattles around Texas employing his horsemanship and Spanish to whatever advantage he can. All are agreed, however, that very soon after Charlie's departure, Robert and Gabriela leave Texas, in May 1881. They sail from New Orleans, not for Britain but for France, docking at Dieppe where they have a brief rendezvous with Missy before moving on to Vigo. Here in Northern Spain they settle for the next couple of years. Their exile, Anne Taylor suggests, continues.

I know that my mother and Anne Taylor corresponded, and possibly met. Both their books were published in 2005. What I don't know is whether Anne Taylor, during the period of her research, had access to the material at that time still in my mother's possession, prior to her donating it to the National Library of Scotland. My mother quotes from a number of letters that are not mentioned by Anne Taylor. She also gives a confident account of the eight months which, she says, Robert and Gabriela spent together in San Antonio; though the absence of any mention of Gabriela in Robert's letters home makes it harder to establish her movements with certainty. Meanwhile, Anne Taylor offers no account of what Gabriela got up to in New Orleans.

My mother, it is fair to say, was not delighted by *The People's Laird*. This was not, I believe, because she doubted its accuracy or saw it in competition to *Gaucho Laird* but rather because it was, if anything, too accurate; it uncovered truths about, or at the very least asked questions of, her hero that she would have preferred to remain unexposed. On the other hand, she approved very much of Alexander Maitland's portrait, *Robert & Gabriela Cunninghame Graham*. She welcomed him to Harden, her home in the Borders, threw open her archive to him and eventually wrote the foreword to the book. His only misfortune was that at the time of his writing, her revelation about Gabriela's true identity was still a few years in the future. Nevertheless, he suggests that whatever actually took place during those eight months in San Antonio, the details are relatively unimportant. What matters – and it frustrates him, as it does me, that there is no hard evidence here – is how Gabriela and Robert were getting on. Was Robert's side-trip to Argentina some kind of turning point? Had things gone wrong on the trail to or from Mexico City? If anything might have strained a relationship only two years old, it was surely a tough and often dangerous fifteen-hundred-mile journey on horseback.

Although neither mentions the other by name in their respective accounts of the Mexican trip, and both wrote about it well after the event, there is nothing in either *A Hegira* or *The Waggon Train* to suggest that they found one another anything other than agreeable travelling companions. Gabriela concludes her story with the companionable image of them on their first night in Mexico City, 'in a comfortable French hotel, luxuriously supping on cotelettes à la Milanaise and a bottle of burgundy'. I know from having written about my own Latin American odyssey, which tested an even newer relationship than theirs, that I could only describe an intensely personal experience of travel; a description that precluded much reference to my travelling companion. Which is not to say that we didn't have the good humour, the youthful sense of invincibility, and the care for one another to help us bear the months of sleeping in tents, hammocks and the cheapest hotels, the frustrations, mishaps and occasional illnesses of life on the road, as well as the inevitable disagreements that arose. We travelled well together. But we also parted company at the end of the journey and it was the best part of a year before we were back together again.

Perhaps Gabriela had simply had enough of travelling. Perhaps she found Robert's restlessness and impetuosity too hard to live with. His closeness to his mother and her disapproval of Gabriela must have been hard for her. Perhaps Robert was having difficulty adjusting to this new commitment; including, as Alexander Maitland suggests, the novelty of marital sex after a decade of finding it, and most likely paying for it, where he could. Both were highly independent-minded and doubtless still learning to accommodate one another. But an eight-month separation, if that's what it was, suggests more than merely a row. Anne Taylor ventures that Gabriela may have been repeating the pattern, begun in adolescence, of simply bolting when faced with circumstances not to her liking; to which I would add that there may have been extenuating circumstances which could explain such behaviour. My mother, without saying as much, blames Robert and has him returning from Argentina full of remorse, to fall into Gabriela's forgiving arms, their happiness together now secured.

Whatever caused the rift, and however long it lasted, Robert and Gabriela survived it. It may even have set the pattern for their future together. From here on, although they were frequently to separate for long periods, it is clear that they would remain the most important people in one another's lives.

Nine

GARTMORE

At the crossroads

A mong pine-wooded hills overlooking Vigo's long, sheltered Atlantic inlet, Robert and Gabriela, with Jack in attendance, found a haven for the next two years. Quinta la Graña was a roughly converted granary with magnolia trees, an old stone fountain in the courtyard, and a sandy garden overgrown with roses. Heaps of maize cobs littered the farmyard and in the stable below their bedroom, oxen fed on freshly cut clover. Gone was the stifling heat of Texas. Here the warmth and sunshine were welcome. Sea breezes and rain squalls freshened the air. Seasonal mists crept in, as they did at Gartmore, and the Galicians, dour in character, reminded Robert of his own countrymen.

In Texas, it seems likely, Robert's physical crises had been echoed in the spirit; he had suffered a kind of breakdown. At the *curator's* insistence, he had submitted to a doctor's examination on their return and was now, again, under orders to rest. Gabriela's health had suffered, too. The weakness in her chest had been exacerbated by a new-found addiction to cigarettes. On the trail, it was the smoke from coarse black tobacco that had kept insects at bay.

They had met with Missy briefly on arrival in Dieppe, as she was returning from a holiday with Malise in the Pyrenees. At this encounter there appears to have been some rapprochement between mother and daughter-in-law. 'Gabriela sends her best love,' Robert wrote afterwards. But the fact that the couple had not stopped over to visit friends and relatives in London had caused eyebrows to be raised. Following a visit to Missy's great friend, Blanche Fane, Malise reported to his mother that he had 'said no more than necessary on the Bob subject'.

Was their continuing 'exile' contrived by the family to keep the lid on 'the Bob subject' – in other words, to keep the unsuitable Gabriela out of public view? Or was it self-imposed? Robert was victim of both his father's illness and his own unconventional impulses. In ordinary circumstances he would have been expected by now to have found some suitable occupation to pursue until he should become laird of Gartmore and, by family tradition, enter politics. But instead, constrained by the *curator's* grip on the Bontines' affairs, dismayed at the family wrangling that resulted, and naïvely believing he could make his fortune, he had opted to become a traveller and adventurer. South America had spoilt him for the conventional life. He was headstrong, impulsive and clever, idealistic, witty and charming, while remaining a natural outsider, an observer; and now he had a wife of dubious provenance. The family still had no idea what to do with him. For his part he longed for Gartmore, to cease being a financial burden on the estate, and to engage actively with the process of discharging the debts first incurred by his great-grandfather, the Swindler, and further amassed by Willy. Most of all, he was physically and emotionally exhausted. A quiet spell in Spain offered him the chance to catch his breath and consolidate his marriage.

The *curator* now applied to the court and, to Robert's great relief, was granted the powers to borrow a sum of £2,000 to settle debts they had run up in Texas. Given that this sum far exceeded anything they would have spent on living and travelling, it can only have been the result of bad investment – in land, livestock or commodities, or perhaps even the putative partnership with the Mexican-Greek. Robert, it was clear to everyone including him, had no head for business. That the same was fortunately not true of Gabriela would in due course become apparent. Meanwhile, the *curator* also increased Robert's annual allowance from £400 to £500 (a skilled worker in Scotland at the time might expect to earn around £50 per annum): in part to cover interest on the loan, in part that he might maintain a position suitable for the heir to the Gartmore and Ardoch estates.

Between summer 1881 and summer 1883, that position was one of expatriate resident of Vigo. Spain then was a world almost unknown to northern Europeans, '. . . unchanged since the Middle Ages, virtually unaltered to . . . when the Moors and the Spaniards lived side by side together in the heart of the peninsula,' as Gabriela wrote later for a lecture. If seclusion was their aim, they could hardly have chosen better. On the sunny terrace overlooking the bay, Robert read, worked on his notes about the Conquest, and began tentatively to write. Gabriela explored the local churches, sitting contemplatively in their cool dark interiors for hours. Back at the *quinta* she sketched, gardened and issued instructions to their new house-keeper, Peregrina Collazo, a young woman from Vigo. Peregrina brought the twin benefits of local knowledge and ease of acceptance by the local community. She was also prone to sulking and refusal to obey instructions she didn't like; which didn't prevent her forming a deep attachment to Gabriela. Their fractious relationship – characterised by frequent outbursts and threats of dismissal – was to endure throughout Gabriela's life. There is a scrapbook of Gabriela's in which a series of photographs of Peregrina at Gartmore have each had the face and part of the body excised, presumably with a razor blade. Beneath, Gabriela has written: 'I would rather any page of this book were destroyed but this.' The fact that one cannot tell whether this was written before or after the photographs were, literally, defaced says most of what one needs to know about their relationship.

An early visitor to Vigo was Mallie, now a student of theology at Oriel College, Oxford. He and Gabriela shared an interest in matters religious. They also shared that weakness of the chest which, in Mallie's case, was to prove fatal within only a few years. Delicate-looking, yet cheerful and good-humoured, Mallie was set on the priesthood and would shortly, on graduating from Oxford, be appointed curate at St John's Church, Winchester, where he had also been at school. The pleasure of his company owed something to the musical gene which appears to have bypassed Robert, who could neither sing nor play an instrument, but had landed in Malise, as it did in me, his namesake, and also my brother Simon. An accomplished organist, he had set to music his eponymous ancestor's poem: 'If doughty deeds my lady please, right soon I'll mount my steed . . .'

Another visitor was George Mansel who turned up unexpectedly on his way back from Argentina to Dorset. He congratulated Robert on his 'excellent taste in wives', though he appears to have found the couple's exile strange, and suggested to Robert that the longer they remained out of circulation, the more tongues would wag at home – an opinion Robert duly passed on to his mother. Perhaps as a consequence of this, the couple returned to Britain in the autumn of 1881. Here Anne Taylor places the visit to the Mansel family in Dorset, following a spell in London and a visit to the aunts in Leamington Spa where Robert was pleased to see that Gabriela's charm was not lost on some of the more elderly members of the family, even if Missy remained generally impervious to it.

At Gabriela's insistence they wintered in Vigo. The following spring they made a trip to Wales where they met Bernard Evans, a painter who exhibited regularly at the Royal Academy Summer Exhibition and also at the Grosvenor Gallery in Bond Street. Evans offered tuition to Gabriela which she readily accepted, and she and his wife Mary quickly became friends and regular correspondents. It may have been through the Evans's that Gabriela and Robert were later to become *habitués* of the Grosvenor Gallery; a stepping-off point to the world of contemporary art and artists that was to become such a prominent part of both their lives in years to come.

In the autumn of that year, 1882, they travelled to Scotland to visit Willy, who was now in deteriorating health. From Dumfriesshire they went on to stay with Robert's Erskine cousins at Cardross, across the Lake of Menteith from Gartmore. Here the Gabriela charm offensive scored another hit, this time with Cousin John, Admiral Sir John Erskine, who from then on wrote to her regularly, his letters chatty and affectionate. It may have been while with the Erskines – the admiral's mother was Missy's youngest Elphinstone aunt – that Robert began to consider a legal challenge to the curatorship. If he could have Jamieson, the *curator*, removed, on the grounds that his costs to the estate were excessive, he could take over Gartmore and go and live there with Gabriela – the thing he most longed for. But Missy was greatly alarmed at the prospect of Robert managing the family finances upon which she depended for her income. Taking her friend Robert Wright's counsel, she and Bobby Cunninghame Graham asked Jamieson to seek legal opinion on the matter. The answer came back that while it would be permissible for Robert to be appointed Tutor-at-Law to his father, and so to control the whole estate, he would forfeit his allowance and could neither charge for his services nor live rent free at Gartmore, which was currently let at £750 per annum to Sir Gerald Fitzgerald. This blow can only have been made worse by his mother's apparent lack of confidence in him. No less hurtful was the fact that she patently doted on the girl Charlie had recently met at Sandringham and was soon to marry. She wrote of her future daughter-in-law, the beautiful Barbara Bagot, daughter of the Reverend Charles Bagot, rector of Castle Rising, that she was 'too heavenly pet and talks incessantly and is always kind and sweet to me'.

Robert and Gabriela moved back from Spain in summer 1883 and rented a farmhouse near Liphook, Hampshire – without informing Missy. But within a matter of weeks everything was to change. On 6 September, aged fifty-eight, Willy Bontine died. The causes given were: (a) Insanity – about nineteen years; (b) Irregularity of action of heart, lungs and stomach, probably due to disease of the nervous system – three months. Four days later, his body was brought back from Eccles House, where he had spent the last solitary sixteen years, and laid to rest in the family burial ground at Gartmore. Robert was now tenth laird and Gartmore, along with the estates of Ardoch and Gallangad, at long last was his.

For several weeks following the funeral, Robert stayed on at Lochend, an Erskine house at the Lake of Menteith, for meetings with lawyers, the factor and tenants. Gabriela, nursing an autumn attack of bronchitis – and perhaps a certain horror at what they were about to take on – retreated to Liphook. Robert might now be free to claim his inheritance, but an avalanche of further woes descended on him.

When all the counting was done, it was revealed that Willy had left assets of £14,000 and debts of £94,000. The latter included

£60,000 of debt inherited from his grandfather. That was not all. There were annuities to be paid to maiden aunts under the terms of his grandfather's will. Anne Elizabeth was to receive £1,200 a year, plus £1,500 for mourning garments, plate and linen for her new establishment as a widow. Brothers Charlie and Mallie were to have £10,000 pounds each, and the Dumfries-shire doctor who had tended to Willie was owed £1,500. There were also £5,000 pounds in fees due to the family solicitor and the *curator bonis* – at today's rate, liabilities to a total of nearly £10 million. Meanwhile, income from rents was estimated at £9,700 against expenditure of £9,040; an annual profit of £660 – but only if no improvements whatever were made to the estate and nothing was done to reduce the heritable debt.

Faced with the impossibility of all this, and following a week riding round the Gartmore farms in bad weather, Robert went down with a violent cough and cold. He wrote to Gabriela that he was feeling miserable, urging that she be careful of her own health – and perhaps her spending, since she had an expensive taste in clothes – and 'think of our future'. Sir Gerald had been given notice, he went on. Now he was in need of a good horse and perhaps a new factor too, since he couldn't afford to give the present one a rise in salary. To the news that Gabriela had been frostily received during a visit to Ebury Street, he added, 'as regards Milly [his new sister-in-law, Mildred Barbara] and my mother, do not bother yourself, and I wonder why you called at all. Both you and I are greatly liked here, and as we shall, I suppose, spend our life between here and Spain, it is all we want, chère petite femme.' He signed himself: 'Ton petit mari qui t'adore, Lob.'

Relations with Missy might be as strained as ever, but his marriage, at least, seemed now to be on a better footing; though it still required careful tending. Throughout these weeks of separation, Gabriela had complained of loneliness and begged Robert to take her to Spain. At one point he had written, somewhat sharply: 'Do try and look matters properly in the face. *All* our future depends on the next six months, as, if we "play the fool" now, not even the sale of Ardoch will clear our debts *then*.' Was he simply reminding her that this was not a moment for self-pity? Or had she proposed a money-making venture of the kind to which she would later, and to good effect, turn her hand? A letter she wrote to Mary Evans reveals that Gabriela was fully aware of the difficulties that faced them. And Robert was stressed and anxious. After the years of over-spending and risk-taking, he had at last begun to regard his financial responsibilities with seriousness and alarm in equal measure. But the health of his marriage was no less serious a matter.

By November it had been agreed that the only way they could afford to live at Gartmore was by selling Ardoch. Arrangements to do so were put in place. Now they could look forward to a few months' respite. They set out for the Mediterranean, taking ship for Valencia in order then to make their way slowly westwards through central Spain towards Vigo. What better balm for their relationship, and what better preparation for what lay ahead, than a winter travelling in the sun?

Shortly before Christmas Robert wrote to Missy reporting that the journey through the centre of Spain had been 'very interesting and exceedingly comfortable, and the food excellent . . .' But the cold had taken them by surprise.

There has been a foot of snow in Valencia which I can hardly realise as there were hundreds of acres of oranges and dates when we left. But there has even been snow at Lisbon, and five degrees of frost in Seville! There is none at Vigo, though the wind is bitter.

In early January he wrote again to say that the weather had turned fine and that they had been out in a boat to see some 'anchors, bullets, jars of indigo, blocks of mahogany . . . fished up from the galleons sunk by Sir Cloudsley Shovel [sic].' In February they travelled inland to visit Madrid for the first time. Here Robert went in search of archives, as was now his habit wherever there might be material relating to the Conquest. Despite having just learnt that there were to be yet more claims on his resources – his uncle Douglas Cunninghame Graham was due a legacy of £3,000 and not the £500 Robert had been led to believe – he wrote home chattily. He had heard from their old tutor, Mr Gulliver, now living in

Auckland, New Zealand – 'the postal authorities in Vigo think that New Zealand is in America!' – and concluded: 'Jack writes to say he is well, but found the Scotch dogs a dour lot! Gabrielle sends her best love. Believe me, your affec. son, R. C. Graham Bontine.'

This was perhaps the last time Robert would sign himself in this way. On 20 April 1884, accompanied by Peregrina and Jack, he and Gabriela arrived at Gartmore. Installed as tenth laird, Robert was Mr Bontine no longer. He would henceforth take Cunninghame Graham as his surname.

As I came to know my great-great uncle's story better it seemed that I was increasingly pursued by coincidence.

Driving over to Gartmore for a reconnoitre, I was looking for something to listen to on the journey from Birnam, where I live, and came across a BBC Radio Three podcast from 2018 by a former neighbour, the poet Kenneth Steven. In *New Ways Through The Glens*, a title borrowed from the social historian ARB Haldane, he looks at the effect on the Highlands of the roads and canals built in the eighteenth and nineteenth centuries.

Just as I left the A9 at Dunblane to head along the Carse of Stirling, he turned to the subject of the mosses that lie along the carse, a great watery no-man's-land between lowlands and highlands, and well-nigh impossible to cross until the start of the drainage schemes in the late eighteenth century. I was intrigued to learn that when they drained part of the Blair Drummond moss they found no stones but a vast quantity of seashells and the complete skeleton of a whale. It was the Dutch who brought with them their drainage skills and lent their name to the Flanders Moss, one of the defining features of the Gartmore landscape that Robert describes so fondly and vividly. These Dutch also lent their name to the many Flemings of Lowland Scotland, one of whom was Robert's maternal grandfather.

Later, having visited the house and grounds – now a centre for arts, crafts and activity holidays – I went to pay my respects at the Cunninghame Graham memorial, on the edge of the Gartmore village football pitch and stood for a while, pondering the inset stones from Argentina and Uraguay. Leaving Gartmore I went on to Aberfoyle for a bowl of soup. I had with me an early edition of *Notes On The District of Menteith* – Robert's first published work, with its wry notice: 'all rights reserved except in the republic of Paraguay', and complete with the word 'Gartmore' in his sweeping hand, along with his brand mark, inscribed in ink on the first page. In the chapter titled *Traditional* I read about Trootie, the old tramp fisherman who haunted the burns and upper reaches of the Forth around the estate, and to whom Robert dedicated the book. The following day my brother, Simon, posted a picture on Facebook. He had been sorting through some Cunninghame Graham photographs and had come across an image of an old man with a big white beard, toes poking out of the end of his boots, and a fishing rod over his shoulder. It was Trootie.

Maybe this is just what happens when one starts researching deeply, inhabiting another life, but I was tempted to take these serendipitous moments as a kind of approving nod from the other side.

From Gartmore on a clear day you can see east along the carse, all the way to Stirling. When the mist is down you can sense the southern ramparts of the Grampians looming at your shoulder.

Gartmore (the name derives from the Gaelic *gart* meaning a field or field of standing corn, and *mòr* meaning big) surveys the border lands like a watchtower. Perched on its eminence, the Flanders Moss and the Lake of Menteith stretching away at its feet, it's a place where cultures, landscapes and languages meet.

To the south the land softens towards the Campsies and the Central Belt, the intervening carse itself a lowland in the most literal sense, site of the sea that once washed inland halfway to Glasgow. Until the eighteenth century, the moss was merely a foretaste of what the traveller would encounter once into the great confusion of hills and woods, rivers and glens that lay immediately beyond. There, in the roadless and lawless Highlands, Gaelic was the only language spoken. Society was organised according to the system of clans and conflict between them was frequent and brutal. Into the borderlands to the immediate north of Gartmore, marauding Highlanders could disappear with their lowland booty, knowing that pursuit and detection were virtually impossible.

McGregors were the Grahams' sworn enemies, and Robert's forebears held out against their depredations for several centuries. Nicol Graham, Robert's great-great grandfather, had had a gibbet erected within sight of the house. Most notable among the McGregors was Rob Roy, the legendary bandit.

Only after the failure of the first Jacobite rising in 1715, a mere eight years after the detested Act of Union, were the first roads built in the Highlands. General Wade was sent north by the Hanoverians to facilitate the building and linking of the garrisons that now peppered the Highlands against the possibility of future insurrection. Ironically, when the second uprising occurred, thirty years later, it was the Jacobite army which benefited most, travelling south to Edinburgh at immeasurably greater speeds than would previously have been possible.

Robert was no stranger to the history of this marginal place. He had read the books in the library avidly as a teenager and he had deeply absorbed the exploits and lineages of his forebears. For all his energy and zest for adventure, he had a studious, reflective side to his nature that stood him in good stead throughout his life. When there were new facts to be ascertained, facts to support his views, he was sure to know them.

Robert was familiar with borderlands too. He was to some extent a creature of them, as his mature character began to show through and the many contradictions in his nature took shape. He himself was a kind of raucous crossroads, where thoughts, ideas, beliefs met and often clashed – the man of action with the observer's eye, the writer's detachment; the European who had gone native in Argentina; the adventurer who deplored the brutality of life in the Wild West; the would-be rancher whose sympathies lay with the Indians who may have burned him out; the beneficiary of a colonial past whose compassionate instinct found its object in those who had been most badly treated by the colonisers; the contemporary thinker who deplored progress. Gartmore offered a physical manifestation of these swirling eddies and counter-currents.

Whatever Gabrielle had been used to, nothing could have prepared her for the monstrosity that was Gartmore, with its 26 bedrooms, the elephant's skull in the entrance hall, the walls adorned with assegais and other curiosities of Victorian travel, the wallpaper faded into patches from the family portraits sold by the Swindler, the bone chilling damp and cold.

Before coming north Robert and Gabriela had spent several days in London, seeing the family and fitting Gabriela out with the clothes she would need in her new role as laird's wife; the sensible, cold- and rain-resistant wardrobe appropriate to life in a damp and draughty Scottish country mansion. Robert had also written to Khāt, now his last surviving grandparent, whom he had not seen since Catalina's death. The old sailor replied fondly from the Isle of Wight: 'My dear old Bob, I am so glad to hear that you had a good crossing and that both you and Gabrielle are O.K. . . . Dear Mallie looks very well in his parson's trappings, and is much liked. I am pretty well for an old one, occasional squeezes of rheumatics upset me, in other respects I cannot complain. I hope, dear Bob, you will be able to run down to give me a hand before you leave London, when we could talk of the probability and the feasibility of a trip to Gartmore. My kind love to Gabrielle, and believe me, your affectionate, J. Katon.' To Robert's great sorrow, he would be dead within the year.

For the present, though, such open affection was a tonic in the face of the challenges that now awaited them. Sir Gerald had used the house only during the shooting season. The grounds were unkempt and the house and other buildings shabby. Roofs leaked and moss grew. Farms and cottages were tumbling down, fences needed repair, waterlogged fields drainage; all for want of working capital. Furthermore, an agricultural depression had been deepening since the sodden summer of 1879. Now rents were poised to tumble, and one Gartmore tenant farmer had already been driven to bankruptcy.

In *Pollybaglan* (*Progress*, 1905) Robert later described the extremes of dilapidation he encountered at one of the outlying Gartmore farms, deep in the Flanders Moss. Here the soil was of thick clay between great banks of moss, the road laid out on faggots which did nothing to prevent carts sinking to their axles in winter, or horses' feet sticking in sun-baked cracks in summer. Fences were constructed from brushwood held in place by rusty wire, broken ploughs and carts served as gates, drainpipes lay scattered across fields. Scanty crops of oats grew like rice in the water that gathered in hollows in the clay, meagre potatoes and turnips turned black with disease. And the tenant himself, though not a Highlander, had become fashioned like one, Robert suggests, by the harshness of the landscape he inhabited and the life he led: 'Tall and shock-headed and freckled on the red patches of the skin which a rough crop of beard and whiskers left exposed, his eyes looked out upon the world as if he had a sort of second sight begot of whisky and of loneliness.'

While Robert rode the marches, talking to the farmers and work-ers and their families, assessing the full extent of the disrepair into which the estate had fallen, Gabriela began to attend to the house. She wrote to Mary Evans in May that she was busier than she had ever been, and plagued by what she described as 'the maid agony'. Demanding and sometimes temperamental, she was assisted by the dour, irascible, non-English-speaking Peregrina. Small wonder that keeping staff proved an agony. Nevertheless, in addition to Peregrina who served as both supervisor and Gabriela's personal maid, the smooth running of things required a cook, two table maids and three laundry-maids who also cleaned the house. Gabriela herself held the keys to the bread room, the paraffin room, the dairy room, the meat safe and the potato room. Most importantly, and to Robert's great relief, she began to take charge of the estate book-keeping and rent roll – a task at which she was to prove more than capable. But to her personal chagrin, maintenance of the garden had to be set aside; it was costing an enormous £350 per annum. Nevertheless, her interest in all things botanical now found a focus in the many varieties of moss that flourished in the damp environ-ments of the house and grounds, and she began a correspondence on the subject with a professor at Glasgow University.

In what leisure time there was, they rode out together, Robert on Pampa, a black Argentine horse he had rescued from the Glasgow trams, recognising the brand mark of a neighbouring estancia from Santa Anita; Gabriela on a small caramel-coloured Icelandic pony called Talla, after one of the islands in the Lake of Menteith where once had stood a small Graham stronghold. Often they visited Inchmahome, rowing across from Port of Menteith to savour its almost other-worldly tranquillity. There Gabriela read and sketched while Robert reflected on both his heritage and his future, this peaceful enclave offering respite from the burdensome responsibilities of Gartmore.

Much was expected of the new laird and his 'leddy'. Robert found that he was obliged to provide a new school, with house and garden, for the parish of Kippen on the southern edge of his land. A plethora of other worthy causes awaited their donations. Village and estate events demanded a supportive presence and gracious words, not to mention the provision of pies and scones, tea and whisky. There was a new village hall at Buchlyvie to be opened, sheep shearing to be celebrated, hospitality to be laid on for local militia units on manoeuvre. As in South America, so here in Scotland, Robert was all the time storing away observations of the landscape and the characters who inhabited it. Frequent funerals – one of the few forms of social gathering in rural communities, and generally all-male affairs at which much drink was taken – proved fertile ground for observation, as well as for winning over the estate folk to whom he was 'Laird', and neighbours to whom he was simply 'Gartmore'. With his charm and easy manner, Robert excelled at cultivating that peculiarly Scottish lack of deference, that familiarity and mutual respect that could pass between a laird and his folk.

Robert's ability to connect with the common folk did not go unnoticed. The Liberal Party had been dominant in Scottish politics for half a century. Now it was looking for candidates who could bridge the gulf between the businessmen and entrepreneurs, beneficiaries of the tremendous industrial growth of recent years, who formed the majority of MPs, and an electorate that was growing increasingly restive and eager for social and political change.

In August 1884, just a few months after Robert and Gabriela had moved into Gartmore, a welcome dinner was held for them in the Gartmore village school-house. As well as employees, tenants and neighbours, the Lord Provost of Glasgow and three local MPs, two Liberals and a Conservative, were present. The *Stirling Advertiser* reported that after the meal, toasts were made and the name of Robert's forebear, the first Robert Graham of Gartmore, invoked as exemplar of the prosperity and order that the speakers hoped young Robert would now restore to the estate. With this went the unspoken expectation – discussion of politics being forbidden by the Lord Provost, who presided for the evening – that Robert would also follow his forebear into politics and represent those present in the wider world.

Back in his ancestral homeland, Robert's left-leaning political heritage was catching up with him. The radical inclinations of his forebears seeped from Gartmore's moss-covered masonry as from the surrounding landscape. In addition to the first Robert Graham, Doughty Deeds, who as MP for Stirlingshire had presented his own Bill of Rights, both Robert's grandfathers had campaigned for reforms including the franchise for all householders, freedom of slaves and the humane treatment of sailors. His father had campaigned against overseas military campaigns. And his mother had encouraged his two brothers to oppose the Disraeli Conservative government. Now she saw in her eldest son a quick wit and a way with words, a willingness to question orthodoxies, and an unshakeable belief in his own convictions. Robert himself, now aged thirty-two, was starting to synthesise all the experiences of his South American years, along with those of his more recent sojourn in the United States and Mexico, and time spent in Spain and France; and to view them all in the context of the homeland to which he had now returned, the heritage that surrounded him, and the uncertain future presented by the challenges that faced not only himself as laird, but the people of Scotland generally, urban and rural alike.

The old Whig sap was rising. Robert was ready for politics.

Ten

COATBRIDGE

On the stump

In the year 2000, a dozen years before Robert stepped from the background to the foreground of my consciousness, I began to write a novel, *The Witness*, which was eventually published in 2007. Returning to live in Scotland in 1990, after twenty years in London, I had settled in a glen in Highland Perthshire. I found myself beginning to wonder about the fact that all the surrounding land was in the hands of three or four landowners. These were my neighbours, people who welcomed me and my family generously and warmly to our new home, people to whose social class I belonged, among whose kind I had spent my childhood and in whose company, as a boy with a gun, I had walked the hills.

Now I couldn't avoid the thoughts of inequity that confronted me in every direction I looked. Land reform was on the agenda of the newly fledged Scottish Parliament, a personal passion of the first First Minister, Donald Dewar, and being a devolved issue, one he could actually do something about. I followed developments with interest, spoke to landowners, interviewed the campaigner Andy Wightman, and ended up developing a story in which, in an independent Scotland in the near future, land ownership had been restricted to a single acre by a One-Acre Act, the rest being owned by the nation and available only to rent. In my dystopian future, this had given rise to armed insurrection in the Highlands, funded by the dispossessed lairds – a kind of reverse Clearances.

From the perspective of today, as we enter the third decade of the twenty-first century, I would have told a very different story. Be that as it may, the uniquely unequal distribution of land ownership in Scotland, and its impact on an environmentally and democratically sustainable future, remains an issue that any government of a fully independent Scotland will have to address.

Imagine my surprise, however, when I came to understand that the issue of land ownership had been one of the key factors in Robert's decision to enter politics in 1885, setting him apart from almost all his landowning peers the length and breadth of Scotland.

In his first recorded political speech, at Coatbridge in Lanarkshire, in August 1885, he would say:

Here, and here almost alone, has the existence of enormous territorial possessions continued, and whilst in other civilised countries we find the land almost exclusively cultivated by the peasants or agricultural labourers themselves, here in Great Britain is still to be found a class of feudal magnates who still enjoy privileges such as no class should enjoy to the exclusion of the rest in a civilised country.

The backdrop at that time was Ireland where unrest was now reaching critical levels. Irish social convention and inheritance law had long forced the sub-division of individual landholdings to unsustainably small sizes, capable of supporting nothing more than a crop of potatoes with which a peasant farmer might feed his family. Poor management of heavily mortgaged estates by absentee English landlords, who had effectively colonised Ireland through the sixteenth and seventeenth centuries, further exacerbated the situation, with tenants subject to summary eviction for which there was no redress. In the 1840s the Great Famine, brought about by potato blight, had killed over a million people and forced a further million to emigrate. Further famines had followed, up until the late 1870s. Now the Irish tenantry had had enough.

Under the banner of the Irish National Land League, such figures as Charles Stuart Parnell, Michael Davitt and William O'Brien had encouraged the rural population to agitate for better rights for tenant farmers, and eventually for wholesale land redistribution – and had been thrown in prison for their pains. Attempted evictions were met with violence which the British government, whose writ at that time still ran throughout the whole of Ireland, put down with equal force. Alleviating legislation had since been passed, but the wounds ran deep and now, partly in reaction to British heavy-handedness, calls for Irish Home Rule by Parnell and his Irish Parliamentary Party were growing at Westminster. With eighty-six MPs he held the balance of power, loosely supporting the Salisbury Conservative government. But when, in 1886, Gladstone changed tack and committed himself to Home Rule and justice for Ireland, Parnell switched allegiance. The Salisbury government fell and Gladstone's Liberals took power.

In Scotland, meanwhile, there had lately been widespread protests at the treatment of crofters in the West Highlands and Islands, and the assertion by certain clan chiefs, notably the Duke of Argyll and MacLeod of MacLeod, that the land was not held in trust for their fellow clansmen, as tradition maintained, but was theirs to do with as they wished. This had led in some cases to strongly resisted evictions and on two occasions naval gunboats and marines, along with police drafted in from Glasgow, had been sent in to quell the disturbances, known as the Crofters' Wars. The government responded by setting up a commission of enquiry under Francis, Lord Napier, whose report exposed the injustices of a system in which crofters were often little more than serfs, with no votes, no security of tenure, no written leases and no protections. These people, already reduced by cold, hunger and disease, had long been vulnerable to being cleared off the land in favour of income-generating sheep, deer and grouse. Meanwhile, the Reform Act of 1884 had enfranchised a further two million adult men throughout the United Kingdom. These included the crofters who were not slow to come together in a crofters' party, The Land Restoration League, which would contest seats in a small number of Scottish constituencies at the forthcoming general election.

Robert had by now put himself forward for selection as a parliamentary candidate in a process that would prove as unconventional as the career that was to follow. He was adopted first as the Liberal candidate for the constituency of Blackfriars in Glasgow's city centre, a maze of closes, lanes, wynds and vennels where the poorest of the city were to be found. Many of them, resident in cramped, filthy, noisy tenements, were Highlanders, forced south in order to support their families. Already well acquainted with the situation in Ireland, Robert at once recognised the parallels on his doorstep and found his sympathies aroused by the plight of these 'men of intelligence, high moral standards, and industrious habits' as the Napier Commission had described the Highlanders. Robert could relate to their dispossession. He had lived amongst just such outsiders in Argentina, the gauchos; had seen the Guarani Indians of Paraguay reduced to poverty and disease by their colonial oppressors; had ridden, laboured and drunk with exiled Highlanders. He understood what it meant to be severed from a place with which ancient connections were deeply felt. And if he needed further encouragement, the *curator bonis*, George Auldjo Jamieson, Robert's old adversary, in his capacity as factor to a number of Highland estates had given evidence to the Napier Commission, arguing strenuously in favour of the *status quo*.

However, shortly after presenting his programme to the Blackfriars selectors and winning their approval, Robert was invited by chance to a meeting of the Land Restoration League, whose candidate, James Shaw Maxwell, was also standing. Impressed by what he heard at this meeting, particularly a speech by an old Skye crofter, Robert with typical generosity decided not to stand against the crofters' candidate. He turned instead to the east end constituency of Glasgow Camlachie, another slum of smoking chimneys and run-down buildings, whose inhabitants – again, many of them Highlanders – earned their pittance spinning cotton or making clay pipes. As the official candidate for Camlachie, Robert was invited to speak at a meeting in Coatbridge, principal town of the newly-formed and heavily industrialised neighbouring constituency of North West Lanarkshire. If Blackfriars and Camlachie were squalid slums, Coatbridge, a kind of Scottish Birmingham, was a vision of hell. Dominated by belching ironworks, its crowded rows of workers' houses shook to the constant pounding of steam hammers and din of heavy machinery, the air laden with the sulphurous stench of spoil, the night sky reddened by furnaces.

Robert had published his manifesto a few days earlier, on 9 September 1885, describing himself as 'a Liberal by both descent and conviction'. For all his omission of the word 'radical', this speech, his first, at Coatbridge's Theatre Royal, left no one in any doubt of his leanings. He launched straight into the land issue, citing the persistence of the feudal system of land ownership as the basis of an invidious class system, and the chief obstacle to any kind of progressive reform. He deplored the present government's aggressive foreign policy and argued for the repeal of the game laws which restricted the right to kill or take game. He proposed the abolition of primogeniture and entail, and advocated free education, graduated income tax, more local self-government and local option on the sale of liquor. The self-styled 'prentice politician', apparently campaigning against his own best interests as a landowner, overcame his audience's suspicions and stirred them to wild applause. He was duly invited to stand in North-West Lanarkshire, which the Liberal Association in Camlachie did not oppose.

Robert's ideas were being formulated partly through his own life experiences, which set him apart not only from his immediate opponents but from almost any other parliamentarian in the country; and partly through his reading, both of William Morris's *The Commonweal*, and the American Henry George's *Progress and Poverty*. The aesthetic in Morris appealed to Robert's own sense of the aesthetic, which he found no trouble in linking to ideas of social justice, as did Morris. George's international best-seller, arguing for a single universal tax on land, chimed equally powerfully. Nor could Robert ignore the Irish cause and the Irish Parliamentary Party leader Charles Parnell's fierce denunciation of landlordism. From the issue of land ownership, it was a short step to that of national identity and the idea of self-determination, a flame that Robert was to keep alive until his last breath.

Duly selected, and now a favourite with voters and also women, who had no vote but warmed in growing numbers to the 'curlyheaded darling' with his fine head of auburn hair, his handsome features and witty asides, Robert began campaigning in earnest. Dressed in well-cut tweeds and a soft hat, a deliberate departure from the more formal attire favoured by most candidates, he was frequently attended by Gabriela, the exotic wife, and Charlie, the dashing young naval officer. It's hard to overstate the impression this trio must have made on the newly enfranchised working men who turned out to hear the eloquent, highly-strung young man and delight in the casual but cutting delivery that was to become his hallmark, the historical references and rhetorical flourishes, the humour and skill at dealing with hecklers that would distinguish him from so many of his more pedestrian peers.

> He comes of an old Scotch family – the Grahams of Gartmore – and is the son of a very clever mother, The Hon Mrs (Graham) Bontine, a sister of the 14th Lord Elphinstone. From her Mr Graham derives the literary tastes which lent a flavour as pleasant as peculiar to his election speeches.

So the *Pall Mall Gazette* later noted in a short biography of the new Member for North-West Lanarkshire.

Robert's chief opponent now was a former contemporary from Harrow, John Baird, scion of the enormously wealthy family of Baird ironmasters who had virtually built Coatbridge. The recent owner of a Highland estate, Baird presented himself as a laird to boot; one who, like Jamieson, had argued before the Napier Commission against the interests of the crofters. As a Tory he should have offered little competition to Robert. But in November, a few weeks before the election, Parnell ordered his supporters, many of whom were employed in the industrial inferno of North-West Lanarkshire, to vote Conservative in any seat where a Liberal or a Radical was the contender, since he believed a Conservative government the more likely to support a united Ireland.

Despite having declared his personal support for Irish Home Rule, Robert fell victim to tactical voting. On 4 December he was defeated by John Baird, with a majority of 1103. Robert was not present to hear the results. He and Gabriela had already left for London where days earlier Mallie had died of tuberculosis, aged only twenty-five. A few months previously he had written to Robert from Switzerland, where he had been sent for his health. He had applauded his brother's decision to stand in the election and signed the letter, perhaps with foreknowledge, 'Goodbye, ever your affec. brother, Malise Graham.'

1886 began badly. Robert retired to Gartmore to lick his wounds. Defeat in the election, and criticism from some quarters for having lost the safest seat in Scotland, was compounded by the loss of his beloved youngest brother and by the effect this had on his mother. She had nursed Mallie through the last stages of his illness and now found herself in mourning for the third time in as many years: first her husband, then her stepfather, and now her youngest son. It was Mallie whose constant company and shared passion for music and theatre had been her greatest comfort; whose obituary in the *Winchester Observer* called him 'this greatly beloved and gifted young clergyman', noting his 'deep and earnest sympathies with the poor'.

Gabriela, meanwhile, had left for Italy, unable to persuade Robert to join her as he clung, 'a limpet', to whatever comfort the old house offered him. 'I don't like to leave him,' she wrote to Mary Evans, but the misery of January in Scotland and its effect on her fragile health overrode even her loyalty to her husband. The quest for warmth and sunshine was to become an ever more frequent theme in her life, although when intellectual and spiritual pursuits demanded she would, until the very end, expose herself to all manner of hardship and discomfort; just one of the many contradictions in her character to rival those of her husband.

As Robert yet again pondered his future, further misery attended him during those dark early days of the year. There was bad news about the estate finances: tenants were seeking rent reductions after a year of rain, there were several hundred pounds of election campaign costs to be found, and the settlement of Malise's estate involved a further, enormous outlay of £10,000. As the constant drip of financial anxiety wore away at him, he consoled himself by riding out on Pampa with the terrier Jack at their heels – in Gabriela's absence his closest companions – and burying himself in the genealogical tomes in the Gartmore bookroom.

The Gartmore finances in early 1886 echoed those of the country. A nationwide industrial decline was being felt most acutely in Scotland where shipbuilding and both iron and coal production had slumped, putting thousands out of work. In such a climate the sale of Ardoch, which would have offered Robert some hope of salvation, was not possible. A new word, 'unemployment', had entered the English lexicon and in London the unemployed were taking to the streets to protest. In February, supported by two rival factions, the Fair Traders and the Social Democratic Federation, the protesters shocked London by attacking properties in the West End, breaking into shops in Piccadilly and smashing the windows of Robert's own club, the Devonshire Club. A few weeks later their leaders stood trial for seditious intention and were acquitted. One of them, John Burns, was later to become Robert's companion-in-arms in Trafalgar Square as they confronted the forces of order arraigned against them by the new Metropolitan Police Commissioner, Sir Charles Warren. Warren's ineffectual predecessor had taken to mingling anonymously with the protesters during the riots in February – to such good effect that when orders needed to be given he was nowhere to be found, and ended up having his pocket picked.

With the plight of the working folk of North-West Lanarkshire sharp in his mind, Robert took due note of the demands of both parties, the Fair Traders – dockers, seamen and other waterfront workers, who argued for the protection of English goods and public works for the benefit of the unemployed; and Henry Hyndman's more radical Social Democratic Federation which argued for the overthrow of capitalism.

Meanwhile Gladstone, the Liberal Prime Minister, was trying to warm the British electorate to the idea of self-government for Ireland and to push his Irish Home Rule bill through parliament. But when it came to it his party split. Union supporting Liberals voted with the opposition to defeat the Bill by thirty votes, leaving Gladstone no choice but to stand down. In June 1886, a second general election was called. Robert roused himself from his gloom and, perhaps with Mallie's dying endorsement to stiffen his resolve, put himself forward again for North-West Lanarkshire, this time going 'the whole Radical hog' as the *Pall Mall Gazette* put it. He stood for the establishment of an Irish parliament – a simple restoration of power which he believed should also be extended to

Scotland and Wales, wholesale land reform and a ten-hour working day. His stance placed him at odds with the majority of Liberals who identified themselves as Unionists under Joseph Chamberlain, and in Scotland were now supported by both the *Scotsman* and the *Glasgow Herald*. These newspapers pledged their loyalty to the Union and deplored the prospect of Irish MPs voting on English affairs. Robert meanwhile remained steadfast and vocal in support of Gladstone who, he declared, had 'more sanity in his little finger than the united brains of the Tory party'.

Alongside its sizeable Catholic population of Irish workers, Coatbridge also hosted a number of Orange lodges whose members, with an election looming and it being July and peak marching season, were more than usually eager to strike up their flutes and drums. Robert was only too well aware of these sectarian tensions and throughout the campaign he skillfully trod the religious tight-rope, dodging awkward questions, any one of which might have derailed him. Privately he deplored the mean and narrow, not to mention hypocritical, view of the world which John Knox had visited on the Scots. Later in life he would speak of the Presbyterian view that a man could lie, cheat, be cruel to animals, but so long as he went to church his place in heaven was assured. Catholicism, however, drew a warmer response from him. His experiences in South America, as well as in France, Spain and Portugal, had acquainted him with Catholics whose company he enjoyed and whose faith he admired, even if he didn't adhere to it himself. Furthermore, it was his wife's adopted religion.

Out on the stump, Robert warned his constituents of the awful alternatives to Gladstone, not just for Ireland but for Scotland also. Ireland he likened to a great bird denied its liberty and bound for eighty years in a cage fashioned of union laws – the key to which, he said, was Home Rule. For Scotland he invoked a putative Graham ancestor, John of the Bright Sword, who had fought and died with William Wallace; two warriors whose names would live on 'as long as the Bass Rock stood sentinel at the mouth of the Forth, and the seagulls circled around Ailsa Craig.' He attacked the hereditary chiefs and other Highland proprietors, accusing them of flagrant abuses of the human rights of crofters:

The unfortunate people starve, and the Tory government, to their cry for meal, answers with bullets . . . Are deer game? Have crofters broken any laws? Have they injured any man? Have they destroyed the work of any man's hand? Scotland is a free country – quite, it appears, for a crofter to starve in, or for a deer to eat his crops in. I wish – and surely there is no harm in wishing – that there were not a deer, a grouse, or a salmon in all the Highlands. If there were not, we might see more sheep, more agriculture, and more men, and fewer Cockneys and German Princelets.

The speeches were rapturously received and on 9 July 1886 he defeated his old adversary John Baird by 335 votes. Following the declaration, bands of Union-supporting Baird followers went on the rampage and there were fears of riots to rival those that had lately paralysed Belfast.

But the riots failed to materialise and the following day, 10 July, Robert awoke, aged thirty-four, the new Liberal Member of Parliament for one of Scotland's most important industrial seats. The fact that the Conservatives, led by Lord Salisbury and supported by the Liberal Unionists, had defeated Gladstone and been returned to power, albeit as a minority government, for the first time in forty years, did nothing to tarnish Robert's achievement. His return to Gartmore was triumphant. The *Airdrie Advertiser* reported that a crowd of five hundred villagers and tenants turned out to welcome Robert and Gabriela at Buchlyvie station. A procession led by the village piper escorted them back to Gartmore where, at the entrance to the policies, the horses were unhitched and a throng of young men scrambled for the privilege of man-hauling the carriage to the house – a direct echo of the reception granted by the Skye crofters to the American author and land reformer, Henry George, on his arrival on the island. At Gartmore, refreshments were served on the lawn and later bonfires were lit. 'We may say that Mr and Mrs Graham have completely won the hearts of the tenantry and the numerous villagers on their estates,' concluded the report.

Mr Graham was 'a good all-round Liberal,' reported another paper, 'one who, having faith in his principles seeks to apply them. Not just a Land Reformer, but one who is in favour of a full and ample measure of local self-government for all three kingdoms. He is in favour of free education, the extension of the franchise to women, and all the prominent questions of the day which show he is an independent and progressive Liberal.'

Quite how independent and progressive, they could have had little idea.

Eleven

WESTMINSTER

Blazing forth

Until quite late in life, I was envious of people with strong political convictions. It seemed like a kind of maturity that I didn't
possess, or perhaps an absence of the kind of life experiences that
bring with them an earnest desire for social change. Unlike Robert,
I was brought up in a resolutely Tory household where politics were
seldom discussed. It seemed a given of our class that the Tories
were right and everyone else – except possibly a few Liberals, Jo
Grimond, David Steel, for example – was not only wrong but also
dangerous. Scot Nats, as we knew them, were simply bearded
loonies.

My father as a young QC, later Scottish judge and ultimately
Lord of Appeal, was a small-c conservative who, outside of court,
found his passions in the countryside and was most in his element
on the river or grouse moor. My mother, for all her adulation of
Robert and embrace of her Whig forebears, was no less conservative in her politics. In the 1963 Kinross and West Perthshire by-election, members of the then Conservative Prime Minister, Alec
Douglas-Home's campaign team, including a young speechwriter
by name of Nigel Lawson, were billeted on my parents at our family
home. By that time, following Robert's educational trajectory, I was
also at boarding school in England where I fared somewhat better
than he had done at Harrow, although it's fair to say that at Radley
I was not generally rubbing shoulders with the 'sprigs of the nobility' as Robert later disparaged his Harrovian classmates. Neither,
despite it being the epoch of Lindsay Anderson's great film of

generational rebellion, *if . . .,* did anything in the experience of public school incline me towards revolutionary thought of any kind. I was a late developer.

At the end of my first year at Aberdeen University, 1969, my mother and father parted. My mother re-married immediately to a prominent Scottish financier, the former Governor of the Bank of Scotland and hereditary peer, Harry, Lord Polwarth, who went on to serve briefly as Minister of State for Scotland in the dying days of the Heath government. For a while their elegant Edinburgh house, and Harry's ancient family seat in the Borders, were the scenes of many receptions and dinners. My stepfather was a committed francophile, also an accomplished francophone, and one frequent visitor was Jérôme Monod, advisor to Jacques Chirac and co-founder with Chirac of the centre-right Rally for the Republic party. He and his wife Françoise became close friends of my parents who holidayed with them several times in the Vaucluse. Harry was also a director of the US oil services giant, Halliburton, where fellow board members included Dick Cheney, later US Defence Secretary and Vice President to George W. Bush. From an earlier era, a cordially signed photograph of George Bush senior and his wife Barbara held pride of place in the Edinburgh drawing room. Another visitor to the house was Birendra, the charming Eton-educated Nepalese crown prince, who succeeded to the throne in 1972 and was assassinated, along with other members of his family, in 2001. With the exception of Tam Dalyell, author of the West Lothian Question and to whom we were obscurely related, the political classes of my limited twenty-year-old acquaintance were firmly of the right.

In Aberdeen, meanwhile, the folk club was the only place I brushed with politics of any kind. The closest I came to activism was when the Springboks rugby tour came to Aberdeen in December 1969 and a small group of friends – I was not among them – went along to protest. The police bundled them into vans, drove them five miles up the coast, booted them out and told them to walk home again. A couple of years later, equipped with a law degree, I headed for London where I eventually settled down for two decades of journalism, publishing and music. I became one of the

Independent-reading, Liberal-voting, South London-dwelling, family-raising middle classes. I instinctively disliked Margaret Thatcher, yet felt no connection with Callaghan, Foot or Kinnock, so plumped without much thought for the safe middle ground. By now in my thirties, my political awakening was still the best part of a further thirty years in the future.

Robert, in his thirties, was already politically galvanised. With Willy's death and the move to Gartmore had come a Damascene surrender to his destiny, an acceptance of his responsibilities and acknowledgment of his heritage, which had coalesced into a furious sense of purpose – the very purpose which had been so lacking since his return from South America, three years earlier; which was now accompanied by a new confidence in his political convictions and powers of persuasion; and which also offered welcome distraction from his financial anxieties. For the next six years the horseman would himself be ridden by an almost manic compulsion that left him no respite.

Home Rule for Ireland, land ownership, freedom of speech, poverty, disease and dire working conditions, women's rights, local democracy, the class system, capitalism, British foreign policy, a complacent political class – these were among the throng of issues that now clamoured for Robert's heart and mind, and most of whose effects, in one manifestation or another, were there to be seen in the lives of his new constituents: men and women whose welfare was now his chief concern and who were hurting more than ever thanks to a reduction in miners' wages of sixpence per day on account of the poor demand for coal.

Following the largely English upbringing and the subsequent years abroad, he was now, through both his ancestral connection with Gartmore and his engagement with the working classes of North-West Lanarkshire, discovering a new, deep and mature commitment to Scotland and her cause as a nation. Robert had long ago understood the question of land ownership to be central to the fair and healthy governance of society. Now he saw how closely related it was to the welfare of those – whether Irish peasant farmers or West Highland crofters – who had in many cases been driven off the land by that new class of landowners, the very industrialists who exploited their labour. This fundamental equation between land, wealth, employment and social justice would inform and motivate almost every cause Robert was to espouse during his six years at Westminster.

All of which set him on collision course with the new minority Conservative government, headed by the Marquis of Salisbury, not to mention the twenty-five Scottish Liberal members who had been returned as Unionists. He was starting his career at Westminster as the outsider he would remain; although not among those in Scotland for whom nationalism was becoming an increasingly attractive alternative to the anticipated oppression of Tory rule, and whose hopes had recently been raised by the creation of a new Scottish Department at Westminster, then swiftly dashed when they learnt that its Minister was to be subordinated to the Home Secretary.

Robert and Gabriela spent the summer of 1886 at Gartmore where they hosted politically themed picnics, including one for the Band of Hope. Given the effects of drink on an impoverished populace, Good Templars, as the Band's followers were known, were numerous among Robert's constituents. Airdrie was home to the largest branch of the Band of Hope in the world at the time. Gabriela was persuaded by the local Free Church minister, Reverend McLean, to become president of a new Gartmore branch, for whom a gathering – whisky absent – was duly laid on. Robert, much against his better judgement, signed the pledge, though history doesn't relate whether he proceeded to live by it. Gabriela was more blatant in the breach. She confided in Mary Evans that she might be 'a teetotaller in theory' but was not one in practice. More than a hundred children attended the picnic, reported the *Airdrie Advertiser*. Strawberries and cream were served and prizes given out for regular attendance at Good Templar meetings. The most favoured prize among the girls was a plush framed portrait of Gabriela. The laird himself led the younger children around the grounds on Talla, his wife's pony.

Throughout the late summer and early autumn Robert was busy with meetings across his constituency, mostly in response to the miners' fury at the reduction in their wages. It was at one of these meetings that he first made the acquaintance of a young former miner turned journalist, James Keir Hardie. Meanwhile, it was noted with some disappointment by his supporters that Robert had yet to take his seat in Parliament. Then, in October, the *Airdrie Advertiser* reported that Mrs Cunninghame Graham was so seriously ill the doctor had ordered her to Spain. Could she have contrived, even sub-consciously, to keep Robert from Westminster, knowing the claims it would come to make of him? She had been very unwell, Gabriela told Mary Evans, later in the year, and was still not fully recovered, but she would resist all attempts to send her abroad again.

Following Christmas at Gartmore, they returned together to London for Robert to take his seat in Parliament in the New Year. Unwilling to join his Unionist colleagues on the opposition benches, he sat down on the cross benches, between members of the Crofters' Party and the Irish MPs; a none-too-subtle hint that while his support for Gladstone may have won him the seat, he was determined to remain independent. As he moved to take his place he was informed that it was Parnell's seat. Robert characteristically refused to yield and Parnell politely gave way. Thus, Robert later wrote, began a 'desultory' friendship with Parnell, based mostly on a shared interest in horses, which nevertheless lasted until the Irishman's death. In *A Memory of Parnell* (*Thirty Tales and Sketches*, 1929) it becomes apparent that it was the Irishman's contempt for England in general and his fellow parliamentarians in particular – amongst whom he stood out 'as the Old Man of Hoy stands out against the sea' – that most endeared him to Robert.

The theme of contempt, a kind of lofty defence against personal injury by all manner of people including his readers, was to make a not infrequent, if sometimes jarring, appearance in many of Robert's writings.

On 1 February 1887 Robert was called to speak in support of an opposition amendment to the Queen's Speech. It was the start of the Queen's Golden Jubilee year, but since she was no longer able to attend Parliament in person, her speech was read by the Lord Chancellor. Salisbury's new government faced many problems, among the most pressing of which remained Ireland where, forty years after the Great Famine, the rural poor were once again in desperate straits. Parnell's steadying hand was now being rocked by more radical forces led by William O'Brien and John Dillon who, in October, and with the support of Irish politicians, had launched their Plan of Campaign. This encouraged tenants to offer what they considered to be a fair rent to their landlords; a sum which, if refused, could then be paid into a special fund to support the victims of eviction. The Queen's Speech sought to outlaw the Plan.

By tradition a maiden speech was expected to avoid anything contentious. Robert waded in with fists metaphorically flying. The royal family were parasites, he declared. The government's desire was evidently to do nothing at all at home while intervening selectively and unconscionably in the affairs of others abroad. There was not a hint of tax relief or relief of any other kind for those who were suffering, no attempt to bridge the chasm between poor and rich, nothing but platitudes and a view of society 'through a little bit of pink-tinted glass'; the society in question being one in which

> one man works and another enjoys the fruits, in which capital and luxury make Heaven for thirty thousand and Hell for thirty million, that society whose crowning glory is London, this dreary waste of mud and stucco with its misery, its want and degradation, its prostitution and its glaring inequalities – the society we call London – that society which, by refinement of irony has placed the mainspring of human action, almost the power of life and death, and the absolute power to pay labour and to reward honour, behind the grey tweed veil which enshrouds the greasy pockets of the capitalist.

The speech caused a sensation. With Gabriela and her mother-in-law looking on from the gallery, Robert rose an unknown and sat down a celebrity, having kept the house 'in continuous uproar for more than half an hour' according to the pseudonymous political correspondent of *Vanity Fair*, 'Sir Rougham Rasper', who noted:

> Advent of the new man. Name: Cunninghame Graham. Description: Scotch Home Rule Visionary. Outward aspect: something between Grosvenor Gallery aesthete and waiter in Swiss café. Person of 'cultchaw', evidently, from tips of taper fingers to loftiest curl of billowy hair, and with sad, soulful voice to match. Draws out some deuced smart things. Effect of speech heightened by air of chastened melancholy . . . Fogeys and fossils eye him askance, and whisper that he ought to be 'put down'; but lovers of originality, in all quarters, hail him with satisfaction.

'A wonderful speech,' crowed the *Airdrie Advertiser*. 'Mr Graham blazes forth, a star of the first magnitude.' Robert had indeed blazed, though not in the manner of a firebrand. This was a study in coolly calculated irony, his passion mediated through caustic wit and scorn for the sanctimonious and greedy. It was a broad call for humanity and social justice made with almost preternatural self-assurance. 'Does the House recognise how a band of marauders is put down?' he asked in relation to the reported 'triumph' of British troops killing native *dacoits* in Burma. 'I do; I have seen it done often,' he continued.

> Surely it can be no great matter of self-congratulation for Britons with arms of precision to shoot down naked savages . . . A native wounded to death, I take it, and tormented by mosquitoes in the jungle, felt his misery as acutely as the best be-broadclothed gentlemen among us, even though he should happen to be a chairman of a School Board.

Turning his fire on the landed classes of Ireland he observed:

It is the pride and the privilege of the Irish landlord to look after the interests, creature as well as spiritual, of his tenants; and, such is the relation of class to class that, so far from turning them out on a bleak, cold winter's night, the landlord has provided his dependents with a fire to warm their hands; only, through a pardonable inadvertence, it was their houses that had furnished the blaze.

'Mr Graham's description of his own qualification to speak on the Irish question was inimitable,' noted the *Pall Mall Gazette*.

He had never been to Ireland, but had gained something of the national colour by sitting amongst the nationalist members, and (here the house went off into laughter) he had once known an Irish commercial traveller who had imparted information to him quite unattainable by the general public. The advent of a new humourist – to newspaper readers as well as the House – must afford in these days of exhaustive Parliamentary reporting, infinite satisfaction.

Another periodical asked if it was

the air of the Western world that has given the Hon. Member the peculiar dry humour which he effects, and which greatly diverted the House for a short half-hour? For Mr Graham has been a cattle raiser in South America, on the River Plate.

Cattle raiser or not – and to the extent that he never corrected such stories he seemed content for them to become part of his personal mythology – if Robert had found physical courage on the plains and in the forests of South America, it was here in Westminster that he was discovering the moral courage that might land him in trouble of all kinds but would seldom in future desert him. To have spoken thus, and as a member of neither of the two main parties, was to ensure that there would be very little prospect of advancement to a political career that had barely begun. But Robert didn't care. His radical blood was up, stirred by what he saw as the complacency, the smug indifference to human misery, that surrounded him on the benches of the House of Commons.

Two days later, on learning that starving miners had looted shops in Blantyre and Coatbridge, Robert dashed north to his constituency.

Mounted police had been brought in to control and intimidate the destitute strikers and their families. The weather was exceptionally cold and arrests were deliberately made in the small hours. A few days later Robert addressed a huge demonstration gathered at Glasgow Green, the large park in the city's east end, where he told the miners that they had as much right to band together to keep wages up as their employers had to band together to keep them down. 'When I took my ticket at Euston and came here, I knew I was leaving behind me every chance of rising in political life,' he told a gathering of his Liberal supporters. 'What had I, a landlord, to gain by championing the working class? I had everything to lose.' But finding his constituents in worse straits than he could have believed possible, 'would you have me say to those poor starving fellows that I could do nothing for them?'

'Roaring on the Green', as he came to call these Glasgow orations, was a habit Robert would regularly indulge in years to come. On this first occasion, for all the rhetoric, he took a pragmatic view of the crisis and recommended that the miners negotiate rather than take the direct action that was being counselled by others who drew their inspiration in part from Irish activists such as Michael Davitt. Released from Dartmoor after serving seven years of a fifteen-year prison sentence for conspiring to overthrow British rule in Ireland, Davitt had lately been speaking at Crofters' Party meetings in support of Home Rule and against landlords. Robert now called for a conference of workers and employers that would draft legislation to end the mineral royalties paid by mine-owners to landowners – 'a shameful tax upon communities' – and agree a sliding scale of wages with employers. Five shillings per day, his recommended wage, was 'hardly gorgeous for men toiling eight hours a day in the bowels of the earth.'

Over the following weeks Robert visited those toiling men, touring the pits and making his first journey underground with James Keir Hardie as his guide. Wherever he went he advised against violence or any lawbreaking that would harm their cause. In the end the miners acknowledged the unequal struggle and agreed to return to the pits on their employers' terms, but having first determined among themselves to strengthen their union, educate their

members and agitate until reforms were achieved. Robert returned
to Westminster, pledging to do his best for them – these miners
whose respect in recent weeks he had earned for his 'openness of
mind, breadth of view, sanity and discipline', as one admirer
declared. He had counselled his constituents wisely through this
first crisis as their new representative. He had drawn energy from
the very real affinity he felt for their plight; yet he had mediated his
anger through a shrewd assessment of what was practicable. He
would not always be so temperate in future.

The plight of the miners was just one symptom of the progress
which brought Robert's feelings into conflict. If progress was an
eight-hour working day that gave the working man an opportunity
to educate himself, then Robert favoured it. But what of industriali-
sation itself, that force that blighted the landscape and created these
new inequalities in the first place? Robert turned to William Morris,
founder of the Socialist League, whose belief that industry was a
threat to man's fragile relationship with the world around him
struck a chord. England, Morris had declared, was 'in part a cinder
heap, in part a game reserve, when it ought to be a fair green
garden.' Robert had seen at first hand the fair green gardens of
Argentina, Uruguay, Paraguay and Brazil. He had lived for the best
part of eight years in landscapes as yet unsullied by progress of any
sort. And where he had come across progress he had tended to
lament its effect on those least able to resist it.

In February 1887 Robert spoke against the building of a railway
line between Windermere and Ambleside. It would destroy one of
the country's most beautiful areas, he said. No one wanted it. Why
not buy the land and preserve it? He cited the recent creation of
Yellowstone National Park in the United States. It was to be another
six decades before such a vision for the Lake District would be realised, but Robert understood the benefits of wilderness and natural
beauty to the wellbeing of individuals and communities, the social
justice inherent in shared use and enjoyment of land. He continued
to advocate the establishment of national parks for the rest of his
life.

A few days earlier, Morris had written in his diary:

. . . a young new MP, Cunninghame Graham by name, called on me by appointment to pump me on the subject of socialism and we had an agreeable talk. A brisk bright sort of young man; the other day he made his maiden speech and produced quite an impression by its brilliancy and socialistic hints.

Despite finding Robert a perplexing character, whose illegible scrawl suggested 'a loose screw', Morris was happy to meet and correspond with him, and soon invited him to chair a socialist meeting in Glasgow. Following this event, Morris wrote: 'Cunninghame Graham MP took the chair for me, which was thought bold on a Sunday and a Socialist meeting: he declared himself not a socialist because he agreed with the Owenite doctrine of man being made by his circumstances' – Robert Owen being the philanthropic Welsh textile magnate who promoted experimental socialistic communities of factory workers.

Owenite Robert may have called himself, at that point anyway, but his personal charisma, his easy manner, his knowledge and wit, won over panel and audience alike. Present at the meeting the journalist and activist, Joseph Burgess, described Robert thus:

One of the handsomest men of his generation, he might have stepped right out of a canvas by Velasquez. He was a tall, lithe young man, browned by exposure on the grassy plains of Mexico where he had spent some years ranching, and generally dressed in a suit of brown Melton cloth. His clothes were fashionably cut; he stood erect on somewhat long feet, and he had a habit, as he spoke, of running his aristocratic hands through a thick crop of upstanding dark hair. His face was long and thin, the length accentuated by the high narrow forehead and the pointed brown beard, and he had intuitive eyes which burned and glowed with animation.

Morris's newspaper, *Commonweal*, hailed the meeting as a unique occasion: 'For the first time in the history of Scotland a Scottish MP took part in a political meeting held on a Sunday, and for the first time in the history of Britain, a British MP presided at a socialist meeting.' Two years later, Robert would come to embody another first as he publicly embraced the need for state regulation of labour, thereby declaring himself the first Socialist in British parliamentary history.

But he had much to do meanwhile.

Twelve

WESTMINSTER

The National Gasworks

For Robert and Gabriela this time of new friendships and connections brought with it a ferment of ideas. They were invited by William Morris to Kelmscott, his Hammersmith residence. Through his extended circle they forged links with other socialists including Eleanor Marx Aveling, daughter of Karl Marx; the artist Walter Crane; the economists and early Fabians, Beatrice and Sydney Webb; Annie Besant, secularist and women's rights campaigner; and Henry Hyndman, founder of the Social Democratic Federation. Yet the ideology which so invigorated so many of his new acquaintances – and at the same time forced them endlessly to reconfigure their alliances: Morris's Socialist League was itself a breakaway group from the authoritarian Hyndman's SDF – was never fully to claim Robert's adherence. Where Morris, who admitted struggling to grasp the ideas contained in *Das Kapital*, embraced socialism from an essentially aesthetic standpoint, Robert came at it as an humanitarian. He felt the wretchedness of oppressed people wherever he encountered them – in the coalmines and ironworks of Lanarkshire or the swamps and forests of Paraguay – felt it deeply and personally, and raged against the society that gave licence to their oppression. Yet he remained too much an individualist to subscribe fully to any single movement, and too hot-blooded to allow much for the influence of political theory on his actions.

Meanwhile, that same loftiness, which emanated from his heritage and upbringing and which could sometimes manifest itself as contempt, held him constantly a little apart from his peers in almost every aspect of his life. It was this that enabled him to accommodate the apparent paradoxes of being a landowner whose politics placed the landowning classes at the top of the radicals' most-wanted list, yet one who flatly refused to divest himself of his own assets when challenged to do so; for he knew that it was precisely those assets that afforded him the position from which he could speak out and be taken seriously. By the same token, Robert detested the very institution which offered him the platform to champion the causes he espoused. He referred to it simply as 'the National Gasworks'.

Gabriela also was now finding a voice and starting to give talks on topics including socialism, women's suffrage and Irish history: one to the Bloomsbury Socialist Club at the invitation of Eleanor Marx Aveling, others in Scotland where she was now Vice President of the Scottish Women's Liberal Association, to whose members she declared:

I believe the entrance of women into the field of politics, although on the outside it seems somewhat alien to their natures, is the only means by which the poor and the women of the middle and lower middle classes may be respected and treated as reasoning beings. I do not think that the giving of the vote to women will practically alter the issue of any election. The only appreciable result will be to increase the number of votes. But I do think it will put women in a more logical and a firmer position in society as at present constituted. And it is from this point of view that I earnestly urge upon women of every rank to join a women's political association.

If this sounds lukewarm it is most likely because, as Gabriela later confided to Mary Evans, 'I take a flimsy interest in politics, more out of duty than conviction, and because everyone seems to have the idea that one cares for nothing else – the least interesting and most repugnant topic to me under the sun.' Gabriela, it seems, was in London on sufferance. In truth, it was the upkeep of Gartmore that preyed on her mind. Her health was fragile, and such energy as remained to her was being drawn increasingly towards Spain and her preoccupation with Catholic mysticism. Meanwhile, she returned to Gartmore whenever she could. She was growing fond of the place and its people, for all the anxieties they represented. Robert wrote to her there from London in April 1887 when a cold spell had laid her low. He was solicitous about her health and sought to cheer her up with news of his visit to Buffalo Bill's Wild West show, which was currently taking London by storm. Robert, who had met William Cody in Texas, and on a later tour of the sell-out show would entertain him at Glasgow's Arts Club, was especially delighted by an encounter with a group of Mexican cowboys with whom he had swapped traveller's tales, he told Gabriela.

The previous year, in May 1886, a bomb had exploded at a demonstration for an eight-hour working day in Chicago, killing seven policeman and four civilians. Eight known anarchists were arrested. On the slender evidence that one may have built the bomb, even though none of them were known to have thrown it, they had now been convicted and sentenced to hang. Robert joined Morris, Annie Besant, the anarchist Prince Kropotkin and others at a meeting to protest the sentence and to petition the US Supreme Court for a reprieve. Robert argued that conviction by association, without evidence, was a threat to freedom of speech, and that an eight-hour working day was the only way for working people to educate themselves in order ultimately to be capable of government. This won him favourable comparisons with Morris as a defender of free speech and fighter for social justice.

At home meanwhile, unemployment was now at record levels and protests were being held throughout the country, none more vigorously than in the capital where the new commissioner, Charles Warren, was determined to exert control by whatever means possible. Cat-and-mouse games ensued as the protesters mobilised in different parts of the city, always keeping one step ahead of the police. When arrests were made the penalties were severe: imprisonment and fines of up to fifty pounds, with the inevitable consequence that families were left destitute. In early May, following the dispersal by police of a meeting of Socialist Democratic Federation supporters, Robert questioned the Home Secretary on whether the police had been given special authority to break up Socialist meetings. This the Home Secretary categorically denied. But when, the following week, a gathering was ordered to disperse before any speaking had begun, this was seen as tantamount to a ban and the ensuing public outcry led to a Commons debate a few days later.

In Ireland the temperature was rising. Prime Minister Salisbury's nephew and newly appointed Irish Secretary, Arthur Balfour, had introduced repressive new legislation, commonly known as the Irish Crimes Act, which gave greater law enforcement power to the authorities. Its principal target was the Plan of Campaign which it effectively outlawed, enabling Balfour to set about suppressing protests. Hundreds were arrested and imprisoned, including no less than twenty MPs, often for nothing more than offering succour to evicted tenants. With these injustices burning in his mind, and in language dripping with sarcasm, Robert rose to speak against what appeared to be similarly coercive measures being brought to bear in London. 'England is a free country – thanks to Heaven,' he declared. 'It is a free country for a man to starve in – that is a boon you can never take away from him – but it appears in the future it is not going to be a free country to hold public meetings in.' These gatherings were being dispersed because the people taking part in them were poor and nobody liked what they stood for or were prepared to speak out for them, he went on. Freedom of speech was under threat, he warned, and it might not be long before there would be revolution in the air.

This was talk of a kind that provoked gasps in the House. Robert's unusual, and to some extent naïve, self-confidence presented a clear target for those who wanted to undermine his credibility. He had an inflated view of his own importance, said some. He suffered from the same manic disposition as his father, said others. And an offhand reference in his speech to Buffalo Bill Cody, whose show continued its record-breaking London run, was seen simply as showing off – which it probably was, suggesting that in times of trouble he, Robert, was a man who knew a thing or two about rough-riding and hostile Indians.

Over the summer at Gartmore, Robert and Gabriela entertained, visited neighbours and tenants, and attended to the house and grounds. Duty was never far away, as Robert made time for his constituents and met further demands as a Justice of the Peace and Deputy Lieutenant for Stirlingshire. Keir Hardie was now regularly at his side in his capacity as agent for the Lanarkshire miners, and their friendship was growing. As the price of coal stayed low, the Scottish miners' wages, having earlier been restored, were docked once again. Robert re-doubled his commitment to his constituents, placing an eight-hour working day at the centre of his proposals. Hardie's new paper, the *Miner*, applauded Robert's commitment to its readers' cause, noting that he emptied the lobbies whenever he spoke at Westminster.

In August, the Coal Mines Regulation Bill came before Parliament, setting out a raft of long-awaited and sorely needed safety measures. As if to underline the urgency, a firedamp explosion at the Udston Colliery in Hamilton had killed seventy-three miners at the end of May. Over the following weeks Robert spoke a total of nineteen times, putting forward amendments on issues ranging from the care of pit ponies to safety equipment, unskilled labour, ventilation, tied houses and the setting up of an accident and insurance fund. His final intervention was to propose an eight-hour working day for Scotland where, he explained, the unions were not yet strong enough to counter owners and workers needed the protection of Parliament. He was putting this before the House, he added, on the very day that eight hundred miners, locked out over the issue of hours, were being evicted.

> Anyone who knows the miners of Scotland will know the miserable conditions those men are in, and little by little they had disposed of their wretched goods and chattels. I appeal to anyone who has seen the eviction of a miner's family, whether a wretched rickety table, a dirty chair, and a few pots and pans do not constitute the whole household goods? In the face of a scene like that they were to have political economy – supply and demand – and the mumbo-jumbo of books thrust down their throats.

To his fury the amendment was roundly defeated. The Home Secretary declared that legislation of this kind was encouraging men to rely on Parliament to do for them what they ought to do for themselves: negotiate with the owners. But Robert saw that they lacked the education to do so; a situation only to be remedied by the shorter working day which would afford them the leisure time necessary for self-improvement. Despite this setback, Robert vowed to continue his campaign for an eight-hour day which, as the *Labour Elector* reported, he believed to be 'the battle ground on which the first real skirmish of Capital and Labour (in our time) will be fought.'

Meanwhile, a Parliamentary sketch from a London paper which found its way into the *Airdrie Advertiser* reported that Robert was to be seen rushing frantically through the lobbies 'always bareheaded, at a pace seldom seen in Parliamentary circles'; the inference being that he was chaotic and ineffectual. The truth, however, was somewhat different. He was desperately trying to secure a reprieve for a young Polish Jew, Israel Lipski, who had been convicted of the brutal murder of a woman, Miriam Angel, also Polish, in London's East End, and sentenced to hang.

Lipski and most of his witnesses barely spoke English. The judge publicly questioned his own judgement almost as soon as he had passed sentence. Robert gathered the signatures of 110 MPs for a petition to the Home Secretary to have Lipski's sentence commuted to life imprisonment, on the grounds that the prosecution had failed to prove beyond reasonable doubt that he was the murderer. When this was rejected, Robert wasted no time collecting two thousand signatures from residents of Whitechapel and the surrounding areas, which he presented the following day. Again this was rejected amid protests that he was interfering with the judicial process by asking questions in the House. An attempt to meet with the Prime Minister met with a closed door. By now there were fears that the execution would cause riots. Widespread calls for a reprieve were led by W.T. Stead, the campaigning editor of the *Pall Mall Gazette*. With less than twenty-four hours to go until the moment of execution, and the Home Secretary still struggling to reach a decision, news arrived that Lipski had confessed. He was duly hanged at eight o'clock the next morning. Robert, who as an MP had been able to visit the young man in prison and had remained convinced of his innocence until the end, was devastated. It has since been suggested that Lipski's confession may have been a bid for suicide, when faced with the alternative of life in prison.

A few days later Robert and Gabriela hastened across the water to Dublin in support of the Plan of Campaign leaders, Michael Davitt, John Dillon and William O'Brien, amid large-scale protests against Balfour's banning of the Irish League. Robert had earlier spoken against the repressive Irish Crimes Act at a meeting in Coatbridge, but once in Dublin he declined to take advantage of the platform this would undoubtedly have offered him as an emerging nationalist politician. Instead of speaking he returned home on the next boat. Many years later he wrote to Wilfred Scawen Blunt, explaining his decision:

> We were so disgusted with that awful deputation (that we joined in Dublin), their vulgarity, their want of tact, their commonness, that I said I had a cold and would not speak (we did not know you [Blunt] were to speak) and after driving once round Dublin . . . came straight home and were sick crossing . . .

The Irish activists were too rough a bunch for a man of his sensibilities, was the excuse. In fairness, Robert always deplored the prospect of violence – he had seen enough of it in his younger days, after all – although he was, by the same token, perfectly used to less refined company than his own. But he was also by now thoroughly exhausted from the exertions of recent months and the Lipski affair had proved the final straw. At his side, Gabriela may have encouraged him to withdraw for the good of his health.

If he needed respite, it was brief. The following week and back in Westminster, Robert became embroiled for the first, but not the last, time in a matter of protocol. The Lords' amendments to the Coal Mines Regulation Bill included a clause aimed at frustrating the appointment of men chosen by the miners from among their number as safety inspectors. Already incensed that recommendations were being made by 'eight or ten old gentlemen who know nothing of the subject,' and already rebuked by Mr Speaker for saying so, Robert again spoke up: '. . . it does seem a curious thing that an Assembly which is not elected by a popular vote should dare to dictate to us, who are elected – ' At this the Speaker intervened, ordering Robert to withdraw the words 'dare to dictate' and apologise. Robert replied: 'I regret to say that as this is a matter of conscience I cannot apologise.' He was duly suspended and left the House to noisy support from sympathisers, having first offered a measured personal apology to the Speaker, along with an adamant refusal to withdraw the offending words.

In the event Robert's suspension lasted only a few minutes, since it was already three o'clock in the morning and this was the last sitting before Parliament rose for the autumn recess. But pleas of conscience were taken seriously in the House and this time Robert won approval for his stance from several quarters. In the following days the sketch writers, among them those of the *Scottish Leader* and the *Edinburgh Dispatch*, remarked favourably on his unconventional approach. He might not model the professional politician, they noted, in fact far from it, but he got people listening and served his constituents, the Scottish miners, assiduously. Furthermore he had good manners, 'an old-world courtliness worthy of Black Rod'.

Aware that his own party, the Liberals, were increasingly unlikely to provide the support he needed to secure his aims, Robert now set out to establish himself as an independent voice for the working men of Scotland. Throughout the early autumn, with Keir Hardie accompanying him, he toured the mining districts with the simple message that the ruling class was intrinsically antagonistic to the working man and that change would only come if they began to elect representatives from amongst themselves. 'Corbies dinna pike oot the een o' ither corbies', he would say, lapsing into the broad Scots which he often used to calculated effect. His meetings were starting to draw large crowds and when he was late, as he often was because of prior engagements, the audience were free to feast their eyes on Gabriela who arrived on the platform before him – so said the ever-present *Airdrie Advertiser*.

In Ireland public resentment of the Irish Crimes Act continued to mount. Early September saw William O'Brien being brought before magistrates in Mitchelston, Co Tipperary, charged under the new legislation with making inflammatory speeches. An angry crowd of protesters gathered and police opened fire, killing three of them. News of the 'Mitchelstown Massacre' swiftly crossed the Irish Sea, further fuelling indignation in Scotland. A month later Robert spoke to the Coatbridge Junior Liberals, his arrival greeted with cries of 'Here comes the gallant Graham'. Here he made his first overt appeal to nationalism. As things were, he pointed out, Irish affairs stood in the way of Scottish progress on social issues such as land reform, the working day and alcohol consumption, since Irish MPs in Westminster were fearful of diverting attention from their own cause. Yet surely the Scots and Irish interests were one and the same and all the challenges facing crofters, miners, factory workers and those looking to tackle the drink problem, would be solved far quicker in Scotland than in Westminster. All four nations should have regional assemblies, and 'the sooner they take the management of English affairs out of Westminster and place it at York or elsewhere, the better,' he declared.

From Coatbridge Robert then travelled east to Broxburn where shale miners had been locked out after eighteen weeks of a wage dispute and now faced strike-breaking action by imported 'black-nebs'. Their only chance against the owners, who had earlier resorted to evictions in an effort to break the strike, was to join the growing movement for unionisation, he told them. He had just attended the annual national coal miners' conference, held this year in Edinburgh. There, a rising group of Scots, Keir Hardie among their leaders, had challenged the presiding faction of English delegates by proposing the introduction of an eight-hour working Bill. This motion was resoundingly carried. The *Pall Mall Gazette* reported that it seemed 'not unlikely that a Scottish Labour Party will be formed before long and that Mr Cunninghame Graham will be their leader. The Hon. gentleman is gaining enormous popularity with the Scottish workers and especially the miners.'

It was now early November 1887. The Irish crisis persisted. The economy remained depressed and unemployment continued to rise. On the streets of London an autumn chill had done nothing to dampen the unrest that simmered on following the sultry summer of the Queen's Golden Jubilee. Robert had now been active in Parliament for a giddy nine months, racing hither and thither to speak on the myriad issues that stirred his passions, rattling the establishment cage as he went. His refusal to conform to the parliamentary mould, his apparently chaotic approach to business and disregard for process, not to mention his distinctive appearance and unconventional rhetorical style, continued to earn him the criticism of eccentricity and dilettantism from some quarters. But events were now looming which would place the seriousness, the authenticity of Robert's commitment to social justice and reform, beyond doubt.

Thirteen

TRAFALGAR SQUARE

Bloody Sunday

In autumn 1974, a year after I returned from South America, I settled back in London with a job as a writer for a small magazine publishing company with the ambitious name of Dominion Press. I remember attending the interview wearing a Peruvian woollen poncho over my Carnaby Street suit – the vestiges of the trip still clung firmly to me. No one batted an eyelid. It was the 1970s, after all.

The business was housed in Grand Buildings, the imposing bull-nosed block that formed the apex of The Strand and Northumberland Avenue. Built as the Grand Hotel in 1870, it overlooked Trafalgar Square and was now being worn away by the droppings of the enormous flock of pigeons which inhabited the square. It was also, at dusk on a winter's day, a roost for the huge murmurations of starlings which swirled above the square before settling noisily on the rooftops to add their corrosive excretions to those of the pigeons.

From our second-floor vantage point we were regularly treated to the sight of marches and gatherings of one kind or another. Directly across the Strand, occupying the whole block between Grand Buildings and the church of St Martin-in-the-Fields, stood South Africa House which later would become the scene of the four-year-long continuous picket by the City of London Anti Apartheid Group in support of the release of Nelson Mandela – a protest of which Robert would certainly have approved. But what I did not know at the time of my sojourn in Grand Buildings was that ninety-five years previously, on the site now occupied by South

Africa House, had for many years stood Morley's Hotel. And it was from Morley's Hotel, on 13 November 1887, that Gabriela had watched the tumultuous events that would unfold below.

Throughout the autumn of 1887, Trafalgar Square and the growing gatherings taking place there had been a magnet for the unemployed men who came in daily from outlying districts to mingle and listen to speakers. These included William Morris, Annie Besant and Bernard Shaw, who addressed the crowd on topics such as the need for self-help and the means to find work. The resulting throng made it difficult for commuters to get to Charing Cross station and the Underground. Shoppers struggled to find their way from the West End to the Strand. Ladies were jostled. Hoteliers and retailers complained that their business was being hurt. Plainclothes policemen mingled with the crowd, taking notes at Socialist meetings and gathering the names of bystanders, all in an attempt to prove that there was a conspiracy against the government or, if no conspiracy, at the very least that the crowd harboured criminals and Irish-style terrorists with bombs.

The middle classes, most of whom had never ventured east of Aldgate, knew nothing of the misery that drove these jobless workers daily through the City and towards the West End, and had little sympathy for them. But for the poverty-stricken dockers and labourers, tradesmen and craftsmen, Trafalgar Square was not only the principal place in the capital for the exercise of free speech but also, being where East and West Ends met, a focal point for the class struggle – which was nowhere more sharply highlighted than at the Lord Mayor's show. Scheduled for 9 November, this was now fast approaching and with it the prospect of a repeat of the previous year's debacle when, to the embarrassment of assembled grandees and onlookers, a raggle-taggle army of the unemployed had attached itself to the tail end of the gilt-spangled mayoral procession. The nervous middle classes now placed their faith in the person of the Metropolitan Police Commissioner, Sir Charles Warren, a former expeditionary soldier and devout Anglican. Determined to take a hard line on maintaining the peace he duly issued a proclamation, without consulting the Home Secretary, which banned anyone from carrying a banner or making a speech at any point along the route of the mayoral procession, which included Trafalgar Square.

In Ireland, meanwhile, following his recent conviction at Mitchelston for inflammatory speech, William O'Brien had been moved from Cork, where his imprisonment was being vigorously protested, to the more secure Tullamore Jail. O'Brien was no stranger to detention, but now he was suffering from tuberculosis and his health was deteriorating. The Metropolitan Radical Federation, an umbrella group of Irish, Socialist and working men's organisations, had planned a demonstration to protest at his treatment. Senior Socialist figures now summoned Robert from Scotland to join a meeting with the Home Secretary to seek assurances that, despite Warren's injunction, the MRF demonstration could go ahead. When they arrived at the Home Office, Henry Matthews, the Home Secretary, refused to see them. Robert, as the only MP, insisted on being admitted and a bad-tempered exchange ensued, exacerbated by the fact that the two men had sparred over the Lipski case. Nevertheless, Robert left the meeting with the understanding that consent had been given. He issued a statement that he would speak in Trafalgar Square, specifically to challenge Warren's right to ban the Lord Mayor's Show demonstration. This went beyond the treatment of O'Brien, he believed, and directly to the most sacred of democratic principles: freedom of speech and assembly. But when his statement was reported in the press it came with the news that the Home Secretary had changed his mind without informing Robert or his colleagues, and that the authorities would prevent the meeting 'by a strong force of police and military'.

Had Robert not spent much of the summer in Scotland he might have gauged the moods of both his parliamentary colleagues and the authorities more closely. As it was he had, typically, dashed back to London to confront the Home Secretary and, as he saw it, to be double-crossed at the eleventh hour; not only that but, as subsequent events were to show, to be let down by his fellow Liberal MPs, not one of whom was to turn up at Trafalgar Square in his support. Now, however, precarious though his position was as someone who

had sworn an oath of loyalty to the Crown, he felt himself committed to challenging the authorities.

Sunday 13 November dawned

a Dickensian Sabbath, the sort that Graham especially loathed,
with the drizzly veiling of outlines all too characteristic of
London in late autumn. The going for the marchers would be
slimy underfoot, as the dirty rain mixed with the inevitable grime
of dirty pavements . . .

So Cedric Watts and Laurence Davies set the scene in their critical biography. Those marchers – many of whom were immigrant
Irish workers – were now setting off from points mostly across
south and east London. To some onlookers they appeared peaceful
and well behaved. Others noted that they seemed half-starved and
listless. Others still feared them for a mob waiting to be unleashed.
As they made their way towards Trafalgar Square, the mood grew
bleak as two items of news filtered through: O'Brien's condition
had worsened to the point that he had been moved to the prison
infirmary; and the Chicago Seven's appeal had failed and they had
been executed the previous day.

Warren, meanwhile, had assembled a huge force of police whose
main objective was to prevent the demonstration gaining access to
the sunken area in the centre of Trafalgar Square and the plinth of
Nelson's Column, from where speeches could be made. He posi-
tioned policemen shoulder-to-shoulder around the edge of the
central space, two deep to the north and west, four deep to the
south and east from where the main assault was anticipated. In
reserve he had contingents of Horse Guards and Foot Guards, with
bayonets fixed, waiting nearby. He also had a magistrate standing by
with a copy of the Riot Act. But first he planned to prevent as many
of the demonstrators as possible from reaching the square at all. To
this end he had police ready to intervene at all access points on a
one-mile radius.

Robert arrived on Sunday morning from Stoke-on-Trent where
he had been speaking at a miners' meeting the previous day. First he
took Gabriela to Morley's Hotel where he knew she would have a

ringside seat, along with the hundreds of other eager spectators – including Bernard Shaw and his mother – who had found vantage points around the square in hotels, offices and even on rooftops. Then he made for the steps of St Martin-in-the-Fields where he was due to meet William Morris and Annie Besant. But that meeting never took place. While marchers from the south and east were met and dispersed by police on Westminster Bridge, Morris and Besant, coming from Clerkenwell Green with the SDF contingent, and marching behind a banner urging onlookers to 'Educate, Agitate, Organise', were set upon by police at Seven Dials and beaten with truncheons. Morris and most of his fellows fled north. Annie Besant, determined to be arrested so that she could challenge Warren's authority in court, continued towards the north side of the central police cordon. There, by the National Gallery, she presented herself and invited the police to detain her. Knowing her capacity for making trouble, they declined.

Robert now made his way from St Martin-in-the-Fields to Charing Cross underground where he met up with John Burns, an ardent trades unionist, leading member of the SDF and an impassioned speaker. He, Henry Hyndman and Robert were all due to address the gathering. According to Robert his meeting with Burns on this occasion was serendipitous, a version of events he stuck to at the trial since a charge of conspiracy would have greatly increased the severity of the penalty they faced. In any event, Robert and Burns passed through the mounted patrols, Robert soothing the horses as they slipped by, and together they approached the police cordon on the south of the square, intent like Annie Besant on presenting themselves for arrest. They were followed now by a solid group of a hundred or more men. It was four o'clock in the afternoon.

Robert and Burns, a burly figure well known to the police as an agitator, walked forward arm-in-arm and with the phalanx of followers behind them pushed their way through the first and second police cordons. But as other officers closed around them, truncheons raised, the followers dropped back, leaving Robert and Burns isolated. According to the police, Robert then threw off his hat, shouted 'Now for the square!', and rushed at their inner line, throwing punches as he went, one of which struck a constable in the mouth, before being restrained with a blow to the head and arrested. Other witnesses say he simply walked forward peacefully and raised his hands to protect his head once the blows began to rain down.

A description of these events appeared the following day in a letter to the *Times* from Sir Edward Reed, Liberal MP for Cardiff who, along with a horrified Gabriela, had been watching from Morley's Hotel. Surrounded by police, Reed wrote, Robert now stood restrained by the arms as two further policemen stepped up behind him and struck him again on the head 'with a violence and brutality shocking to behold'. Then, as he was being manhandled into the space behind the cordon, 'another from behind seized him most needlessly by the hair (the abundance of which perhaps tempted him) and dragged his head back and in that manner he was forced back many yards.' Even in the melée, Robert with his shock of auburn hair was conspicuous amid a sea of flat caps and helmets. Gabriela, having seen him fall with blood streaming from his head, was convinced he must have suffered a fatal blow. However, once he and Burns were held in the centre of the square he was able, despite feeling faint from the blow, to clean himself with water from the fountain, brought in Burns' hat.

At this point Warren, who was overseeing events from his horse, ordered the troops in. A full-blown cavalry charge ensued and pandemonium erupted as screaming protesters fought to get out of the way of the horses and flailing police truncheons. Within moments the crowd was in full retreat. The magistrate who had been standing by to read the Riot Act turned disappointedly for home. By six o'clock the square had been cleared. A total of 300 arrests were made and 150 protesters were treated at various hospitals. William Morris later pointed out that it could have been worse had the protesters made it through the cordons into the centre of the square. Then there might have been a massacre to rival Peterloo. In any event, it was bad enough for Robert. He and John Burns were taken to a small, windowless cell at Bow Street magistrates' court, furnished with nothing but a covering of straw for the floor. Denied bail, and Robert with his wound still untreated, they spent a miserable night, listening to the harsh songs of drunks and prostitutes

and the pleas and groans of a prisoner being bullied by his gaolers .
– as Robert later told the House.

Next morning, Monday, Missy arrived with her nephew, Adrian
Hope. In a letter to her daughter-in-law, Barbara, she described
Robert as being 'in good spirits . . . making even the police inspector
laugh'; though knowing what a blow to the head had done for her
husband, she must privately have been deeply alarmed to see her
son pale and drawn, his luxuriant hair matted with blood from the
large wound to his now-bandaged skull.

Robert and John Burns were kept waiting in their Bow Street cell
until two o'clock when the case against them was finally heard and
adjourned for a week. R.B. Haldane, a rising young barrister, had
rushed from his chambers to represent them as William Morris,
Walter Crane and Oscar Wilde all looked on. Gabriela had also
arrived at Bow Street sometime during the morning and had been
present at the hearing, along with Robert's aunt Margaret and
husband William Hope, the speculating VC, whom Missy had not
seen for twenty-five years and 'should not care if I ever saw him
again.' Hope, nevertheless, had stood bail for his 'misguided'
nephew, making it clear in a letter to the *Times* the following day, 15
November, that he had done so not from personal conviction but
out of loyalty to an injured member of his family; the irony escap-
ing him that had he not meddled in the family finances a decade
earlier, the injured family member might have had the wherewithal
to stand his own bail.

In her letter to Barbara, Missy described the scene in court:

> Poor Robert looked so worn and ill . . . but so handsome notwith-
> standing his bandage. One of his eyes is shut up. Gabrielle who I
> really was sorry for was in one of her best moods. I asked her to
> come back to lunch with me but she was too busy, she said.

Busy, perhaps, with the furious letter she was writing to the
Times. A perfectly orderly gathering had been turned into a riot,
Gabriela wrote, by the 'imperial and autocratic warrant of the
Home Secretary and Sir Charles Warren'. 'Now Sir,' she went
on,

how is it that he, a Scottish MP, was not accompanied by Metropolitan MPs, by those Liberal MPs who, holding the same views, talk loudly when they can do it with safety but the moment it is to be put to its logical conclusion, they vanish. My husband acted nobly and bravely. The first steps to the fearful coercion and tyranny which has embittered Ireland for so long have now been taken in London. The people are to be coerced. Their rights of open-air demonstration; their expression of indignation at a man dying of consumption in an Irish jail is to be suppressed by the Riot Act and charges by cavalry and mounted police. The Government has gone too far now, and I'm sure my husband will have the sympathy of all brave Scotchmen who hate injustice and coercion.

When Gabriela's blood was up she, like her husband, did not hold back.

Released from Bow Street, Robert went first to see a doctor. From the surgery he issued a press statement asserting that he had not been part of the Socialist demonstration, but had gone to Trafalgar Square solely to affirm his right of free speech there and to support the MRF resolution regarding the treatment of William O'Brien. He felt no ill-will towards the police, merely pity for the dreadful job they had to do.

Back at Morley's Hotel, Robert and Gabriela were besieged by well-wishers, while out in the lobby plainclothes policemen loitered. The press were now splashing their front pages. The *Pall Mall Gazette* described events as a *coup d'etat* by the police and the Horse Guards. The *Times* congratulated Warren on prevailing against the forces of chaos. The ever-attentive *Airdrie Advertiser* told its readers that Robert was now the most talked-about man in London, with wild claims circulating about his past: that he had ridden the plains for years with Buffalo Bill before striking gold and becoming a millionaire, for example.

At the Home Office, meanwhile, Matthews was feeling the pressure of public opinion. He needed an opportunity to air and preferably dispel claims of police brutality. Given Reed's letter describing Robert's assault from behind by two policeman, the forthcoming trial of Robert and Burns offered just such an opportunity. The date for the case was set for 22 November, but when the accused came to Bow Street it was adjourned for a further week in order that the prosecution could prepare.

Robert returned swiftly to Scotland and a hero's welcome at Central Station in Glasgow, organised by the local branch of the Irish National League, of which he was president. 'The Hon gentleman looked pale and weakly and on removing his hat in acknowledgment of the loud cheers that greeted him, it was noticed that his head was still covered by a dark silk bandage,' reported the *Airdrie Advertiser*, which forbore from remarking on the Hon gentleman's innate sense of theatre. A crowd of several thousand mobbed his carriage as it made its way down Hope Street. When he and Gabriela eventually reached Balfron, another large crowd of tenants and neighbours greeted them and escorted them up to Gartmore.

A week later, on 30 November, Robert and Burns were back at Bow Street on remand. Robert's defence counsel was Herbert Asquith, Liberal MP for East Fife. John Burns defended himself. Prosecuting was Harry Poland, as Treasury Counsel. Robert's defence was that he had been exercising his legitimate right of public assembly. He called Sir Edward Reed in his defence. But Reed's eyewitness account of events was to no avail. Neither was the sensational testimony of another witness, Charles Bradlaugh, a fellow activist and founder of the National Secular Society. Bradlaugh claimed that the authorities had fully intended to stir up the riot; a fact evidenced by their actions at the violent meeting the previous February, 1886, when the Tory party had paid the Fair Traders to discredit the SDF, payment having been made with a cheque which Bradlaugh himself had seen.

Unconvinced, the magistrate sent Robert and Burns for trial on three counts: riot, unlawful assembly and assaulting the police. The trial date was set for 16 January 1888.

Christmas at Gartmore was a subdued affair. The penalty for riot and assault was two years in prison with hard labour. 'An English prison is torture and meant to be so,' noted William Morris to a mutual friend. For all their apparent bravado, Robert and Gabriela can only have been worried. The Hogmanay weather was cold and tempestuous. While Robert attended a few meetings – despite having not yet fully recovered from his injury, he drew comfort from the abundant sympathy with which he was met – Gabriela spent as much time outdoors as she could, walking, riding, planting fruit trees and planning a new formal garden; anything, one can only imagine, rather than hanging around in the large, gloomy house where every crack in the plaster reminded her of debt. Her mood quickly spiralled downwards and she ended up yet again berating the staff, perhaps as a substitute for the members of Robert's family upon whom – as we know from the only volume of her diary to have survived – she brooded constantly. On the first day of the trial she was to lunch with 'my dreadful M in L'. The following day she would sit in one part of the court, showing a brave face to friends and well-wishers, while Missy, with Charlie and Barbara, sat in another.

They returned to London on 13 January. It was cold and foggy with a biting east wind. Gabriela took immediately to her bed and was shortly diagnosed with pleurisy. But by Monday 16th she was up again and at the Old Bailey in time for the trial to begin. Even before it started, the trial had become a legal and political *cause célèbre*, the newspapers already dubbing the battle of Trafalgar Square 'Bloody Sunday'. Now the gallery was filled to bursting with supporters. Curious barristers thronged the well of the court as the parties lined up: the Attorney General for the prosecution; Herbert Asquith, future Prime Minister, for Robert; and John Burns, with advice from a friendly barrister, for himself. Burns entered the dock first, concluding his case several hours later with a cross-examination of Sir Charles Warren, during which he landed enough punches to leave the Metropolitan Police Commissioner 'flushed and annoyed'. Now came Robert's turn. The new radical paper, the Star, described the scene:

> He coolly took off his hat, laid down his stick, pulled off his over-coat, struck his fingers through his hair and settled down to have a calm survey of the historic courtroom. Graham is a striking figure as he stands in the dock with his fine breezy head of hair

undivided by a parting – in the artistic disorder of which his opponents would see a touch of revolutionary unkemptness – and his moustachios to match. He is over middle height and although not strongly built is decidedly wiry. His features are clear-cut – his nose sharp and his eyes keen.

Robert's purpose had been simply to attend a lawful meeting in a public place long recognised as such, argued Asquith. The cry ascribed to him by the police had not been intended to encourage anyone to follow him into the square, merely to announce his presence and intentions. This stretched the credulity of the jury which eventually, with guidance from the judge, found the two defendants not guilty of the more serious charges of causing a riot and assaulting the police, but guilty of the lesser and rarely used charge of unlawful assembly. For this Robert and John Burns received six weeks gaol each, mercifully without hard labour. Sir Charles Warren, meanwhile, was entirely vindicated of all suggestions that he had acted unlawfully.

Pentonville Prison in 1887 was not a pleasant place to be. It had been built in the 1840s to serve the principle that prisoners were most likely to see the error of their ways when locked up alone for most, or all, of the time. Robert disagreed. In *Sursum Corda* (*Success*, 1902), he wrote:

How crass it is to shut men up in vast hotels, withdrawing them from any possible influence which might ever change their lives and to confine them in whitewashed cells with windows of Dutch glass, gas, and the Bible, table, chair, little square saltbox, wooden spoon, tin pan, schedule of rules, hell in their hearts, a pound of oakum in their hands, condemned to silence and to count the days, pricking them off under the ventilator with a bent nail or pin.

Clad in his arrow-marked jacket and trousers, Robert settled down to the tedium of a routine devoid of stimulating activity. Complaining of hunger and cold, he was awarded cooked beef twice a week, an extra blanket and mattress. But a bladder infection brought on by a kick in the stomach on Bloody Sunday, and which caused him constant discomfort, earned Robert no remission. Nor did his family's pleas direct to the Home Secretary grant them the right to visit. John Burns, diagnosed at the outset with jaundice, was luckier. He was transferred to the infirmary where he was allowed to be visited by his wife.

'Day follows day with "skilly", exercise, with Chapel, with dreary dullness and with counting hours,' Robert continued.

Night follows night and when the light goes out the tramping up and down the cells begins, the rappings and the mysterious code by which prisoners communicate sound through the building like an imprisoned woodpecker tapping to be free: tremendous nights of eight and forty hours, twisting turning rising oft and lying down to rise again, of watching, counting up to one million, walking about and touching every single article; of thinking upon every base action of one's life, of breaking out a-cursing like a drab; then falling to a fitful un-refreshing sleep which seems to last but a minute and then the morning bell.

The irony of the title of the piece, *Sursum Corda*, meaning 'Lift up your hearts', refers to the moment each week when the prisoners in chapel find release in the singing of a hymn.

Like an earthquake the pent-up sound breaks forth, the chapel quivers like a ship from stem to stern, dust flies, and loud from every throat the pious doggerel peals. And in the sounds the prison melts away, the doors are opened and each man sits in his home surrounded by his friends, his Sunday dinner smokes, his children all clean washed are by his side . . . Old lags and forgers, area sneaks, burglars, cheats, swindlers, confidence trick men, horse thieves, and dogs stealers, men in for rape, for crimes of violence, assault and battery, with 'smashers', swell mobsmen, blackmailers, all the vilest of the vile . . . made human once again during the sixteen verses of the hymn, and all the miseries of the past week wiped out in the brief exercise of unusual speech.

In the world beyond, meanwhile, Robert and Burns were alternately lauded for their defence of free speech and excoriated as troublemakers, Robert in particular for being a lawmaker who had broken the law. William Morris wrote: 'Graham must expect for some time to come to be a pariah among MPs. To do him justice he is not likely to care much about that.' This proved prophetic. More than two years later, in June 1889, the Observer would opine that Robert was 'undoubtedly the most unpopular man in the House of Commons.'

Following Robert's imprisonment Gabriela took to her bed again for three days with pleurisy. Socialists and radicals now rushed to support her, the wife of a political prisoner. Chief among these was William Stead, editor of the *Pall Mall Gazette*, who had himself been jailed for three months in 1885 for buying a little girl for three pounds, having her certified a virgin and put to bed in a brothel, then alerting the Salvation Army, in order to expose juvenile prostitution.

Gauche, eccentric, but passionate about the injustices of Victorian society and the need for change, Stead considered himself as a newspaper editor to be the 'uncrowned king of an educated democracy'. He was indeed one of the most influential people of his time. Now he latched onto Gabriela, showing solidarity with her and Robert as a way of vicariously reliving his own 'noble' incarceration. 'I often think of you, my dear widowed heroine,' he wrote to her. For her part, Gabriela may have felt a little more ambivalent. In her novel *Beautiful Lies*, Clare Clark suggests that Gabriela was terrified Stead, the dogged investigator, would uncover the secrets of her past and use them to ruin Robert's and her reputations. On the other hand, he also represented an opportunity to get into print. Stead proposed she write an article for his new magazine, the *Link*, journal of the newly formed Law and Liberty League. Although it initially attracted attention from socialists and radicals such as the Socialist League, the SDF and the Fabian Society, their support ebbed away when it became clear that Stead harboured some deeply undemocratic intentions: the creation of what he called Ironside Circles, which would monitor the activity of prominent citizens and report them via the *Link* for behaviour that failed to meet strict requirements. On receipt of Gabriela's article, Stead offered a luke-warm response. It was 'very nice and bright', he said.

Recovered from her illness, Gabriela had by now returned to Gartmore where she spent the remaining four weeks of Robert's incarceration working on the estate accounts and applying to the *curator* for cash which, humiliatingly, had to be paid first to Grant, the estate factor, before being passed on to the laird or his wife. She also stood in for Robert at a meeting of the local Liberal Association in Coatbridge, attended by a large number of working men for whom their MP's wife had become an attraction to rival his. This time, Stead and the *Pall Mall Gazette* were more enthusiastic.

On 18 February 1888, at seven o'clock in the morning, Robert and John Burns walked out of Pentonville Prison to be met by William Morris, Annie Besant and Michael Davitt, who had all been waiting there already for an hour. They repaired to a coffee shop on Caledonian Road where they feasted on meat pies, bacon and eggs. A little later Charlie and his wife arrived, followed shortly by Missy who, as the *Standard* reported, fell wordlessly into her son's arms. Finally, Gabriela appeared to cheers and applause and embraced everyone present.

Fourteen

CRADLEY HEATH

'I never withdraw'

It was now early spring 1888. Robert was thirty-five years old and it was little over a year since he had first taken his seat as a Member of Parliament, a tumultuous twelve months into which he had crammed more emotional intensity than many of his fellow parliamentarians would experience in their entire careers.

His injuries from Trafalgar Square, added to the strain of the trial and his six weeks in Pentonville, had left him exhausted and weak. He continued to suffer from the painful and debilitating bladder complaint which had required the issue of a catheter while he was in prison. But the condemnation of both his peers and influential voices in the press, the fact that even his mother, while admiring his courage, acknowledged that he had brought this public odium upon himself, seemed merely to fuel his indignation, his passion for progress and change. 'Are you thinking where to put your guillotine?' enquired Salisbury, the Prime Minister, as he passed Robert in the House of Commons lobby. 'In Trafalgar Square, of course,' Robert replied.

One thing Pentonville had afforded him was time to think, not least about the misery of the lives of those in whose company he had found himself. In an article for the *Contemporary Review*, published a couple of weeks after his release from gaol, he asked provocatively: *Has the Liberal Party a Future?* This was his first venture into print and it set the tone for a career as a commentator that would bring him even greater notoriety than his brief parliamentary one. Relations between the state and the people had never been more strained, he argued. So long as the Liberal Party stood for progress and against social inequity and the stigma of poverty, for good laws and mediation between poor and the police, employees and employers, tenant and landlord, it should last a thousand years. Otherwise let it go. The party had no future under its current leadership and was turning into a Gladstone personality cult, while working people were waking up to the fact that with a more equal distribution of wealth there would be plenty for everyone. But most Liberals – 'timorous, miserable, invertebrate animals' – were really Tories at heart.

Unsurprisingly, the article infuriated the party. Robert almost immediately compounded the injury with an exculpatory speech in the House of Commons. If to be revolutionary was to wish to ameliorate the condition of the poor of the City, to wish for a more democratic form of government, to wish that Members of Parliament should be paid for their services . . . then he was a revolutionary, he exclaimed. He closed with the warning that the time would come when he would hold a meeting of as many men as Trafalgar Square could hold and the government, of whatever stripe, would happily help him to preserve law and order, so greatly would public opinion have changed by then. 'You never heard such a noise,' he told John Burns proudly of the commotion that ensued, 'even at the roughest meeting. I was ill but managed to get it all out.'

Pilloried in the right-wing press, blackballed by even the radical Brooks' club, he returned to Gartmore for a few days of badly needed recuperation. But absolute rest was beyond him. He closeted himself in the bookroom to write the letters needed to advance the cause so rudely interrupted by Bloody Sunday – that of the Scottish working men. Sooner than he could have expected, an opportunity for action arose in the shape of a by-election for the safe Liberal seat of Mid-Lanark. Robert wasted no time in proposing Keir Hardie as candidate. Miners in recent years had sacrificed causes dear to them, such as the eight-hour working day, in order to return the Liberal Party. Now, that party could repay the debt by helping the party of labour to return the first working man's representative in Scotland. But in the face of a nervous Gladstone's wish to moderate the activities of his party, Robert and Hardie's vocal support for Irish Home Rule, along with Robert's overt socialism and recent infamy as a rioter, alarmed the selectors. J.W. Phillips, a young English Liberal from 'the top drawer' – Oxford-educated, heir to a baronetcy – was duly selected, and received Parnell's endorsement.

Hardie, however, refused to stand down and went forward as an independent candidate, though he was little helped by Robert whose behaviour throughout the following weeks of April was to become increasingly erratic, with explosions of temper in private meetings and outbursts at public ones. The natural conclusion was that he was suffering from the Bloody Sunday blow to his head, a worrying echo of his father's affliction, and so a possible source of concern about his future career. Hardie's agents warned him to steer clear of Robert for the rest of the campaign, while Liberal Party officials tried to persuade Hardie to stand down and avoid splitting the vote, even offering him money and the promise of a safe seat at the next opportunity.

Robert now set off to London with a reluctant Gabriela who had been happily gardening during a spell of fine spring weather at Gartmore, then promptly left her to her own devices as he went off to drum up support for Hardie. On 27 April the future leader of the Labour Party threw his hat in the electoral ring for the first time. He came third with 617 votes. To the Liberals' immense relief, J.W. Phillips saw off his Conservative competitor with a majority of some nine hundred votes. But Hardie had gained important support from the non-Irish Liberal voters of Mid-Lanark.

Despite the defeat both Hardie and Robert were upbeat. Robert spoke animatedly about the prospect of breaking away from the Liberal Party and forming the Scottish Labour Party, whose arrival was already anticipated by readers of the *Glasgow Evening News* to whom Robert had recently given an interview. An initial meeting was held on 19 May, attended by representatives of the crofters, miners, land reformers, and local members of the Irish National League. Three months later, on 25 August, the Scottish Labour Party formally came into being at a public meeting in Glasgow. Robert was appointed president in recognition of his leading role. James Shaw

Maxwell was voted chairman, and Keir Hardie secretary. Dr Gavin Clark and John Ferguson were appointed vice presidents.

The new party's platform was a mixture of state socialism and ordinary radical reform, so William Morris's *Commonweal* reported. It was in the first instance a pressure group, its primary intention to win support for labour reform among existing MPs and to field independent candidates in certain seats. Membership was small but it was a start, foreshadowing the founding of the Independent Labour Party four years later, which in turn offered a model for the modern Labour Party. And at its head, the most radical of all those involved, the one who had argued for the nationalisation of land to be included in its manifesto but had been overruled, was Robert, owner himself of several thousand acres. How was that to be squared? How did he claim the right to speak for the working man? If the contradiction troubled him, he kept it to himself. The practical answer was this: given that the funding of labour candidates was a continual challenge and subject to intense Tory scrutiny, Robert was almost the only person in Parliament available to speak for the labour cause and it was his assets, or rather the borrowing they facilitated, that allowed him to remain there.

Meanwhile he remained steadfast in his opposition to any form of concession to 'Liberal humbug or Tory reaction' as Henry Hyndman, leader of the SDF, observed. As president Robert held firm, the moral compass of the new party. 'Scotland, by far the best educated part of the United Kingdom, would . . . take the lead in the political arena on behalf of the disinherited class,' Hyndman opined.

Robert had by now enjoyed a long association with Henry Champion, a leading figure in the socialist movement and, like Robert, a moneyed, educated and landed Scot. Champion had recently launched a monthly magazine, the *Labour Elector*, whose aim was to expose unfair practices by employers. Most famously it had brought to public attention the plight of the Bryant & May match girls in London's East End, among whose many miserable and unsafe conditions of employment was continual exposure to the risk of phosphorus poisoning. A strike, marches and protests throughout London swiftly brought the company to heel and the match girls' wages were raised.

Robert had spoken at meetings and on street corners in support of this campaign, and his behind-the-scenes involvement with Champion's magazine was now giving him a taste for campaigning journalism. Another of Champion's reports soon offered Robert a new cause to ignite his sense of injustice: that of the nail- and chain-makers of Cradley Heath in the Black Country.

The desperate conditions of these workers, men, women and children, had been known about for decades yet no one had done anything to alleviate their misery. Now, following an abortive strike attempt, an official report was commissioned by the Board of Trade and presented to the Commons in early November. The domestic workshop system, whereby the nail-makers worked in their own dwellings, was 'the root of all evil' the report concluded. Robert now published a pamphlet, putting flesh on the description of the place which Disraeli, many years previously, had called Hell Hole.

'Let me try to place it before you,' Robert wrote.

A long straggling poverty stricken redbrick Worcestershire village. Houses all aslant with the subsidences of the coal workings under-neath. Houses, yes, houses because people live in them. But such dens. Ill ventilated, squalid, insanitary, crowded; an air of listless-ness hanging on everything. Not a pig, not a chicken, not a dog to be seen . . . something picturesque withal about these wretched houses, something old world about the shops where the people slave. Something of pre-machinery days in the deliberate tenacity with which the chains are made. The crowded little workshop, with its four or five 'hearths', its bellows, its anvils, its trough of black water, its miserable baby cradled in a starch box. The pile of chains in the corner, the fire of small coals, the thin, sweating girl, or boy, or old man. The roof without ceiling, the smell of bad drainage, the fumes of reeking human beings pent in a close space – such is a Cradley Heath workshop.

Robert proposed that the only way the wretched workers could be properly protected in future from the depredations of capitalists

– who would surely extract the marrow from their bones, given the chance – was for the establishment of a factory system controlled by a government-appointed local authority, elected by the nail- and chain-makers themselves.

But he was frustrated in his wish to bring this proposal before the Commons. 13 November saw the first anniversary of Bloody Sunday and the news, rapturously received by radicals and socialists, that Charles Warren had resigned. His unwillingness to cooperate with the Home Secretary was weakening the effectiveness of the Metropolitan Police to do what the Government wished. The public, meanwhile, were more dismayed by the police's failure to make progress with their investigations into the horrific murders committed in Whitechapel by Jack the Ripper earlier in the autumn. At a meeting at Clerkenwell Green to commemorate Bloody Sunday and celebrate Warren's departure, a minor fracas ensued between the crowd and the police, some of whose horses had grown restive. Robert spoke the following day in the Commons. He seemed unusually agitated, warning that police brutality would lead eventually to uprising and events like that which had resulted in the execution of the Chicago Seven. He even hinted at the fact that he had on several occasions headed off a threat to the Home Secretary of assassination. Whether true or not, this was all quite disproportionate to what had actually happened the previous day, and the Home Secretary wisely ignored it. Others reflected that Robert had been reliving his own experiences on Bloody Sunday.

A fortnight later Robert moved that the Board of Trade report on Cradley Heath should be debated. Brooke Robinson, Tory MP for Dudley, which included Cradley Heath, blocked the motion. Two days later Robert raised the matter again. This time W.H. Smith, First Lord of the Treasury, refused on the grounds that the government had already referred the matter to the Lords Committee on Sweating (the practice of outsourcing labour to underpaid workers toiling long hours in their own cramped and often insanitary dwellings). Robert replied furiously that this was a dishonourable trick.

The Speaker intervened: 'The Honourable Member is conducting himself in the most unusual and unparliamentary manner in making use of language of that kind. I must request him to withdraw the expression.' 'I never withdraw,' Robert replied. 'I simply said what I mean.' The speaker asked him to withdraw twice more. Robert refused. 'Then I must ask the Honourable Member to withdraw from the House.' 'Certainly sir, I will go to Cradley Heath,' Robert retorted.

A week later Robinson brought on his motion at two a.m., and rebuked Robert for not being present. A colleague rose to explain that Robert had been called to Scotland where his wife was very seriously ill. Robert later wrote to thank a well-wisher, reporting that Gabriela was so ill they were leaving for Spain immediately, and that he feared she might never recover. He regretted that his sudden departure meant he would not be able to continue his fight for the people of Cradley in Parliament.

What had really happened? Parliamentary life was taking its toll on Robert and Gabriela equally, though for different reasons. For Robert, in addition to the lingering effects of the Bloody Sunday beating, there was simple exhaustion compounded by worry about the Gartmore finances and the cumulative effect of a life-time of equestrian injuries. For Gabriela it was the frequent chest infections with their threat of pneumonia, exacerbated by her heavy smoking, and equally frequent bouts of diarrhoea, that left her weakened – both the symptoms of a disease that had at that point yet to be diagnosed: diabetes. She, like Robert, was irritable, her maid Peregrina bearing the brunt of her temper as she fought the loneliness and resentment of life in London as a parliamentary widow.

We now know that diabetes ran in the Horsfall family. Grace Stevenson suffered from it. Dorothy, Gabriela's youngest sister, died from it, as Gabriela herself would. But in a letter to a friend written from Gartmore on Christmas Eve 1888, she made no reference to illness or plans to be abroad. So was Robert indeed suffering some kind of post-traumatic stress from Bloody Sunday, exacerbated by the anniversary, his increasingly fragile emotional and physical state undermining him to the point where he could no longer take the strain of his work? Had he used Gabriela's health as a pretext for taking the steps he deemed necessary to safeguard his own?

For all her disavowal of politics to her friend, Mary Evans, Gabriela shared her husband's sense of outrage at social injustice. Lately it had driven her to speak at socialist meetings, attend rallies and marches in the East End, write pamphlets and letters to newspapers, and on at least one occasion to speak in the lecture hall at William Morris's London house, Kelmscott. Following Bloody Sunday, the 'poor little widow', as W.T. Stead had described her in the *Pall Mall Gazette*, had been seen as a possible heir to Annie Besant; yet in truth the disease was sapping her spirit. The *Times'* sketch of the strong, determined young woman who stood by her husband after Bloody Sunday contrasts markedly with the ethereal, mystical portrait of a pale, intense young woman of hispanic appearance, painted at around the same time by Percy Jacomb Hood.

An awareness of her own mortality might well have sharpened Gabriela's concern for Robert's wellbeing. In the circumstances, a retreat to Spain, the country to which she was increasingly drawn for reasons of both physical and spiritual comfort, would have been an obvious course of action.

Fifteen

CAMLACHIE

Defeat and release

Even in Spain, rest seemed beyond Robert's grasp. Over the Christmas period he visited the Chamber of Deputies in Madrid, made contact with Spanish socialists and other activists, and reported to the *Labour Elector* on the frequent arrest, imprisonment and sometimes torture of Spanish, Italian and French activists by governments alarmed at the perceived threats they represented to social order.

Back in England his mood remained volatile. In January 1889 a new acquaintance, Friedrich Engels, wrote to Karl Marx's daughter, Laura Lafargue, that Robert was 'a nice fellow but always in want of a manager, otherwise bows to foolhardiness, altogether much of an English Blanquist'; Blanqui being a much-imprisoned French Communist, widely known for his journalism and activism.

Through this connection with Engels, Robert, Keir Hardie and John Burns were invited to attend the centenary of the storming of the Bastille. By now Robert had clearly raised his colours in an exchange with the president of the Local Government Board. Asked if his insistence that there was some kind of state regulation of labour was the doctrine of pure socialism, he replied 'Undoubtedly'. So was Robert asking the House to raise the conditions of the working classes by adopting the tenets of pure unmitigated socialism? 'Undoubtedly,' Robert repeated, thus making history as the first person ever to declare himself a Socialist in the British parliament.

The Bastille centenary was marked by two congresses hosted by competing international workers' organisations. Robert was honoured by being invited to preside over the final day of the Second

International, where calls were made for the eight-hour day to be made universal, and for 1 May each year to be the day for demonstrations in its favour. Robert admired the speeches he heard in Paris. They were fierce, sturdy and workmanlike. They addressed practicalities such as hours of work, safety, wages and so on. He contrasted them favourably with what was to be heard in the 'National Gasworks'.

A shakeup at the *Labour Elector*, resulting from the need for more transparency in funding and management, led to a place for Robert on its board alongside a number of trades unionists. Robert and John Burns were now dispatched to Canning Town where the dockers' anger at their working conditions were starting to boil over. The two persuaded the regular hands to form a union, but could do nothing for the casual labourers who began a series of daily protests to win public support.

Throughout that summer of 1889, whenever he could get away from Parliament, Robert would turn up at the dock gates first thing to encourage the pickets to hold firm against the blackleg labour drafted in to keep the docks working. He was not, however, the agitator his detractors wished to portray him as. Addressing crowds so large – thirty thousand on one occasion, he claimed – that his voice frequently gave out, he urged the strikers to avoid provoking the police or soldiers at all costs. He was often accompanied by Gabriela and sometimes joined the protest leaders in their headquarters, the snug behind the bar of the Wade's Arms, where his attire – and doubtless everything else about him – marked him out as a 'West End dude' among the working men. A dude, nonetheless, 'with an eye keener than a hawk's and a voice and manner that riveted attention as he drove home his satirical points,' as the trade unionist, Tom Mann, wrote in his *Memoirs*.

September found Robert and Hardie in Dundee for the annual Trades Union Congress gathering. There they argued for unskilled workers to be brought under the TUC umbrella. But most of the delegates, who belonged to long-established craft unions of skilled workers, disagreed. Beatrice Potter (later Webb) wrote of his performance that Robert was 'a cross between an aristocrat and a barber's block . . . a poseur but also an enthusiast, above all an unmitigated fool in politics'. Yet what poseur would have stayed five minutes in late-Victorian Coatbridge, let alone gone back there time and again? So asked Cedric Watts and Laurence Davies in their critical biography.

While they were still in Dundee news came through that the Liberal MP for the city, J.B. Frith, had died. Robert, Hardie and Gabriela, plus Eleanor Marx and Edward Aveling, now threw themselves into the task of persuading the working folk in Dundee that John Burns was their man. At the meeting to propose Burns' nomination, Robert, in the chair, lost his temper and stormed out, berating the audience as being 'fit only to be governed by capitalists'. By the time he had calmed down and returned to the hall, Burns had been unanimously elected. However, to Robert's great disappointment Burns later withdrew and announced that he would instead contest London's Battersea, the constituency in which he had been raised and where he had founded the Battersea Labour League, which had funded his election to the London County Council in 1888.

Robert was now losing favour both in the press and among his constituents, accused variously of giving up on politics and of trying to split the Liberal vote in return for Tory gold, as the Glasgow Daily Mail suggested. For some, his aristocratic appearance and demeanour was simply too great an obstacle to the belief that he could genuinely be a fighter for the working man's cause. And he himself was constantly frustrated by those very working men's apparent unwillingness, or inability, to grasp the opportunities he and others were working so hard to create for them. 'I fear the English working classes are born slaves,' he told John Burns in a dispirited moment.

Meanwhile, Robert's financial situation was growing increasingly desperate. He confided in friends that despite his determination to stay until he saw enough working men elected to make a difference, he could ill afford to remain in Parliament. In addition to his domestic anxieties, the fee to Herbert Asquith for defending him in the Bloody Sunday trial was an enormous £2,000, somewhere around £250,000 in today's terms. 'If my constituents can't pay my expenses I can no longer go on in Parliament', he had written to fellow

Liberal, Sir Charles Dilke, in April 1889. Dilke had offered to bail him out, an offer Robert politely declined.

Exhausted again from rushing up and down the country to make the case for the eight-hour working day, and suffering from bouts of rheumatism, the legacy of his many arduous journeys in South America, Robert retired to Gartmore during the autumn of 1889. There he kept a low profile, trying to recover his strength and energy and keeping clear of his constituency where he left it to Keir Hardie to keep an eye on things. Yet he was still capable of delivering a speech that raised the roof at a Scottish Labour Party gathering in October, the audience hailing him as a Scottish Parnell. Gabriela, meanwhile, was absent in Spain where her research into the life of the mystic Teresa of Avila would take her away for increasingly long periods over the next five years. Parliament was still sitting in November 1889 when Robert left for Valencia to join her. From there they travelled to Lisbon, where Robert interviewed Portuguese socialists for the *Labour Elector*. A month later they were in Morocco, spending Christmas in Tangier.

Perhaps it was the break from Westminster, the change of scenery, that now prompted a shift in Robert's journalistic tone. What he had found so difficult about his early attempts to write, on his return from Argentina, was resolving itself without him having to think. 'I could write plenty more if I was not right over a stable in which two mules are fighting, and if I had not, for want of blotting paper, to get up at the end of each sheet and take a little sand out of the wall with a knife to dry what I have written,' he reported from Lisbon. And later, from Tangier: 'I have seen what England was like in the Middle Ages.' After the months of sometimes dry, sometimes polemical political reportage and commentary, his relief at, and delight in, the discovery of a gift for simple observation was almost palpable.

They returned to London in January 1890 to find the whole country gripped by scandal. Captain William O'Shea, petitioning for divorce from his wife Kitty, cited Charles Stewart Parnell as co-respondent. A few days before, Parnell had met with Gladstone and they had agreed that Home Rule for Ireland would be introduced as soon as the Liberal Party returned to power. Now he assured Gladstone and Irish colleagues like Michael Davitt that the accusations against him were baseless.

Divorce was not a subject for discussion in polite society at that time. Unabashed, Robert waded in through the pages of the *Labour Elector*.

> Yes I know thou shalt not commit adultery. That is to say, thou shalt not be found out . . . If he *has* been found out, look around the House of Commons, look at the well fed, idle, rich men in it and then ask me to believe they are all earnest practitioners of social purity.

The hypocrisy was breathtaking, he suggested, 'in a state of society where marriage itself is too often a clerical absolved prostitution . . . in a society where we see a Prince marry his daughter to a boon companion and no one raises a note of disgust or contempt.' This was a reference to Princess Louise, daughter of the Prince and Princess of Wales, recently married at the age of 22 to the 40-year-old Earl of Fife, and observed to be in tears throughout the ceremony.

O'Shea's divorce hearing took place in November and he was granted a decree nisi. Parnell's detractors were vindicated. Now the Irish leader was not only the guilty party in the divorce, but also was seen to have lied to colleagues about his culpability. Correspondence with John Burns reveals that Robert was one of the very few to whom Parnell had personally asserted his innocence. Yet Robert seemed unperturbed. Later in the month, having been re-elected leader of the Irish party, Parnell entered the chamber. 'I walked forward and shook hands with Parnell before the whole House. Not a man of them all would speak to him,' Robert wrote to Gabriela.

Robert's behaviour provoked almost as much indignation as the events prompting it. An acquaintance of his mother's, Lady Monkswell, wrote that Robert was 'a sort of wild creature who has been making himself most offensive in the House, more Irish than the Irish themselves.' He had been observed to shake hands with a man 'upon whose head rests at least a hundred murders,' she went on. For those who abhorred the idea of Irish Home Rule, the fall from grace of the man whom they held responsible for the deaths of many representatives of the British authorities was a gift.

Throughout the year, 1890, Robert continued to throw himself into the causes that most preoccupied him. Support for the striking dockers of Liverpool in their struggle for wages was one. Trying to rein in John Burns, who was increasingly proving himself to be a man of his own mind, and who now seemed to be veering from the labour movement to the Liberals, was another. Support for Hardie was a third. 'The ablest man beside yourself in the whole labour movement is Keir Hardie. Do help him in West Ham both for your own sake in Parliament and for his,' Robert wrote to Burns, having first declared that he would not be standing in another election since he had no money.

In the wake of the scandal, and following Parnell's failure to disclose to his party Gladstone's threat that were he to be re-elected Irish party leader Home Rule would be withdrawn, the Irish party now split. Parnell and Gladstone became bitter enemies and the fate of Irish Home Rule hung in the balance. Robert understood only too well the consequences for Scotland. 'The Parnell split has I fear killed the Labour party in Scotland,' he wrote to John Burns. Suffering from a crippling bout of rheumatism, Robert had to be carried onto the platform for a meeting in Glasgow, and failed to make the opening of Parliament in January. By March he was back in Tangier where he hoped to recuperate. The clear air and empty spaces of Morocco gave him time to gather his strength and consider the dilemma of Gartmore. If he was to save it he had to find a way to make money and soon, something his Parliamentary activities precluded. But how could he relieve himself of those responsibilities?

Back in Europe in May 1891, he dashed between Paris for a protest march, to London to speak at a rally in Hyde Park, and back to France again to join a protest in Calais on the first anniversary of the killing by the authorities of nine supporters of an eight-hour working day, women and children among them. He was immediately arrested and marched to the ferry by a troop of chasseurs. 'I was expelled from France yesterday,' he wrote to Gabriela, adding that while the foreign minister, Castres, remained in office he would be arrested again the minute he set foot in the country.

The general election was due in June 1892. In summer 1891 a friend had offered to pay his expenses and Robert agreed to an invitation to stand for the Liberal Party in Camlachie, Glasgow. But his disenchantment with the party rose to the surface in the autumn when Parnell died, less than a year after his fall from grace. Robert was quick to blame Gladstone, 'that hypocrite', for throwing Parnell to the wolves and in doing so 'shutting off Home Rule for 100 years'. A confrontation with Gladstone himself ensued the following summer in the run-up to the election. Gladstone refused to see a delegation from the London Trades Council who wanted to discuss the eight-hour working day – an expression, Gladstone considered, of the socialist tendency of which he so disapproved. Furious, Robert demanded an audience. Gladstone relented and the delegation was admitted, but the meeting was a miserable failure as Gladstone harangued the delegates and ridiculed their demands. Robert, however, later remembered with pride the moment he had faced down the Grand Old Man.

A few months earlier another confrontation had taken place. In April 1892, Robert was present in the Commons as Herbert Asquith argued that it was iniquitous that unearned income for landowners should, for capital gains purposes, be treated the same way as unearned income for shareholders. This was a favourite Liberal theme, and one whose apparent double standard infuriated Robert. Unable to contain himself, he leapt to his feet to harangue Asquith. Ignoring the Speaker's demands that he desist, he was told he would be suspended. 'Suspend away,' he cried, and when a colleague attempted to calm him down: 'Oh leave me alone, I do not care a damn.' Suspended for that 'single damn' was Shaw's verdict on the incident. Robert himself maintained that he was 'standing up for Socialism'. In truth he was out of order, the suspension well deserved. But he was also out of support and sympathy from his fellows; the weary, exasperated 'leave me alone' an expression of how he already felt about Westminster.

'Yo contra todos, y todos contra mi,' he wrote to Sir Charles Dilke, who had earlier offered to bail him out. 'Me against every-one, and everyone against me.' It was an unpleasant position to be in and one could do no good there, he went on. The 'grocer radicals', having got one down, would not let one up again.

Come June 1892 and campaigning underway, Robert's contempt for the 'grocer radicals', the party that sponsored him, boiled over. Defecting from the Liberals he stood for the Scottish Labour Party along with two other candidates, one in Glasgow Tradeston and one in Dundee. But with five candidates now standing for Camlachie – Robert for Scottish Labour, a Gladstonian Liberal, an Independent Democrat and a Liberal Unionist, there was a real danger that a split vote would let in the fifth, the Tory. Robert was savaged in the Glasgow press: 'a strange mixture of English pluck, Scottish determi-nation and Spanish temper,' and his wife 'a helpmeet as volatile as himself.' Gabriela had compounded Robert's sin with a speech to the Irish National League's Glasgow branch, describing Liberals as 'miser-able, piddling, party hacks, heavy beery brained dullards, who would sell their souls if they had any.' Her audience, she seemed to overlook, was mainly composed of supporters of Michael Davitt, who had lost faith in Parnell over the O'Shea affair. Yet Parnell was the man she now praised, insisting that he had been murdered by Gladstone.

In the event Robert took just over ten percent of the vote. The Irish voted as one man for the Liberal Unionist candidate, Cross, who carried the day. The Gladstonian Liberals fared almost as badly as the Scottish Labour Party. The press again turned on Robert. He knew he had no chance of winning, remarked the *Glasgow Observer*, so why had he stood? Was it revenge on the Liberal leaders, or had he taken Tory money? He was glad to have split the vote and brought the Gladstonian era to an end in Scotland, Robert told his support-ers. But had it really been so calculated? Or had he sub-consciously sabotaged his chances in order to be free of the Westminster knock-about with which he was becoming so disenchanted? In his old constituency, Northwest Lanarkshire, the Tories won narrowly and Robert again was blamed, as the defector.

In London, where he and Gabriela had spent a good deal of time during the campaign – to the undoubted detriment of Robert's performance in Camlachie – things turned out rather better. Keir Hardie won West Ham by a comfortable majority over his Tory opponent. There is no doubt that Robert's support, and his reputation in the East End following Bloody Sunday and the dockers' strike, played a large part in Hardie's victory. For Friedrich Engels it meant that 'the spell which the great Liberal party cast over the English workers for almost forty years is broken'.

West Ham, to Robert's eye, may have been as miserable a place as Coatbridge or Cradley Heath:

> street upon street of half crooked brick abominations called houses, here and there a little 'Bethel' chapel . . . row upon row of stalls at night when the stale vegetables are sold . . . on one side lines of endless docks, and on the other lines of endless misery.

But it was where the future leader of the Labour Party would represent his first constituency – and Robert, at times despite himself, had helped him there.

In doing so, had Robert accomplished his crowning political achievement? At the time of his departure he might well have believed so. Exhausted and disillusioned, he questioned whether he had accomplished anything during his time at Westminster. 'I have been foolish enough to soil myself with the pitch of politics,' he wrote to a friend, 'and to have endured the concentrated idiocy of the Asylum for Incapables at Westminster for six years . . . Now I think I may do my fooling alone, and leave the stage for younger fools . . .'

The furious energy that had driven him there had, like a summer storm, passed on. Now the campaigner who never withdrew had, after only six short years, withdrawn from parliamentary life.

Sixteen

ORENSE

Fool's gold

The Gartmore finances continued to become more alarming as every week went by. Robert and Gabriela had had the misfortune to be living through the worst agricultural depression for a century. Krakatoa's explosion in 1883 had created a five-year drop in global temperatures of 1.2 degrees centigrade. Cold grey summers and hard winters led to meagre harvests around the world, while produce from other parts of the world, including fresh meat, made its way into British markets. Pressure to reduce rents led to falling land values.

Somehow they had to find £1,200 per year for Missy, plus £200 per year for each of the two maiden Cunninghame Graham aunts, Charlotte and Anne. Interest on loans was £1,000 pounds per annum, leaving them with £2,000 for everything else. Out of this had had to come the cost of three election campaigns at around £1,000 each, plus Asquith's fee of £2,000. There were also outstanding mortgages on the estate, the legacy of Robert's forebears' improvidence.

In 1885 Robert had put Ardoch on the market at £100,000 for the house, the estate and two farms. There were no takers, so in 1887 he reduced the price to £85,000 and eventually sold the estate in a number of smaller lots. By now they had both begun to sell rare objects acquired on their travels. From Spain, Gabriela imported furniture, carpets and *objets d'art*. Robert bought leather in Morocco and tapestries in Seville. In correspondence with the Glasgow University botanist, Gabriela began to explore the possibility of commercially exploiting the Flanders Moss. Robert tried to find out what had become of the £5,000 his father Willy had invested in the reclamation scheme in Majorca. Needless to say, the scheme had failed and all the investors' money had drained away into the Mediterranean. In desperation Robert had resorted to selling feus (a form of land tenure) to his tenants. This raised immediate cash and relieved Robert of his responsibilities as feudal superior, but it also meant lower income in future and less control over what happened on the Gartmore lands.

The first time he had thought seriously of selling Gartmore was 1891. He and Gabriela had no children to pass it on to, they were both in poor health, and the strain of trying to keep the place afloat was not making things any easier. On learning of their plans, and alarmed at the prospect of losing her annuity, Anne Elizabeth wrote at once to her long-standing advisor, Mr Wright, now a judge in Leeds. Robert's brother Charlie weighed in in support of their mother, reminding Robert of 'such a miserable life as she has had'. Two years later, in a further, though unintended, rebuke to his childless brother, Charlie would oblige his mother with the distraction of a second grandchild. The first, a girl named Olave, had been born in 1883, nearly ten years previously. I remember her in old age, visiting from Knightsbridge. By then she was an admiral's widow, though in earlier years she had enjoyed a brief flirtation with Hollywood and had sat as the Venus de Medici for a portrait known as the Red Shawl by the Australian artist, George Washington Lambert. Perfectly coiffed, scented and mink-coated, she was known in the family as 'Purr', which may account for my recollection of her as having a feline air about her – although in fact the name derived from Aunt Purdie, a character from Wee Mcgreegor, a popular book of comic tales about working class life in turn-of-the-century Glasgow. But there were no nicknames or diminutives for her new brother, my grandfather. He was solemnly christened Angus Edward Malise Bontine Cunninghame Graham; 'Edward' at the insistence of his godfather, the Prince of Wales, to whom Charlie was now a courtier, and whose famously roving eye was said to have alighted on Charlie's wife, the beautiful Barbara or 'Milly'.

That year, 1893, free of his parliamentary obligations, Robert resolved to free himself of another, more longstanding burden. He finally dispensed with the advice of George Jamieson, the former *curator bonis*, partner in the Edinburgh firm of Lindsay, Jamieson and Haldane, and now a figure of some influence as a director of the Royal Bank of Scotland and advisor to the owners of many estates. After twenty five years, Robert wrote politely, he could no longer afford the fees; though he must have been delighted at last to see the back of the man who had inflicted so much humiliation on him in earlier days. But having said to Jamieson that he would manage without professional support, he then appointed another solicitor to manage the estate finances. When he complained about the amount of work expected of him for a modest fee, Robert rebuked him and shortly sacked him for trying to take over the estate by calling in the mortgages. The time had come to sell Gartmore, he declared. Gabriela now wrote to Anne Elizabeth giving vent to her anxieties and frustrations. Ruin stared them in the face, she said, insisting that she would not become a 'holocaust to hereditary prejudices'.

And yet, the sale did not materialise for another seven years. Were they simply overwhelmed and overwrought during those early months of 1893? During their remaining years at Gartmore Gabriela was assiduous in her care of the accounts, often to be found sitting on the bookroom floor surrounded by papers and encircled by overflowing ashtrays, her unregulated tobacco consumption – up to a hundred cigarettes a day, it was said – doing little for her already poor health. She even went so far as to be present at the twice-yearly collection of the monies due from the remaining feuars, a practice that caused tongues to wag disapprovingly in the neighbourhood. They lived like church mice, ensuring that one of them was always there, she had written to Missy in 1885. 'We have two women servants, no horses, no carriages, no shootings, no society. Everything is regulated by the strictest economy.' A decade later, Robert would write to his friend, the artist Will Rothenstein:

You have no idea of my finances, I am driven to desperation with debts, & troubles & am trying hard to sell all I possess, & even then should probably manage to save only a few hundred a year.

The sins or follies of my ancestor have been visited heavily indeed on me.

Nevertheless, there were moments of contentment to be found at Gartmore with *la familia*: Gabriela, the two horses, Pampa and Talla, and Jack the fox terrier. Unshackled from Westminster, now he had the time and inclination to start looking around him through the eyes of a writer; to experiment with the more observational style he had first adopted in his earlier reports from Portugal and Morocco for the *Labour Elector*.

He began with what was literally on his doorstep. Published in 1895, *Notes on the District of Menteith* was a slim guide to the geography, history, flora and fauna of the place closest his heart. 'Ben Lomond dominates the land,' he wrote of its presiding peak,

a sort of Scottish Vesuvius, never wholly without a cloud-cap. You cannot move a step that it does not tower over you. In winter, a vast white sugar-loaf; in summer, a prismatic cone of yellow and amethyst and opaline lights; in spring a grey, gloomy pile of rocks.

But this, as the publishers A&C Black recognised, was no mere guide for visitors. This was a series of meditations on Scotland and the Scots, of such novelty that readers were surprised and delighted by it. The *Saturday Review* enthused: 'the wittiest little book to come out for a long time'. What was it, Robert asked, that made a Scottish graveyard so different from its English counterpart where the rector's pony grazed, the grass grew long and swifts wheeled overhead? It may be the knowledge that the sleeping souls are all in torment – for none could possibly escape the penalties so liberally dispensed to them in church in life. The *Saturday Review* hoped that Mr Graham 'should cease to "fash" [trouble] himself with politics and give us many another book.'

Robert was entering middle age when this first book was published. Late literary development has continued to run in the family since. His nephew and great-niece, my grandfather and mother respectively, both came to publication in later life, the admiral publishing his *Random Naval Recollections* when he was well into his eighties, my mother being in her mid-sixties when she published her childhood memoir, *Sailor's Daughter*, and seventy-six when *Gaucho Laird* came out. In my case, for all my youthful avoidance of my great-great uncle, one thing I knew and clung to was the fact that he had not published a book until he was over forty (although I was unaware then that he endured lifelong doubts about his literary ability). I assumed that he had started late because he needed to live life fully before he was ready to reflect upon and write about it. I was not entirely wrong; although in truth this was more a projection of my own fears at the time (my thirties) that I had not yet properly unlocked the mysteries of the adult world and had nothing interesting to say. My first novel, a teenage thriller was published when I was forty-one. The fact that I then continued to write what my publishers deemed to be young adult fiction suggests that perhaps I never did unlock those mysteries – or at least not until very much later, and that is another story.

A year after *Notes on the District of Menteith* came out, Frank Harris bought the *Saturday Review*. A gifted and influential man of letters, Harris saw to it that his new weekly was now to be found in every drawing-room in the country. When Harris and Robert met riding in Hyde Park, Robert's reputation preceded him, both as a speaker and political commentator. Harris was in the process of assembling a glittering cast of writers including G.B. Shaw and H.G. Wells, to whom he now readily added Robert, with a first commission in May 1896. From the backwaters of the *Labour Elector* and the *People's Press*, Robert now found himself thrust into the mainstream of national journalism, where his notoriety from Bloody Sunday did him no harm. 'I was the *Saturday Review*er in the theatre,' Shaw wrote, '. . . Cunninghame Graham was a *Saturday Review*er in the universe.' Robert's debut articles, *A Survival* and *Salvagia*, continued the Scottish themes he had explored in *Notes on the District of Menteith*, introducing a new note of realism to Scottish writing. *A Survival* railed against the romanticism of Scott and the sentimentality of the 'kailyarders', writers such as J.M. Barrie and S.R. Crockett, with their homespun tales of couthy country folk. *Salvagia* is set in the fictional village of Gart-na-Cloich – which was clearly

Gartmore – where there were *two churches and two public houses, and a feud between the congregations of each church as bitter as that between the clients of the rival inns.* Scotland had never recovered from the damage done by John Knox, who had taken all pleasure and warmth from life, he proposed.

That year, 1896, A&C Black published Robert's first collection of sketches in *Father Archangel of Scotland*, which he co-authored with Gabriela. She drew on her travels in Spain for three sketches of the remote towns, monasteries and convents she had visited during her research into the life of Saint Teresa. Robert returned to the theme of Knox and the damage he had wrought on the national psyche. 'No one in his wildest fits of patriotism ever talked of Merrie Scotland,' he wrote. 'Did Knox kill merriment even as Macbeth did murder sleep?' Another theme to which he would return time and again was the baneful effect of progress and a nostalgia for an older, simpler, poorer Scotland. In this collection he also turned his attention to South America where many of the same themes pertained; although he swam against the tide of contemporary opinion with his suggestion that the Jesuits had been good for the Indians of Paraguay, being the only group whose presence had not brought death to them. Support for indigenous people against their exploiters and oppressors was a further recurring theme, and one Robert had already explored in a sequence of three memorable articles for the *Daily Graphic*, published between November 1890 and January 1891.

The first, *The American Indians: Ghost Dancing*, reported on the phenomenon that had recently taken hold among Indian tribes throughout the western United States who believed that by dancing they could summon the ancestors to their aid and halt the white man's westward expansion. Thousands of Sioux were now gathering on tribal lands in Dakota, to the consternation of local settlers and authorities. It is worth quoting extensively from this, and the two articles that followed, for the fury that simmers through Robert's reportage.

It was the Sioux themselves who were the ghosts dancing, Robert wrote in the first article:

Ghosts of a primeval race. Ghosts of ghosts who for three hundred years, through no crime committed by themselves (except that of being born), if it be not a crime to love better the rustle of the grass than the shrieking of the engine, have suffered their long purgatory . . . The buffalo have gone first, their bones whitening in long lines on the prairie, the elk have retired into the extreme deserts of Oregon, the beaver is exterminated to make jackets for the sweater's [industrialist's] wife, the Indian must go next, and why not, pray? Is he not of less value than the other three? Let him make place for better things – for the drinking shop, for the speculator, for the tin church . . . Better that they should come and smoke and dance, dance for ten days without food and water, better far that they should die fighting, than by disease or whisky.

Once they were gone, he concluded, the Darwinian theory of weakest to the wall would be further strengthened in the minds of those who wished to turn it against the weakest in Europe.

In the second piece, *Salvation by Starvation: The American Indian Problem*, Robert reported one month later on the death of the Lakota chief, Sitting Bull, an influential figure who had taken part in the Battle of Little Bighorn at which General Custer's forces had been annihilated, and whom the authorities now feared was going to offer his support to the ghost dancing movement. Robert wrote:

The first act in the concluding drama of the existence of the Sioux Indians is played out. Apparently in direct violation of the President's orders, the Indian police arrested Sitting Bull, with the natural consequence that a rescue was attempted and a fight took place. In the fight, Sitting Bull, who was heard giving orders in a loud voice, fell pierced by a bullet. This is an old trick well known in Spain and Mexico, and throughout the frontiers of the United States. The escort appears at the frontier town without the prisoner. Officer reports prisoner endeavoured to escape and, in the struggle that ensued, was accidentally shot. Quite so: that is to say one of two things happened – either the prisoner was offered a suppositious occasion to escape, and shot in the attempt, or else he was deliberately murdered in order to save time, legal expenses and the problematical Spanish-American or Uncle Sam's justice [sic]. This would seem to have been the end of Sitting Bull – deliberately murdered to stop him for asking for food for his tribe.

The latter was a reference to the straitened circumstances of the reservation Lakota Sioux during an exceptionally harsh winter, and the reluctance of the US authorities to provide succour. Robert went on to conclude, presciently, that those who called most loudly for the extermination of the Indians, the Dakota settlers, would in time come to be as dependent for their livelihoods on the forces of capitalism as the starving Indians had been on the US government. Society will always replace one underdog with another.

A week after the second article was published, US government troops killed 150 men, women and children of the Lakota and injured many more at the infamous Wounded Knee Massacre, on the Pine Ridge Reservation in South Dakota. In his response, *The Redskin Problem: "But 'twas a famous victory"*, Robert wrote:

> I see that our 'brave troops' remorselessly slaughtered all the women and children, and our special correspondent, in estimating the 'bag', remarks that by this time probably not more than six children remain alive out of the whole Indian camp. Can anything more miserable be conceived . . . We are told that the Indians planned an ambuscade but it would seem a curious kind of ambuscade that 120 men should allow themselves to be surrounded by 500, backed by artillery.

The reality – of which Robert may not have been fully aware at the time of writing – was a botched attempt by the US Army to disarm the Lakota in the course of which, according to one version of events, a misunderstanding by a deaf Indian and the accidental discharge of his rifle led to the troops opening fire.

But for all his palpable outrage, it seems that Robert's articles did little to sway public opinion. Indians continued to be regarded as 'hostiles', a view that was reinforced by the appearance of whooping, tomahawk-wielding, be-feathered braves in Buffalo Bill Cody's *Wild West* show, which at the time was drawing huge crowds as it toured Europe.

Gabriela had beaten Robert into print by eighteen months – a fact which may have been instrumental in motivating him to pick up his own pen. Her study of the sixteenth century Spanish mystic, Teresa of Avila, had been published also by A&C Black, in March 1894. This massive work, eight hundred pages in two volumes, was the fruit of five years' research involving trips into some of the remotest corners of northern Spain, accompanied only by her ill-tempered but long-suffering and aptly-named Galician maid, Peregrina. Many of the convents and monasteries founded by Teresa and now ruined, lay in high mountains, accessible only via dried-out riverbeds. Up these, Gabriela laboured on donkey or horseback, often in ill-health, her only company – apart from Peregrina – the goatherds she encountered, whose fireside tales of wolves and boar reminded her of the perils of these high, wild places in which she found herself.

Gabriela had come to this unlikely subject by way of a number of circumstances. Her own Catholicism, which she had embraced as a young woman, was a natural progression from the High Anglicanism that she and her clergyman brother William had adopted, in defiance of their father's evangelical fervour. Put simply, she liked the bells and smells, though her devotion to the faith, rather like her commitment to temperance, was less certain. The theatricality of Teresa's visions appealed to her. So undoubtedly did the fact that Teresa had run away from home as a teenager. Furthermore, the saint possessed a practical side, as did Gabriela, which came to the fore in her skillful and efficient founding of convents and dealings with the church authorities.

The climate was right for such a biography, as the Blacks were well aware. Unorthodoxy was fashionable. Spiritualism had captured the public imagination, so too Eastern ideas and beliefs, along with mediums and séances. The Theosophical Society, founded by Madame Blavatsky, was gaining followers by the day with its ideas of ecstasy and reincarnation.

However, Gabriela was most interested in Teresa's own belief that her visions were attributable to ill-health. Gabriela took this thought a step further and suggested that their origins were in fact of a sexual nature. This caused the Blacks some consternation and they advised Gabriela to tread delicately with the subject, but she was insistent. She had by now shared the idea that physical conditions had psychological effects, and vice versa, in conversation with the ground-breaking Spanish feminist and novelist, Emilia Pardo Bazán, whom she had met in La Coruña. The two women struck up a friendship which extended to Emilia assisting Gabriela with her export of expensive antiques and even the transfer of funds to England, a labyrinthine process in the absence of local banks. Emilia's essays and fiction embraced a holistic view of the human condition, with all matters of body, mind and spirit related. She also gave Gabriela much advice on the practicalities of her research, where to go and who to meet. Furthermore, she seems to have arranged for Gabriela to take a role in a play in Madrid, directed by a friend of hers, a prospect at which Gabriela was clearly ecstatic, the childhood dream of the stage still burning within. But it came to nothing.

The book was published under the name Gabriela Cunninghame Graham. While the family continued to refer to her as Gabrielle, this was the first time she had used the Spanish variant of her name, perhaps in homage to her subject. It also revealed the elasticity of the story she had constructed about herself, the French or Chilean origins adaptable to the circumstances in which she found herself.

Santa Teresa: being some account of her life and times, together with some pages from the history of the last great reform in the religious orders, a title whose length may have alerted the unwary reader to what was to follow, was not well received. The *Saturday Review* – not yet in Frank Harris's hands, worse luck for Gabriela – savaged it while grudgingly admitting that it was a good story. The popular appetite for mysticism was not shared by the literary press. Her style was not free from turgid sentences while her powers of description ran riot, remarked the reviewer, whose other charges included the use of language that was obscure and sometimes invented, and that 'she has a peculiar system of mixing her past and present tense.'

Gabriela was deeply hurt by this rejection. Unexpectedly, Missy came to her defence, advising her that 'every book worth anything has been severely rejected', and after listing eminent authors who had suffered similar injury, advised her to 'sit tight and stick to your guns'. This episode represented a temporary thawing of the *froideur* between mother-in-law and daughter-in-law; though later Missy came to refer to *Santa Teresa* as 'that weary book'.

Unsurprisingly, the church in Spain did not approve of the book and an earlier plan that Emilia would translate it came to nothing. As that friendship soured and petered out, Gabriela came to suspect that Emilia had been one of a group of Spanish writers who had conspired to have the book put on the Spanish government index of prohibited works.

Welcome distraction from this literary setback appeared in the pages of an ancient copy of a Spanish edition of Pliny the Elder's *Historia Naturalis*, which they came across in the bookroom at Gartmore. Here there was a reference to a goldmine in a northern part of Roman Lusitania, now Galicia, with which they were famil-iar; a place in what had once been the most important gold-mining region of the Roman Empire, but was now so remote that the mine would surely have lain unnoticed in the two millennia since it had been worked out.

Robert later described what followed in *A Page of Pliny* (*A Hatchment*, 1913). By the time of writing he had lost both Gartmore and Gabriela, and this characteristically colourful travelogue serves as both an exercise in nostalgia and an insight into the dynamic between husband and wife. Writing as an anonymous narrator who recounts a yarn told by an acquaintance – a device Robert frequently employed – he portrays Gartmore as a curious, lonely old house, far from the world, where damp exudes from the walls, furniture exhib-its a moist, bluish bloom, and grates turn red with rust. Here, the acquaintance (who is Robert) 'and his wife, a studious woman, but yet with an adventurous strain, lived quietly as befitting their narrow circumstances, due to the fall in agricultural values, which in those days had just begun.' In the recesses of the bookroom, a long low Adams' room with its four pillars, double fireplaces, and five windows looking out on steep terraces and rushy parks, stand two upright bookcases where, one idle, firelit evening, he comes across the Pliny.

> The book in question (two volumes folio) was bound in sheep-skin with the name on the back done with a thick quill pen, a rose below the lettering as an adornment, and a small piece of sheep-skin gone from near the top of Volume II, leaving the threads that bound the leaves together exposed to daylight.

For all his love of history, old books and maps, Robert soon tires of the Spanish translator's dull commentaries. He passes the book to Gabriela who persists, reading and annotating after her custom. A rainy day or two later she comes across the reference to the mine and their memories of the place are piqued.

> 'Well, well, my wife in half a moment had perceived the connec-tion, intimate and quite complete, between the page of Pliny and the tales the Spanish peasantry had told on the River Sil.' He said this, proud of his clever wife, not that for a single moment he appeared to have been deceived by her quick jump to the end of a long chain and her omission of the links. These he saw clearly were all wanting; but yet he knew his wife's perception and quick intuition were superior to his own, and he was Scotch enough to know when he was outclassed, although no doubt in the realm of things that can be acquired he thought himself omniscient after the fashion of his race.

Robert may on this occasion be the rational Scot, outclassed by his intuitive wife, but the prospect of a horseback journey to a remote place in search of gold, the solution to the ever-present anxi-ety about money, is still irresistible. They will be able to find the place, of that they are in no doubt. But they need technical assis-tance. Robert and Gabriela travel to Madrid where she contacts T.J. Barnard, a mining engineer of her acquaintance, who agrees to help on the basis of a favourable assay of a sample of earth from the region, which she has somehow come by. In the story Robert is soon on his way to the Galician town of Orense to meet up with

Barnard, and thence to the village of Caraceido in Val de Orras (Valley of Gold) where locals, after heavy rains, still take their pans to the River Sil to wash out a little gold, and where the mine supposedly lies. But the story omits the fact that in reality the original plan was for Gabriela and Peregrina to travel to the mine, sending Robert home to hold the fort at Gartmore; however, correspondence reveals that Barnard became so forward in his admiration of Gabriela's 'pretty shoulders', so transparently enthusiastic at the prospect of accompanying an attractive young woman alone into the wilds of Galicia, that she conveniently succumbed to an illness and Robert took over as expedition leader.

So, the story relates that on a day of searing heat in summer 1894, Robert and Barnard leave Caraceido on mule-back, accompanied by a guide leading a provision-laden donkey. For several hours the stony trail leads them upwards through chestnut woods and huge banks of white-flowering cistus, all the while assailed by the scents of thyme and rosemary. As the light begins to fail they hear the Angelus ring out from the village, far below. The moon rises and at length they halt in a forest glade. The guide hobbles his donkey, strikes flint on steel and soon has a bright fire going.

When we had made some tea and smoked a cigarette, we strolled across the little clearing and a most wondrous view, made still more marvellous by the moon's glittering beams, lay stretched beneath us, for the green glade ended abruptly in a precipice. Sheer down it went and seemed unfathomable. It looked as if a monstrous bowl had been dug out of the red earth, about a quarter of a mile across. A chestnut wood, dark and mysterious in the moonlight, covered the floor of the bowl. The depth and false perspective that the moonlight gave everything, made it look like a carpet. Here and there in patches you could see the ground, and from the patches towered great pinnacles of dark red earth, three or four hundred feet high.

Upon their tops grew bushes, making them look like some fantastic vegetable. The moon-beams played upon them, magnifying and distorting them, and striking here and there upon a pebble in their sides, which sparkled brilliantly. So still was everything that we stood looking, awestruck, till the guide, advancing cautiously up to the edge, held out a lean, brown finger and said, 'That is the Roman mine.'

This was a placer-mine (the word deriving from the Spanish *placer* for a shoal or sandbank) where the constant washing-down of alluvial soil for panning had created these strange, termite hill-like earth forms in the valley bottom. Here, where armies of slaves had toiled and died underground, boring watercourses through the heart of the mountains, Robert and Barnard spend several days panning to get enough earth for a scientific assay. Bending at the stream gives Robert back-ache, and boredom soon turns to hatred of the interminable washing of mud from a tin pan.

Eventually they return to Caraceido tired, eaten by mosquitoes, sun-burned, with their hands blistered, 'and in that state of mind in which a man will quarrel with his dearest friend about the colour of a mule.' They have with them two sackfuls of red earth in which Robert maintains his hopes to the last. He looks on anxiously as they are eventually fired in a crucible at the Mining College of Madrid – and reduce to worthless dust.

For Robert, as yet another mirage faded, the adventure and its lingering dreams had been sufficient reward. For Gabriela the disappointment was more acute. Receiving his news of the final assay, she replied that his *descorazonado* (disheartened) letter had given her a 'sorry downcome'. Nevertheless, she encouraged him to put the whole affair behind him and not to hurry home if he was enjoying himself; a generous response given that she was now back at Gartmore where the evidence of their deteriorating circumstances lay all around her.

Seventeen

TAROUDANT

The far west

Robert and Gabriela seemed well adapted to separation. From early on, absences, sometimes of many weeks, had been a regular feature of their marriage as they pursued the separate interests that kept each stimulated, and enlivened the time they spent together at Gartmore or in London. Robert recognised that Spain, its climate and culture, nourished Gabriela in a way that Scotland never could, while she understood, even if she didn't fully share, the deep attachment that Gartmore held for Robert. In adolescence, both had weathered severe ruptures to family life, and both had learnt to be self-sufficient: Robert at boarding school, later in South America, Gabriela after fleeing Yorkshire. Time apart may well have been a necessity for them, which is not to suggest that it facilitated or encouraged other liaisons. Robert's acquaintance with the *demi-monde* is well documented in his own writing, and according to the *mores* of his era and class would not have been much frowned upon. Gabriela formed close attachments with a small number of women friends. But there is nothing in their correspondence, or other accounts of what might at the time have been deemed an unconventional marriage, to suggest that their deepest affections were not reserved exclusively for one another. To the end, no matter the duration or distance, letters flowed regularly and fondly back and forth between 'Chid' and 'Lob', the lisping diminutive Gabriela had bestowed on her husband.

Travel was the panacea for most of their ills. Within a couple of months of Robert's empty-handed return from Val de Orras,

Gabriela was off again to Spain, this time via Switzerland – to which she did not take kindly. It was 'abominable, crowded by shopkeepers & *canallas* [scoundrels] of all sorts,' she wrote to Robert in September 1894.

> I will never go to Switzerland again, nor to any tourist infested country. I have seen enough of France to last me my lifetime & want to see no more. Rough as Spain is, it is still the best & pleasantest, & certainly the most picturesque country I have seen. Everywhere else, I miss the vivid colouring, & the savage odour . . . I am glad to see Spain again, to see the red hills & the stunted olive trees & the broken ground edging the sea; to be awakened by the crowing of a cock instead of the odious whistle of the railway train.

The landscape, history and, above all, the mystery of Spain, not to mention its savage odour, had furnished Gabriela with a spiritual home which might in certain respects – its ruggedness, the dour character of its northern people – have echoed her native Yorkshire, but in most others could not have offered a more welcome contrast.

Despite the good fortune of primary education at a school where a knowledge of France and well-spoken French was considered a key attainment, a stronger connection with Spain and the hispanic world is one I share with both Gabriela and Robert. Arriving in Argentina in 1972 without a word of Spanish, I felt an unexplained but immediate affinity for the language and everything it evoked, which I had never felt for French. Having since visited Spain many times, I now understand this to be a matter of heredity for which I hold Doña Catalina, Robert's and my mutual ancestress, responsible.

While Gabriela sought the healing warmth of the Iberian Peninsula, Robert's compass was set further south. He had first visited Morocco in 1889 and continued to do so almost every year until 1906, and intermittently thereafter. Already familiar with the language and culture as experienced through the prism of Moorish Spain, he found much about North Africa that appealed to him. On that first visit he had written home that Tangier had given him a glimpse of how medieval England would have appeared. The feeling of time travel, the absence of progress, excited him – as always. So too did the opportunity for adventure, the wildness of the landscape, the native love of horses, the characters and intrigue that abounded at all levels of society. South America, whose language, customs and religion he knew more intimately than he would ever know those of the Arab world, would always claim his heart. But here in Morocco there was action aplenty and an embarrassment of material on which to train his writer's eye – and it was a lot easier and less expensive to get to.

'Thirteen miles from Europe as the gull flies, millions of miles in feeling and in life . . . less spoiled with European ways than is Crim-Tartary,' he wrote in *Tanger la Blanca* (*Writ In Sand*, 1932). But it was not to remain unspoilt for much longer. Morocco in the 1890s was fast becoming a potential flashpoint as the European powers, racing for naval supremacy, vied for influence with the corrupt and unstable sultanate of a country whose position at the gateway to the Mediterranean was of increasing strategic importance.

Tangier was the terminus for the host of Europeans who visited or lived there for purposes of diplomacy, commerce, travel, art or the gathering of information on behalf of their national authorities. It had more Ministers, Secretaries of Legation, Consuls, Consuls-General and Vice Consuls per head of population than anywhere else in the world, Robert wrote, and it offered him a plethora of opportunity. At a time when the Gartmore finances were stretched to the very limit, it seems unlikely that he would have abandoned his post as laird had it not been for financial reward of some kind. There are no known records of payments received for any kind of services rendered by him during the 1890s, but it is probable that during this period Robert acted as an agent, both for the British authorities and for certain commercial interests.

His reputation as a politician and journalist, also as an adventurer and master horseman, preceded him as he began to make friends in Tangier's colourful and decadent society, bristling with diplomats, agents and traders, obscure and indigent European aristocrats, phoneys, con-men and fixers of all stripes. Robert's many acquaintances included Dino, Duke of Frías, an immensely wealthy Spaniard with estates the length and breadth of the country. Together with the celebrated painter of birds and animals, Joseph Crawhall, the duke ran the grandly named Tangier Hounds, a rabble of dusty dogs and riders, with whom Robert frequently rode out, echoing his grandfather, Charles Elphinstone Fleming, who had founded the famous Calpe Hunt in Gibraltar, a few miles across the water. Pig sticking was another pastime which attracted a host of preposterously titled Europeans to a wooded region outside Tangier for mounted sport.

But there was serious business to attend to in Tangier as well. As the Sultan's grip of his country grew weaker, the European powers jostled for influence and intelligence. Britain had Gibraltar and control of access by sea. France had Algeria to the east and Senegal to the south. Spain had nothing but the fervent belief that Morocco should be hers. With a combination of alarm and expectation, all anticipated the vacuum that would follow the collapse of the sultanate.

Travellers, particularly adventurous ones such as Robert, were greatly valued by their national legations. In 1891, two years after first visiting Tangier, Robert began a series of journeys into the interior with friends including the painters Will Rothenstein and John Lavery. For the latter, this was the start of a love affair with Morocco, leading later to the purchase of a house outside Tangier where Robert would often stay. Over many years of frequenting the Grosvenor Gallery, often in the company of his mother, Robert had grown knowledgeable about art and it seemed fitting that he should experience this new world in the company of artists, who challenged him to sharpen his powers of observation, finding new ways to see and write about things.

> Whitewash and blinding sunlight on the walls; upon the beach, white sand; the people dressed in robes of dusky white, a shroud of white enfolds, a mist as of an older world hangs over it . . . he wrote of Tangier. As in the time of Jacob, women draw water from the well, the camels rest beside their burdens in the marketplace, the grave-faced men sit selling trinkets, squatted in their little shops, whilst around the public writers covering their yellow

slips of paper stand knots of people wondering at their skill, for writing of itself has something sacred which attaches to it, for all believers know the Cufic alphabet was sent direct from God.

He concludes, approvingly, with an image of 'the white Arab town sleeping peacefully as it has slept for ages, and looking out at Europe with an air of wonder tempered with contempt.'

Robert's guide on several occasions was a young Englishman called Edward 'Bibi' Carleton who had been brought up in Tangier, spoke perfect Arabic, and was one of the few foreigners, or *roumis* (a corruption of 'Romans'), to be generally trusted by the Arabs of Morocco. His family's straitened circumstances obliged Bibi to make a living by guiding Europeans into the interior. This called for the stamina to endure hours on horseback in terrain almost completely devoid of roads or bridges. Robert was Bibi's dream client, not only because of his expert horsemanship and long practice in the rigours of life on the trail, but also because of his habit of courtesy, which won him the approval of all he encountered, be they goatherd, merchant or sheikh. After all, Robert observed, in Morocco all men were equal under Allah.

Robert was in his element as they roamed the dry mountains and dusty ravines of the interior, although he complained to Gabriela that, unlike in South America, in Morocco one could never completely get away from people; while the Arab practice of always sleeping in a tent felt to him like a confinement. 'One never sleeps so soundly as on a fine night beside a fire, one's head on a saddle,' he wrote. He carried a revolver at all times, though he would not countenance the presence of guards.

Robert and Bibi were joined in their adventures by a third companion, young Walter Harris, son of a Quaker shipping magnate, who had gone native to an even greater extent than Carleton, and was known throughout Morocco for his uncanny ability to take on the personality of an Arab. The first time they met, Harris was dressed in local costume, shaven-headed apart from a lock twelve inches long, dangling from the centre of his crown, and accompanied by two greyhounds with feet dyed yellow. He was also, aged only twenty-two, North African correspondent for the *Times*. This for Robert was the start of a forty-year friendship.

In December 1892, a mere six months after Robert had put Westminster behind him, this formidable trio travelled inland to 'great, noisy, dusty Fez'. Robert found it claustrophobic, lying in its deep ravine with its dark, twisting, often waterlogged alleyways, its citizens openly hostile to roumis. One of the few images of Fez to please him were the storks he witnessed as he was leaving the city, like ghosts in the still morning air, asleep on one leg atop the towers of its dazzlingly white, crenellated walls. From here a further twenty days' riding brought them to Morocco City, modern-day Marrakech, where the contrast could scarcely have been greater. One of the few Europeans to travel this far into the Moroccan interior, Robert was instantly captivated. On its high plateau, ringed to the south by the great snow-capped wall of the Atlas Mountains, this sprawling city of empty spaces, the size of Paris, reminded him of Mexico City yet was unlike anywhere he had ever been.

> Sand, sand and more sand, in almost every street, in the vast open spaces, in the long winding narrow lanes outside the walls, up to the city gates; sand in your hair, your clothes, the coats of animals. Streets, streets and still more streets of houses in decay . . . No noise, the footfalls of the mules and camels, falling into the sand as rain falls into the sea, with a soft swishing sound . . .

he wrote in *Bu Gidri* (*Faith*, 1909). For all the encroaching desert he grew to welcome the narrow streets arched over with grape vines, the ever-present sound of water, as he returned to Morocco City time and again in the years that followed, pursuing whatever business it was that brought him to this great meeting place of dignitaries, traders and wandering tribesmen from northern coast and southern desert. Comparing it to Morocco's other cities, he wrote: 'none of them enter into your soul as does this heap of ruins, this sand-heap, desert town, metropolis of the fantastic world which stretches from its walls across the mountains through oases to the Sahara.'

Over the next decade, Robert's knowledge of Morocco and the Arab world grew and grew as he travelled, reported on what he saw, and conducted lengthy and labyrinthine negotiations with local potentates for trade concessions which he could bring back to London and sell. All the while he stored up material for the numerous Moroccan sketches he would later come to write; his exploits meanwhile attracting the attention of other writers such as John Buchan, who drew largely on Robert for the character of Sandy Arbuthnot, the hero of Greenmantle. Tallish, with a lean high-boned face, hair like a fox's pelt and brown eyes, Arbuthnot was 'the wandering Scot carried to the pitch of genius'. As Anne Taylor notes in *The People's Laird*, the resemblance was not only physical: both Arbuthnot and Robert were highly strung, sensitive, proud and volatile, and both were expert horsemen.

One destination to which Robert was drawn for unspecified purposes was Cape Juby, on Morocco's southwest coast. Here a Scot, Donald MacKenzie, had managed to extract a grant for a strip of coastal land from one of the region's most important sheikhs, establishing a factory there to make Manchester cotton goods for sale to the Arabs; but with the ultimate and wildly implausible aim of breaching the coastal dunes to flood the interior and allow trading ships to sail through to Timbuktu and the River Niger, many hundreds of miles distant. Now MacKenzie was negotiating with the British government for the protection of a Royal Charter, failing which he threatened to enter talks with Spain. The only independent harbour for several hundred miles of African coastline, Cape Juby, or Tarfaya as the Arabs called it, represented a significant headache for the Foreign Office. Sovereignty over the land acquired by MacKenzie would be implicit in the charter, should it be granted, a prospect that caused great alarm to Spain, France and the Moroccan sultanate, all of whom were deeply suspicious of British motives.

Here at Cape Juby the desert, flat, sandy and overgrown with low bushes, reminded Robert of Texas, while behind, the desolate and empty sea thundered ceaselessly on the shore. But it was the factory and compound that caught his attention and featured in a number of sketches, including *At Torfaieh* (*The Ipané*, 1899).

A portion of Scotland erratically dropped in Africa . . . [it was] as Scotch, or even still more Scotch, than Peebles, Lesmahagow, or the

Cowcaddens, for the setting went for nothing in comparison with
the North British composition of the place. Decent and orderly the
Scottish clerks, the tall, red-bearded manager; Scotch the pioneer,
known to the Arabs down into the Sahara as 'M'Kenzie' . . . Order
and due precision of accounts, great ledgers, beer upon tap, whis-
key served out 'medicinally', prayers upon Sunday, no trifling with
the Arab women ever allowed, a moral tone, a strict attention to
commercial principles, and yet no trade . . .

This last being a reference to the fact that the company was forbidden to trade while the British government deliberated the grant of
the charter. As a result, incomprehending traders from the interior
were turned away at gunpoint and had to bury the wool they had
brought for sale in the sand. The most important sheikhs were even
paid to stay away, while those that came empty-handed were allowed
to camp outside the compound walls – a state of affairs that left the
local populace, for all their trust in the will of Allah, scratching their
heads at the apparent madness of the Christians.

A great snow-capped rampart, the Atlas Mountains run slantwise
from the Mediterranean to the Atlantic, separating northern
Morocco from the Sahara. Where they approach the southwestern
coast, they split like a lobster claw, the High Atlas to the north and
the Anti-Atlas to the south. Between these pincers the lush, green
Sus valley runs inland from the port of Agadir for a hundred miles.
Here, the local chiefs were eager to collaborate and trade with
anyone who could help facilitate their insurrection against the
sultanate.

Into this pleasant and fertile region appeared a character whom
Robert had previously come across in Argentina, posing as consul
of the fictitious state of Araucania. Captain Geyling was an Austrian
doctor who also, disguised as a Turk, frequently went by the name
of Abdul Karim Bey. With the support of investors including Daniel
Sassoon and Cecil Rhodes, Geyling had set up a company called the
Globe Venture Syndicate to sell rifles, bibles and cotton goods to the
Sus chiefs, also to work the mines rumoured to be there. But these
activities threatened further destabilisation in the south of the

country and attracted the close attention of the Foreign Office, which now advised all British nationals to stay away from the area.

Ignoring this advice, Robert made up his mind to visit Taroudant, a town some thirty miles up the Sus Valley from Agadir. It was this journey that would become the subject of *Mogreb el Acksa* (1898), the book described by his friend Joseph Conrad as 'the travel book of the century'. (*Mogreb el Acksa* translates as 'The Far West', a style of description used by Muslim historians for northwestern Africa and the kingdom of Morocco in particular.)

Robert had heard Taroudant described as a 'land of vines, of orange gardens, olive yards, plantations of pomegranates, Roman remains, and rich mines' and, according to his early biographers, a city where no Christian had ever before set foot – which for Robert would have been incentive enough. While this is almost certainly an exaggeration, Robert persisted in maintaining that it was a forbidden city, which was true to an extent: the sultanate had declared the whole country south of the High Atlas closed to foreigners, although Taroudant did not enjoy the religious or political significance of some other Moroccan cities.

As was the case at Cape Juby, the purpose of Robert's journey to Taroudant has never been made clear. Was he an emissary to the tribes from the Globe Venture Syndicate? Before setting out he would stay at the International Palm Tree Sanatorium in Mogador (modern-day Essaouira), whose proprietor, Peppe Ratto, was known to be an agent for the Globe Venture Syndicate. Or was he information-gathering for the British government? Sir Arthur Nicolson, British Minister at Tangier and a distant cousin, whom he had visited before departing, did nothing to stop Robert despite his government's advice to nationals. These possibilities were not mutually exclusive, nor was the third: that he was simply indulging his natural curiosity and propensity for adventure.

Nevertheless, to travel there was still a risky proposition. Given current political and commercial manoeuverings by European interests, Robert, who spoke little Arabic, could just as easily have been taken for a spy as fallen prey to bandits or been exposed to zealous believers as an infidel – all of which could have proved fatal. Tensions in the region had lately increased due to the activities of

Major Spilsbury, an English adventurer with links to the Globe Venture Syndicate, whose attempt, a few months later, to supply a large quantity of guns to the insurgent tribes of the Sus would end in the interception of his steam yacht, the *Tourmaline*, at Agadir – an incident which Robert later described in an article for the *Saturday Review*. Spilsbury, whom Robert knew and, curiously, admired – for his pluck if not the nature of his enterprise – escaped but was later arrested in London and deported for trial on charges of gun-running to Gibraltar, where a sympathetic jury acquitted him.

Against this backdrop of mounting instability, Robert arrived by ship at Mogador in October 1897. Ignoring the British consul's warnings, he began preparations for the journey. His companions were Haj Mohammed es Swani, 'a Moor of the Riff pirate breed, short, strong, black bearded', who also spoke Spanish and had accompanied Robert on previous journeys; and Hassan Suleiman Lutaif, a poetry-reading Syrian Christian, as interpreter. For a guide they chose a Berber muleteer, Mohammed el Hosein, who would also interpret once they entered Shilha-speaking, Berber territory. Reviewers of *Mogreb el Acksa* would later make comparisons between Robert and the explorer, Sir Richard Burton, but Burton was an accomplished Arabist who readily passed as a native on his *Pilgrimage to Medinah and Mecca*. Robert was not, and knew that he would need to rely heavily on whatever camouflage was available, including that provided by his companions; a necessity heightened by his friend Bibi Carleton's last minute withdrawal from the expedition. This news caused Gabriela to write anxiously from Gartmore, imploring Robert to take care.

It was not unusual for European travellers in the interior to adopt local costume. It was comfortable and practical and helped to close an otherwise yawning cultural gap, while not requiring the wearer to dissemble about faith or nationality. Nevertheless, with some misgivings Robert decided to take the extra precaution of disguising himself as a Turkish doctor. But once outfitted as such, all agreed that he so closely resembled a Moroccan *sherif* that with an appropriately lofty and taciturn demeanour, 'Sheikh Mohammed el Fasi' would pass readily for a man of Fez. *Sherifs*, as descendants of the prophet, were considered holy men, a convenient dispensation for Robert; though he noted that they were as numerous in the Muslim world as the 'ancestors came over with the Conqueror' people in England, and comported themselves with a similar air of entitlement.

Equipped with horse, high Moorish saddle covered with red cloth, dressed in white, but with a blue cloak to cover all, a fez and turban, head duly shaved, and yellow slippers, with, of course, a pair of horseman's boots (called temag by the Arabs) buttoned up the back with green silk buttons, embroidered down the side with silk and silver thread, a leather bag to sling across the shoulders and act as pocket, I was ready for the start.

He had bought the whole outfit, including a horse and saddle 'like a bag of stones', for twenty-nine dollars, a third more than a local would have paid. As further precaution, and with a backwards nod to the Turkish doctor, he equipped himself with quinine, mercury, laxative Seidlitz powders and eye-wash for ophthalmia.

The shortest and least arduous route to Taroudant went south by the coast to Agadir, skirting the mountains to approach the city through the Sus Valley. But shortly before leaving, Robert learned that this was closed due to a local insurrection. He now chose the shorter of the two alternatives, which went by Morocco City and the town of Imintanout, before following a pass through the High Atlas Mountains.

Setting out from Mogador on 12 October, the party kept to the safety of cattle tracks and dried-up watercourses while Robert adjusted to the accoutrements of his new identity, the voluminous white robes and the short Moorish stirrups which required the rider to adopt a semi-kneeling position. This caused him such agony that after he had suffered in silence for some time, Mohammed es Swani took pity on him and when they next dismounted seized him by the legs 'and pulled them violently, and rubbed the knee-joints after the fashion of a shampooer in a Turkish bath.'

Only once satisfied with his performance – holding himself more seemly, not letting his hooded cloak hang too low, not talking English, and when dismounted walking 'as befitted an Arab gentleman, to whom time is a drug' – did his companions allow him to venture onto the main road from Mogador to Morocco City. They carried few provisions:

a kettle and an iron pot, no forks, no spoons as being dressed as Moors we had to eat after the Moorish fashion with our hands, our only luxury being a rather gim-crack brass tea tray, a pewter German teapot, and six small glasses to drink green tea flavoured with mint, and made as sweet as syrup.

As befitted his status as a sherif, Robert shared a small tent with Lutaif, while the others slept with the mules. When hospitality required him to forsake the tent for a stranger's dwelling, he feigned sickness or mumbled incoherently. This appeared to work, though he suspected that given the taboo on Christian company, his hosts more likely felt obliged to collude in the deception and may even have been amused by it; for Arabs, 'like other men, delight in doing what they know they should not do, with the full consciousness of doing wrong . . .'

Reaching Imintatout they learned that the pass ahead had been closed by the local sheikh. Although it would prolong the risk of discovery, Robert now had no choice but to follow the longer, higher and more arduous route via the town of Amsmiz, which they reached a day or two later.

At dawn on 19 October, a week after leaving Mogador, they set out from Amsmiz. The road led steadily up a narrow mule-track towards the shoulder of Tizi n'Test, the Atlas peak that lay in their path. It followed the course of the Wadi el n'Fiss which

at a great depth below . . . boiled furiously among the stones, winding and rewinding like a watch spring and forcing us to cross it many times, when its swift current proved so formidable that, although not more than three feet deep, we had to enter altogether in a group to keep our feet.

Toiling up the narrow and precipitous trail, they passed travellers whose wretched state attested to the long drought that had afflicted the region:

First, father, a fine old Arab, gaunt, miserable, grey-headed, ragged, hollow-cheeked, without a turban, shoes, or waist-belt, carrying a child which looked over his shoulder with enormous black and starving eyes; the mother on foot, in rags and shoeless, and still holding between her teeth a ragged haik to veil her misery from the passer by, a baby at her back, a branch torn from an olive-tree to switch off flies; then three ophthalmic children, flies buzzing about their eyelids; lastly, the eldest son stolidly sitting in despair beside a fallen donkey, carrying salt, and rubbed by girth, by crupper, and by pack ropes, and an epitome of the last stages of famine and of overwork.

Which was worse, Robert asked himself, returning to a familiar theme: an old-fashioned, drought-induced famine, or a modern economic famine where the rich die from an excess of food while the starving poor work themselves to death?

As Robert suspected, his disguise had not proved entirely effective. Less happily still, neither had the anticipated collusion. Word now went ahead of them that an infidel was abroad. On the second day after they had left Amsmiz, they were intercepted by men of the Caid of Kintafi, governor of the mountain province through which they now travelled. When they were within a few hours of the summit of the pass, men rushed at them brandishing guns and fingering daggers. In a tense interrogation, Robert was asked to swear that he was a true believer. Unable to answer convincingly in the Berber tongue 'and so knowing we should be taken back before the Caid and then found out, I answered "Yes, I am the Christian," and began to feel my horse's mouth ready for what might come.'

What came, eventually, was a ten-day stay at the Caid's pleasure in his summer palace, Talaat n'Jacoub, which they had passed earlier, a short distance down the mountain. This was a large mud-built, yellowish-red castle with flat roofs and flat-topped flanking towers, surrounded by gardens, woods and cultivated grounds. Behind it loomed the snow-capped Tizi n'Test, beneath its walls flowed the Wadi el n'Fiss. Following their arrest, and after a long and anxious wait in the shelter of the castle gateway' – it was now pouring with rain – Robert and his companions received word that the Caid would offer them his hospitality while he decided what to do with them. This, Robert suspected, would depend on the outcome of an exchange with the Sultan, from whom the Caid maintained a fiercely independent stand, yet to whom he was answerable for peace and security in the whole region south of the Atlas, and therefore bound to report the presence of Christians.

A tent was now placed at their disposal on the maidan, a flat, open space in front of the castle gates where locals practiced their horsemanship. Here, closely watched by guards, they settled down to wait.

Audience with the Caid proved unforthcoming. 'The 24th still found us, so to speak, in Poste Restante, the Caid invisible, tobacco running low, food not too regular' – they received intermittent deliveries of couscous –

and our animals becoming thinner every day. But still the example of the prisoners, the Sheikhs from Sus, and a tent full of miserable tribesmen, all almost without food, and glad to eat our scraps, kept us for shame's sake patient. So we talked much to everyone . . .

'Everyone' meant the Caid's officials, servants, slaves, various other guests, voluntary or involuntary, hangers-on, travellers, wide-eyed passing tribesmen, and the prisoners – captive rebels who every morning were winched up from the foul-smelling pit in which they had spent the night. Conversation with this company, which included an itinerant Persian singer, a Jewish peddler of Algerian tobacco, a Negro who had once worked for a Scottish trading company which had never transacted a single piece of business in 16 years, and the Sheikhs from Sus – whom Robert was to discover had already waited more than a month for an audience with the Caid – sustained him throughout the following days and provided rich material for later writing.

At length a letter, painfully composed by Lutaif, secured Robert an audience. After a lengthy conversation and an invitation to examine a bullet wound in his host's thigh, which Robert declined to treat, the Caid concluded that he was not yet ready to release them. Nevertheless, the conditions of their detention improved at once. Fruit appeared. A whole sheep was delivered and roasted. News that the roumi was a doctor prompted a queue of the halt and lame to whom Robert dispensed the contents of his medicine chest.

On the tenth day of their captivity, orders arrived at last from the Sultan. The exact nature of the terms, Robert never learned, but the Caid's chamberlain informed him that it was now the pleasure of the Caid that they should be on their way. Determined to the last, Robert offered the chamberlain a hefty bribe to let them pass on for Taroudant. 'What is the use to me of a hundred or a thousand dollars without my head?' came the reply. With that, Robert and his companions set off back down the mountain for Morocco City.

While the intrepid British explorer of popular imagination might bravely have fought off the Caid's interception party and continued over the pass for a triumphant entry to Taroudant, his disguise holding up to the last, Robert had achieved the opposite. He had fooled no one – no one that mattered, at any rate; he had failed to reach his destination; and he had been taken captive into the bargain. On all three counts, *Mogreb el Acksa*, published the following year, 1898, broke the mould of nineteenth century travel writing. Half a century later, in his centenary study of Robert's life, Hugh MacDiarmid would describe it as 'one of the best books of travel ever written'.

In the foreword Robert apologises for offering up

> the history of a failure to accomplish what I tried; and having brought together a sack of cobwebs, a pack of gossamers, a bale of thistle-down, dragon-flies' wings, of Oriental gossip as to bygone facts, of old-world recollections, of new-world practices half understood . . .

Ever since, *Mogreb el Acksa* has been held up as the cardinal example of Robert's belief that failure was more interesting than success; a view which has sometimes been misinterpreted to suggest that he prized failure as a goal in itself. He did no such thing.

During his time spent at the Caid's pleasure Robert had managed to smuggle out letters, both to the British authorities in Tangier and to the London press. In one, to the editor of the *Daily Chronicle*, he makes much of his captivity and begs the editor to put pressure on the Foreign Office to help secure his release. Another, to the editor of the *Saturday Review*, archly offers an apology for being unable to review a book on account of being a prisoner 'at the above address', which he gives as 'Thelata el Jacoub, Kintafi, Atlas Mountains.'

But was this public posturing, a deliberate, almost theatrical over-playing of the danger he faced at the Caid's hands, in order to conceal a different purpose? By most standards the journey had been irresponsible and reckless; it had achieved little of interest; and it had proved an embarrassment to all concerned – the Sultan, the Caid and the British authorities. On learning of Robert's arrest, Sir Arthur Nicolson had written to the Marquess of Salisbury, the Foreign Secretary, pointing out that the consul in Mogador had 'warned Mr Graham of the risks he would incur; but the latter is an adventurous traveller and difficult to dissuade from making journeys which he thinks will be interesting.' Nicolson went on to reassure the Foreign Secretary that no mishap would result from Robert's detention, and that he, Nicolson, would request the immediate release of the travellers.

In the final chapter of *Mogreb el Acksa* Robert describes the return journey, in apparent disarray, to Morocco City and thence to Mogador. En route he stops with a number of local sheikhs who are known to oppose the country's ruling faction. In Morocco City he meets with a previous acquaintance, Sidi Abu Bekhr, a murky character of great wealth and influence who has been British consular agent in the city for thirty years. At first, Bekhr will not believe that Robert 'was not an agent of the Globe Venture Syndicate, or had a mission from the British Government to try and establish some sort of undertaking with the chiefs of Sus.' But did Robert protest too much? Anne Taylor notes these encounters and goes on to suggest that his real objectives may have been to reconnoitre the northern end of the Tizi n'Test pass, and to gain audience with the Caid, his arrest and detention being a blind for the discussions that actually took place. Since the Caid was answerable to the sultanate for peace and security south of the Atlas Mountains, the British government was keen to ascertain where his allegiance really lay. Meanwhile, the Globe Venture Syndicate was eager to know how the Caid would look on a British attempt to gain trade concessions and establish a sphere of influence in the south of the country; an ambition which would shortly come close to being destroyed by Major Spilsbury. Any such information from Robert would have been highly valued by both parties, as Sidi Abu Bekhr well knew.

My copy of *Mogreb el Acksa*, whose flyleaf bears a Spanish proverb in Robert's handwriting, has an envelope glued to the inside back cover containing several intriguing and, perhaps, in respect of Robert's story, mutually contradictory, items. A newspaper cutting of an obituary by Robert in the Tangier English-language newspaper, *Al Moghreb Al-Aksa*, marks the death in 1906 of the English journalist and Morocco specialist, Edward Budgett Meakin. There is a short typed letter, dated September 1908, from Johnston, the British consul in Mogador who had earlier advised Robert not to proceed to Taroudant. Johnston refers to a widely-circulated letter Robert has written and congratulates him 'for allowing the truth to be told about poor Morocco'. He goes on to insist that the French will not have things all their own way – this, presumably, in the aftermath of the Algeciras Conference of 1906, from which Robert reported, and which tried, but failed, to resolve the dispute between Germany and France over France's attempt to establish Morocco as a protectorate. Then there is an undated letter in Arabic script on lined notepaper, with accompanying hand-written translation, informing the indecipherable recipient that certain tribes of Morocco's coastal north now recant their previous hostility towards the recipient and his people (meaning the English) and are ready to do whatever the recipient may wish or please. And finally, in an undated newspaper cutting from, perhaps, the *Airdrie Advertiser*, there is this letter from Robert with his brand mark inked in the margin: *Sir* –

> It has come to my attention that whilst a prisoner in Morocco, an absurd report appeared in a Stirling paper, copied, I understand, from a London paper, that I was perambulating Morocco at the head of fifty men. I did not wish to conquer that country, and, as a matter of fact, had three men and a boy to look after our horses.

I was endeavouring to reach a city almost unknown to Europeans, to verify the reported existence of rich mines, and in my humble way to study the flora, fauna, etc., of the country. As for the fifty men (in buckram, I suppose) I know nothing of them. – I am, yours faithfully, R.B. Cunninghame Graham.

People could ascribe to his adventure whatever purpose they liked, but Robert was having none of it. Back in Britain he continued unabashed, not only to write about the Spilsbury incident in the *Saturday Review*, and later in *Mogreb el Acksa*, but also, in the months and years to come, to maintain contact with both the Globe Venture Syndicate and the Sus tribes, as he continued to seek trading concessions and other development opportunities in southern Morocco.

In mid-life, Robert had found in North Africa what South America had offered him in his youth: adventure, intrigue and the lived experience of other peoples and cultures. No matter what, if any, Robert's clandestine objectives, it was as Nicolson remarked his impulse to make journeys 'which he thinks will be interesting' that makes *Mogreb el Acksa* the book it is. Unlike so many of his European contemporaries who travelled for hard-won goals and observed those they encountered along the way as curiosities, Robert travelled to understand the human condition wherever he encountered it, to immerse himself fully in whatever stream he swam. He admired the Arab dignity and courtesy, the dogged fatalism which seemed to go hand-in-hand with a relentless mercantilism. He found a certain nobility in the simplicity and hardship of life for the many. And, characteristically, he applauded their relationship with animals, noting that an Arab herdsman leads his flock, where his European counterpart drives it. Acknowledging that it was he who was the outsider, Robert travelled with an empathy and respect that enabled him to make meaningful connections with people at all levels of society; and in the process to explore his own understanding of the world around him, to reach a deeper knowledge of himself.

I have not been drawn to the Arab world as Robert was. The language and customs which he strove to assimilate seem insurmountable to me. The nearest I have come to the North Africa of

Robert's experience was the Tunisian coastal town of Monastir, where in 1978 my brother-in-law was working on the set of *Monty Python's Life of Brian*. A costumier, his principal challenge was to ensure that no wristwatches or trainers were visible during crowd scenes. He arranged for us to stay in the cast hotel where I had the surreal experience of having my ears syringed, when they became blocked after swimming, by Brian himself, the Python Graham Chapman, who had also taken on the real-life role of set doctor. During our week's holiday we watched the filming of a number of memorable scenes in the town's fort, transformed into first century Caesarea using sets from Franco Zeffirelli's *Jesus of Nazareth*, which had been shot there the previous year. The crumbling masonry, the white robes, camels, donkeys and flocks of sheep echoed much that Robert describes in *Mogreb el Acksa*. Many years later, on a family holiday to Marrakech, we took a day trip to the mountains. Stopping, inevitably, at a tearoom-cum-carpet warehouse we were ushered onto the roof for refreshments and a view of the snow-capped heights ahead. I pictured Robert doggedly leading his horse up some dry, winding gulley and thought how he would have deplored the corrupting influence of modernity on a country which he had discovered still, for the large part, in an almost pristine state of antiquity; the vulgarity and clamour that tourism had brought to his city of sand; the asphalted road that now made it possible to follow his route from Amsmiz to the Tizi n'Test, and on to Taroudant, in a little over four hours.

Yet again, in Morocco, Robert found himself reporting from a place on the cusp of great and irrevocable change – of which he himself, paradoxical as ever, was an agent.

Eighteen

LONDON

The writing life

'The book arrived by this evening's post. I dropped every-thing – as you may imagine, and rushed at it paper knife in hand . . .' Conrad exclaimed,

> A man staying here [H.G. Wells, suggests my mother in *Gaucho Laird*] has been reading over my shoulder . . . We have been shouting, slapping our legs, leaping up, stamping about . . . I do not know really how to express the kind of intellectual exultation your book has awakened in me; and I will not stay to try; I am in too much of a hurry to get back to the book. My applause, slaps on the back, salaams, benedictions, cheers. Take what you like best of these, what you think most expressive. Or take them all. I can't be too demonstrative.

'Ever yours with yells – Conrad.'

Robert and Joseph Conrad had met in 1897, one year before Conrad wrote excitedly on receipt of *Mogreb el Acksa*. Robert's natural expansiveness found expression, among other things, in his generosity towards other writers, his often-unfettered delight in their achievements. He had written to Conrad the previous year to introduce himself after reading and admiring Conrad's short story *An Outpost of Progress* in Cosmopolis magazine. It was the start of the closest, most enduring literary friendship of both their lives. Although Conrad's career would come to eclipse Robert's many times over, at the start it was Robert who commanded attention, not only for his public prominence but also for his personal presence, which Conrad found dazzling.

In some ways they had much in common, in others they were opposites. A large number of Conrad's letters to Robert survive though sadly, very few of Robert's to Conrad since every so often Conrad would destroy most of his inbound correspondence – perhaps a sailor's habit of avoiding clutter, suggests Laurence Davies. In his introduction to *Joseph Conrad's Letters to Cunninghame Graham*, Cedric Watts notes that both men were described as 'aristocratic' in their bearing, appearance, and in their sense of chivalry, honour and justice. Five years younger than Robert, Conrad had been born in Ukraine to a family of Polish nobles. Like Robert, Conrad had travelled widely and adventurously, serving for nearly twenty years as a mariner on merchant ships. Both tended to approach the present through the lens of an irretrievable past. But where Robert was flamboyant, confident and energetic, Conrad was reticent and prone to illness, anxiety and self-doubt. Where Robert was an idealist, Conrad was a pessimist. And where Robert was a self-declared enemy of the establishment, Conrad was deeply conservative – although with a conservatism that despised wealth. 'By Jove!' he wrote to Robert in October 1907, 'If I had the necessary talent I would like to go for the true anarchist – which is the millionaire. Then you would see the venom flow. But it's too big a job.'

Yet their differences merely fuelled a connection akin to brotherhood. The Conrad scholar, Richard Curle, reported a meeting between the two men in later life: 'In each other's company they appeared to grow younger; they treated one another with that kind of playfulness which can only arise from a complete, unquestioning, and ancient friendship. I doubt whether the presence of any man made Conrad happier than the presence of Don Roberto . . . ' Conrad himself once remarked that he could not go on existing were Robert to die.

No sooner had they met than Robert set about championing Conrad, commending his work in print and in letters to friends; a habit Robert would continue throughout his life with emerging writers whose work he admired, among them John Masefield and

Axel Munthe. Conrad, for his part, began to look to Robert for inspiration for his fictional creations. *Nostromo* was published in 1904, seven years after they met. Aspects of Robert and his personal circumstances are there to see in the character of Charles Gould, owner of a mine in the fictional Latin American republic of Costaguana, and one of the novel's central protagonists. Further, since Conrad himself only ever spent a few days ashore in South America, it's very likely that Robert was one of his primary sources of information about the continent. 'Conrad tells me he has used a story I told him in Nostromo,' he grumbled to his editor, Edward Garnett. 'Nostromo is a dammed [sic] bad name. He ought to have called it Costaguana.' Other characters in *Nostromo* came from Robert's South American recollections: the hotelier Giorgio Viola, based on the bottle-throwing Garibaldino bar keeper in *Cruz Alta*, Enrico Clerici; and Don José Avellanos, the Costaguanan elder statesman, based on Robert's Colombian friend, the writer and diplomat, Santiago Pérez Triana. There are other echoes, too. Anne Taylor notes that the Sao Tomé silver mine, an inheritance to which Gould becomes enslaved, could well be Gartmore; and the Goulds' marriage, one of frequent separation in which the wife, Emilia, eventually accepts that she will not bear a child, mirrors Robert's own. Emilia's increasing independence, as the novel progresses, is strikingly similar to Gabriela's, as is her management of the burden her husband has inherited. And it is not only *Nostromo* where Robert's footprints can be seen. *The Secret Agent, The Inheritors, Heart of Darkness* – all bear traces of his influence; while the inspiration for *Typhoon*, which he dedicated to Robert, may have come directly from correspondence between them when Robert was in need of technical information for the story *SS Atlas*, his account of crossing the Atlantic in a tramp steamer.

For a quarter of a century, Robert and Conrad wrote and visited frequently. They challenged one another in matters literary, political and philosophical, raged together at injustice, admitted one another to their inner lives: Robert confessing to despair at his ever-deteriorating finances, Conrad to his intermittent episodes of depression. To the last, their letters were frequent, wide-ranging and candid. When Conrad died in 1924, aged only sixty-six, Robert was among the chief mourners at the house in Kent where he had earlier amused Conrad's young sons by climbing trees and, with a revolver, shooting thrown apples out of the air. His presence at the funeral, kind and calming to the other mourners, in particular to Conrad's devoted secretary, Lilian Hallowes, is imagined in David Miller's short novel *Today*.

Robert was now approaching fifty and the legend of Don Roberto, the quixotic half-Spanish adventurer, the dashing *hidalgo*, was blossoming. Colourful, confident, a man in his prime, he was happy to allow his Hispanicised story to eclipse the Scottish one, where financial difficulties still dogged him, and aspects of both his father's and his wife's pasts were best kept quiet. His literary star was in the ascendant and his circle of friends and acquaintances included the most prominent writers and artists of his day. To some extent he owed this to his mother. At seventy, still lively, attractive and sharp-minded, The Hon Mrs Bontine was regularly to be seen at galleries, the theatre and musical events, including the Bayreuth Wagnerian Festival which she attended every year. For some years now she had hosted regular gatherings at her house in Chester Square, cultivating gifted young men who perhaps reminded her of Malise. The artists Max Beerbohm and Will Rothenstein had fallen under her spell while still undergraduates, along with a young publisher's reader, Edward Garnett. Other artists, Percy Jacomb-Hood and James Whistler, along with two of the Glasgow Boys, John Lavery and Joseph Crawhall, were regular visitors. Aubrey Beardsley and Oscar Wilde, John Galsworthy and W.B. Yeats put in appearances. But W.H. Hudson, the Anglo-Argentine naturalist and author of *Green Mansions* whom Robert came to admire more than any other writer, and with whom he loved to reminisce about South America, declined an invitation on the grounds of penury. He had emigrated from Argentina in his thirties and now lived in Bayswater, eking a living as an author and naturalist. 'I could no more dine at Chester Square with you and your friends than with the fairies or the angels!' he wrote.

One visitor to whom Missy had taken a particular shine was a young playwright with a blossoming reputation named George

Bernard Shaw. Fascinated by Robert's paradoxical character, in particular the conflict between his idealism and realism, Shaw cast both Hector Hushabye, in *Heartbreak House*, and Sergius Saranoff, the Byronic hero of *Arms and the Man*, in Robert's mould, giving Saranoff the famous line from Robert's parliamentary outburst: 'I never withdraw'. Later, in his notes to *Captain Brassbound's Conversion*, set in Morocco, Shaw acknowledges his debt of gratitude to Robert for detailed descriptions of Mogador and Kintafi, which he had requested on first reading *Mogreb el Acksa*. He goes on to say:

> Cunninghame Graham is the hero of his own book; but I have not made him the hero of my play, because so incredible a personage must have destroyed its likelihood – such as it is. There are moments when I do not myself believe in his existence. And yet he must be real; for I have seen him with these eyes; and I am one of the few men living who can decipher the curious alphabet in which he writes his private letters.

Anne Taylor raises the possibility that there are echoes of Robert and his relationships in *Pygmalion*. Could Robert be the professor, educating his socially inferior bride, Carrie, under the watchful eye of his formidable mother, Anne Elizabeth? Were it to be true, Robert is unlikely to have welcomed such an intrusion.

Conrad and Shaw were not the only people to draw on Robert's character and activities for creative inspiration. For Ford Madox Ford, who deemed Robert the most brilliant writer of the day, he was Don Collar in his novel *An English Girl*, a man torn between the desire for social reform and a hankering after a romanticised past. His friend W.H. Hudson, wrote: 'you are rather like an Arthurian knight abroad in the great forest of the world, in quest of adventure and ready at a moment's notice to lower your lance and joust at any evil-minded person that may turn up.' In similar vein, another friend, Will Rothenstein, painted him as a conquistador, *The Fencer*, hair and moustaches swept up, hand on the hilt of his sword. The Edinburgh engraver, William Strang, chose him as the model for a series of thirty etchings of Don Quixote.

Beyond Chester Square, Robert's circle had widened further under the aegis of Frank Harris and his *Saturday Review*. Now Edward Garnett stepped forward. Emerging London publishers such as T. Fisher Unwin, Gerald Duckworth and Jonathan Cape had begun employing a new breed of editors and readers, young men with a nose for new talent and an ability to anticipate the public appetite. Garnett was one such, destined to become one of the most celebrated editors of his day, and he had been quick to spot Robert's potential.

In May 1898, Garnett proposed to Robert that the first volume of a new series from Unwin, to be called *The Overseas Library*, should feature his writing from the *Saturday Review*. The following year he published the first collection of Robert's work, *The Ipqné*, the title taken from a sketch about a ramshackle cargo boat plying the waters of the Paraguay River. Other sketches ranged from Mexico to Morocco, Scotland to Iceland, as well as an account of William Morris's funeral, *With the North West Wind* – somewhat incongruous in a collection of travel writing, yet it moved Garnett so much that he felt compelled to include it.

This was the start of another long friendship and literary correspondence, lasting until Robert's death nearly forty years later. But for all his editorial acuity Garnett, like so many others, remained a little awed by Robert and it was only once his 'dear Amigo' was dead that he was able to write, with a hint of envy and perhaps the tacit acknowledgement that he might have exercised his editorial authority more firmly:

Absolutely independent of public opinion and class times, Graham was in the delightful position of social observer without any fish to fry but with means and leisure to speak his mind freely. The charm of his manner, his fine breeding, his gleaming wit, his savoir-faire, Spanish courtesy, combined with his Scotch blood to make his personality unique.

In other words, Robert wrote what he damned well pleased, and anyone who tried to make him change his mind was going to be charmed or stonewalled into submission.

Robert worked 'rapidly in white heat, afterwards losing all interest in the fruits of his creations,' according to Alexander Maitland in *Robert and Gabriela Cunninghame Graham*. But while the indecipherable handwriting and slapdash drafts were a source of constant frustration to Garnett, he was excited by Robert's ability to capture the spirit of exotic places and their people, and appreciative of the anti-imperial lens through which he tended to view them. Further, Robert could write things that would in other hands have seemed unacceptably maudlin or salacious: the stories of failed expeditions such as *Cruz Alta*, for example, or the erotic spectacle of a gypsy flamenco dancer in Seville in the sketch *Aurora la Cujiñi* (*Charity* 1912). But Garnett was not entirely satisfied. An admirer of the master storyteller, Turgenev, he urged Robert to develop the characterisation and plot necessary to turn his sketches into short stories. While Robert also admired the Russian, this would have required him to enter territory into which he had never been prepared to go: those deep personal feelings which, with very rare exceptions, made no appearance in what he wrote. 'Now you must understand that I am a man of action and have passed most of my life outdoors,' he wrote defensively, 'I am really, pas de blague, extremely diffident of all I write. I never put pen to paper until I was 37.' Even the company he now kept in Garnett's stable of new writers – Joseph Conrad, John Galsworthy, W.H. Hudson and D.H. Lawrence to name but four – was not enough to reassure him.

Nonetheless, between 1899, when Garnett published *The Ipané*, and 1936, the year of Robert's death and the publication of his final collection, Mirages, he produced more than twenty-five books. The majority were collections of essays, tales and sketches – close to two hundred individual pieces in all. The remainder were biographies and histories, mostly relating to the Conquest of South America. In his memoir, Farewell to Yesterday, Ford Madox Ford declared of Robert that 'He was, all in all, the most brilliant writer of that or of our present day.' Yet despite critical acclaim Robert's books were not widely read, and have long since fallen from whatever modest popularity they enjoyed at the time. They are stylistically of their era. They require the casual reader to indulge what might sound to the modern ear like undue verbosity and a tendency towards discursiveness and philosophical meandering. But as Garnett and others recognised, the form which suited Robert best, the sketch, was ground-breaking in its day for the way it combined personal experience and reminiscence, ironic reflection, and close observation of both the human condition and the natural world. Although Robert is palpably present in almost everything he wrote, either in the first person or as narrator, he writes without judgement of his subjects – unless to make a broader point – and largely without sentimentality, though with evident empathy for the huge cast of underdogs, outsiders and eccentrics that populate his work.

From time to time in younger years I tried to read him and quickly gave up. Only once I began to engage with the man and his life did I discover that persistence paid off. For all Garnett's urging that he should develop his craft, he was, despite his own diffidence, a natural storyteller – as the inscription on the dedicated seat at the Scottish Storytelling Centre in Edinburgh attests. The more I read, the more I found he could hold me with his ability to evoke landscape and atmosphere; to bring characters alive on the page; to draw a simple narrative from what he had heard and observed in real life, with little or no attempt at plotting; to weave a simple tale with a glinting thread of humanity.

I have not read everything he wrote, and this is not a book of literary criticism, but rather the story of a life. In recent years the Scottish publishers Kennedy & Boyd have produced *The Cunninghame Graham Collection*, a complete collection of his essays, tales and sketches in five volumes, excerpts from which I have used here to summon his voice and illuminate his story. His meticulously researched biographies and histories of the Conquest – tasks he could never have undertaken without fluent Spanish and the patience to seek out contemporary accounts in dusty Spanish and South American archives – are long out of print, along with his biographies of other more recent South American figures, the nineteenth century Paraguayan dictator, Francisco Solano Lopéz, for example. It has been suggested that he turned to the conquistadors as biographical subjects in reaction to the late nineteenth, early twentieth century vogue for literary celebration of the British

Empire. But that is to overlook the fact that these histories of the Conquest are themselves a kind of celebration of imperialism, albeit of an earlier order, and fully cognisant of the brutality and avarice of the conquerors; just one of the many paradoxes to be found in Robert's writing.

Also out of print is *Doughty Deeds*, the biography of his great-great-grandfather, the eighteenth century landowner, poet and politician, Robert Graham of Gartmore. Known as Doughty Deeds from the opening line of one his poems, much later set to music by Sir Arthur Sullivan, it was to him, it could be argued, that Robert owed the encumbrance of Gartmore and its accompanying debt; since it was his fortune, acquired in the plantations of Jamaica, that gave subsequent less continent generations a taste for luxury and the habit of extravagant spending that would eventually bring the family to its knees.

For all that, Robert felt a particular connection with this ancestor, the sixth laird of Gartmore (1735-1797). Like Robert, his great-great-grandfather had gone abroad in search of a fortune at the age of seventeen, following an education at Glasgow University. But where Robert strove fruitlessly for financial stability, Doughty Deeds prospered swiftly and easily thanks both to a position as Receiver General for Taxes in Jamaica and marriage to Anna, sister of Simon Taylor, the wealthiest man on the island. In due course, Doughty Deeds came to own two sugar plantations, Roaring Rivers and Lucky Hill.

On his return from Jamaica, around 1770, he was given the small estate of Ardoch by a relative, which came with the entail relating to the name Bontine. Twenty years later the inheritance of the Finlaystone estate from his first cousin, the Earl of Glencairn, required him to add the second barrel, Cunninghame, to Graham. Finlaystone stood more or less directly across the Clyde from Ardoch – the house to which Robert would later retire, and in which my mother spent part of her childhood – which Doughty Deeds had built in the style of a colonial bungalow or cottage. By this time he owned properties in Renfrewshire, Lanarkshire, Stirlingshire and Perthshire, as well as his plantations in Jamaica. It was said that he could walk on land he had inherited, all the way from the Clyde to the Forth.

Doughty Deeds followed family tradition and entered Parliament as MP for Stirlingshire. A political reformer, he proposed a Bill of Rights which failed to be adopted, but nevertheless foreshadowed the great Reform Bill of 1832. He was a friend of the Irish Whig satirist and playwright, Richard Brinsley Sheridan, and was painted by Raeburn with one raised hand pointing to the bust of another friend, the leading radical, Charles James Fox. As Rector of the University of Glasgow, he donated £100 to establish the Gartmore Gold Medal for an outstanding discourse on political liberty. A few years previously his inventory had listed fifty-one enslaved people described as 'my property' on Lucky Hill and valued at £3,604; a fact noted in the 2018 report *Slavery, Abolition and the University of Glasgow*. Robert Burns, who wrote his abolitionist poem *The Slave's Lament* in 1792, and whose patron was Doughty Deeds' cousin, the Earl of Glencairn, said of him: '. . . the noblest instance of great talents, great fortune and great worth that ever I saw in conjunction.'

That the sixth laird could be both a radical and a slave-owner was a contradiction of his times – a contradiction echoed, perhaps more surprisingly, by Robert himself. For all his championing of the oppressed, in writing *Doughty Deeds* he seems to have been little exercised by the fact of slavery in the family history. The earlier Robert, Doughty Deeds, had noted that he had helped quell a slave rebellion by 'Burning, Hanging and Gibbeting the prisoners'; while at the same time maintaining 'I am one of those who in a Land of Slaves, struggle for Liberty.' His descendant justified the contradiction by pointing to the trades unionist who protests against overtime, but takes the extra wage when it suits him; the Labour leader who speaks out against capitalism, then drives away in his motor car; the communist who invests his savings in a company if he is certain it will yield five percent. '. . . and so we ripen and rot' he concludes. Was this a blind spot, an aspect of Robert's ancestry that he found too hard to reconcile with his otherwise burning awareness of social injustice? Did he, for example, in later years overlook the fact that he was living and writing in a house that had, to all intents and purposes, been built with the proceeds of slavery? Or did he prefer to believe that the matter had now been dealt with, and that the injustices of the past were not his concern? Much of what he wrote would point to the contrary. In the face of such a paradox, admittedly one of many in Robert's character, the Scottish poet and academic, Alan Riach, believes that we should look at men such as Robert in the round. That he appeared, uncharacteristically, to tolerate, or at least not to condemn, slavery does not make him a wholly bad person; rather one who, like most of us, is multifaceted and subject to many influences. In these days of binary distinctions, it is difficult to disagree.

All one needed to know about Robert was there in what he wrote, he reminded anyone who enquired. And it is the breadth and depth of his lived experience, the places to which he travelled, the events he witnessed, the languages he spoke, the quite extraordinary circle of friends and acquaintances across at least three continents, that furnished him with such a wealth of material for his essays, tales and sketches – the envy, surely, of every writer of his era. As Conrad, a man whose own life had not been uneventful, said: 'When I think of you, I feel as though I have lived all my life in a dark hole without seeing or knowing anything.'

Robert may have resisted Garnett's exhortation to develop his storytelling craft, but as Frank Harris, who had published his work in the *Saturday Review*, wrote: 'In his stories are the painter's eye and a superb painter's talent. One or two of his sketches of Paris life de Maupassant would gladly have signed, but in spite of their mastery, his best work is found in pictures of Spanish South America or Scotland, land of his heart and home.' In his introduction to *The Cunninghame Graham Collection*, Alan McGillivray notes that it was Robert's reading of the European writers, Guy de Maupassant and Ivan Turgenev in particular, that encouraged him to present these experiences through the lens of an unsentimental, often ironic realism, at odds with the work of many of his British contemporaries. Robert himself might well have dismissed such analysis: he simply wrote what he wrote. But it is certainly true that he had little time for what lay at the opposite end of the literary spectrum – the nineteenth century kailyard school of Scottish writers. That said, Robert was not entirely innocent of the charge himself: there is a certain nostalgia, a misty-eyed romanticism to some of his Scottish sketches, as he returns to the well-worn theme of the *status quo ante* versus modernity.

No account of Robert's writing is complete without mention of his prefaces. These he developed almost into a literary form of their own, writing innumerable prefaces not only for his own work but also for books by his friends and acquaintances: Conrad's *Lord Jim*, *Tales from Maupassant*, Pérez Triana's *Down the Orinoco* to name but three. He used these not only to introduce the work in question, but as platforms for his own philosophy and, it often seems, his outlook on whatever happened to strike him in the moment. Frequently they are ironic. In his first collection, *Father Archangel of Scotland*, he addresses his preface 'To The Respectable Public' and begins: Why the adjective 'respectable' should be applied to the public rather than 'gullible', 'adipose' or 'flatulent', I am unable to determine . . . In the following collection, *The Ipané*, he writes:

> For the most part all books are written from vanity, for hope of gain, pecuniary or of some other nature, and now and then to please the writer . . . Few men know why they write, and most of them are ashamed of all they do when once it stares them in the face in moulded type.

In his tone there is a disdain for his readers that returns time and again. Either this is false modesty, or he seems to be suggesting that they are fools for being taken in by what he has to say. In either case, it reveals something of the underlying defensiveness, the ironic wit verging on sarcasm, that he cultivated in his youth when faced with an apparently hostile world in which his father was a violent madman, his family was broke, and he had to maintain composure in face of the casual cruelty of his schoolboy peers. His friend, the Irish poet W.B. Yeats, whose interest in mysticism and the occult brought him close to Gabriela, cultivated a similar tone of disdain for his readers in which the lofty, poetic sensibility seemed to sneer at its bourgeois admirers; although this was more the product of cultural snobbery than of the self-protective cynicism employed by Robert.

All one needed to know about him was there in his writing. And yet . . . Robert's guard was seldom, if ever, completely lowered. In the preface to *Writ in Sand* (1932) he wrote: 'It is a natural instinct for the majority of men to keep a secret garden in their souls, a something they do not care to talk about, still less to set down, for other members of the herd to trample on.' Even Garnett, who was privy to much of the detail of Robert's life, including his anxiety over affairs at Gartmore, was apparently ignorant of the tragedy of Willy's ill health. And when, after Missy's death in 1925, Garnett complained that he knew nothing about her or her mother, Doña Catalina, and suggested to Robert that he should write about them, Robert refused. For all that he remained close and attentive to Missy until the end, nowhere in his writing is there any trace of her. Family portraits were confined to sketches of the two admirals – his grand-father, Fleeming, and step-grandfather, Katon – along with an assortment of more or less eccentric aunts and uncles. But when it came to his private, personal relationships, they were simply off limits.

Robert liked women. He related to them, admired them and championed their cause. In 1908, foreshadowing by half a century the women's movement of the 1960s, he wrote in the left-wing magazine, the *New Age*:

My real sympathy is with their [women's] social and economic freedom. Almost every institution, economic, social, political and religious (especially religious) is designed, or has become with-out designing, a means to keep women dependent upon men. A woman will be truly emancipated, he continued, when she can look a man squarely in the eye and say, 'I have done this because it was my pleasure', and the man, looking back at her, will see she is an equal, for in the freedom of the will lies true equality.

His relationship with Gabriela bore this out to a large extent: they functioned together as mature individuals, bound together by affec-tion, yet each with their own responsibilities in the relationship and each with their own passions to pursue.

Yet with one notable exception, women feature scarcely at all in

17. Robert's friend, the 'Glasgow Boy' John Lavery, painted him on a number of occasions and as Lavery's fame grew, Robert often stayed with him in Morocco. This sketch may be a preliminary to the full-length portrait which hangs in Glasgow's Kelvingrove Gallery and forms the frontispiece to this book.

18. Gabriela in pensive mood, as captured by Frederick Hollyer, mainly known as the photographer of William Morris and his circle to which Gabriela and Robert peripherally belonged. She was by now travelling frequently to Spain, despite the onset of the diabetes from which she would eventually die.

19. Robert and Gabriela spent sixteen years at Gartmore, from 1884 until it was sold to the shipping magnate Sir Charles Cayzer in 1900. There were moments of great happiness, but an ever-present shadow was anxiety about debt. Willy had died leaving liabilities in today's terms of some £10 million.

20. In 1887, disguised as 'Sheikh Mohammed el Fasi', Robert set out to reach the city of Taroudant in Southern Morocco. Captured en route by a local warlord, he failed in the attempt but the resulting book *Mogreb el Acksa* was described by Joseph Conrad as 'the travel book of the century'.

21. This portrait, painted by John da Costa in 1901, came to be owned by the family of French artist, illustrator and theatre designer, Jean Hugo, great-grandson of Victor Hugo. Jean Hugo's wife's family were direct descendants of Robert's uncle by marriage, William Hope, the speculating VC.

22. Ardoch, the house on the Clyde where Robert retreated to write in later years. It was built in the style of a colonial cottage by Doughty Deeds in the late 18th century. Robert and Gabriela sold Ardoch in 1887, only to buy it back sixteen years later, shortly before Gabriela's death.

23. Robert cut an elegant figure in London's Rotten Row as he rode his beloved Argentine mustang Pampa, which he had rescued from the traces of a Glasgow tram. He would often be accompanied by his new companion, Elizabeth 'Toppie' Dummett, so called for the top hat she wore when riding.

MR. JOHN GALSWORTHY, MR. CUNNINGHAME GRAHAM AND MR. J. B. PRIESTLEY
AT THE WINDMILL PRESS GARDEN PARTY

24. Robert flanked by John Masefield (left) and J.B. Priestley (right) at the Windmill Press garden party, circa 1930. The journalist and SNP leader, William Power, described Robert at a private literary function 'going round the room talking delightfully with everyone he thought was in the slightest danger of being overlooked.'

25. Robert met Aimé Tschiffely in the early 1930s and was captivated by the young man and his epic, three-year journey on horseback from Buenos Aires to Washington DC. The two became close friends and Tschiffely published his biography, *Don Roberto,* in 1937, the year after Robert's death.

26. Robert sat for the Scottish painter James McBey in 1934. Aged eighty-two he chatted constantly about South America throughout the sitting. 'My dear McBey,' he later wrote, 'THE picture looked splendid in the Academy this afternoon and was admired. Being hung rather high shows it off.'

27. Robert remained politically active until the end. Here he is pictured speaking in support of Scottish independence on the anniversary of Bannockburn in 1930. His kinsman, the Duke of Montrose, looks on. In 1934 Robert would be elected Honorary President of the newly formed Scottish National Party.

28. Robert's last journey was a pilgrimage to the birthplace of his great friend, the writer and naturalist W.H. Hudson, in March 1936. Here, sitting in Hudson's dilapidated home at Quilmes, just south of Buenos Aires, Robert writes to Hudson's biographer, Morley Roberts. Within a few short weeks Robert would be dead.

29. Robert died of pneumonia in Buenos Aires on 20 March 1936. Before being shipped home to Scotland, his body lay in the Casa del Teatro where mourners included the President of the Republic. Tschiffely's two horses, Mancha and Gato, are seen here leading the funeral cortège to the docks.

30. Newsreel footage of the funeral shows a small launch conveying Robert's coffin across the Lake of Menteith to his final resting place. He and Gabriela lie in the tranquil ruins of the thirteenth century Augustinian priory on the island of Inchmahome, burial place of Robert's Graham ancestors.

31 & 32. Robert and Gabriela looked on from the walls during the writing of this book, following their rescue from a family attic by the author. The two portraits, which were painted by an unknown artist in 1884, languished for many years in the stables at Ardoch, being deemed insufficiently good to hang in the house. The frame of Robert's portrait bears the Graham motto: *For right and reason*, along with the Spanish proverb which is inscribed on Gabriela's memorial plaque on Inchmahome: *Los muertos abren los ojos a los que viven.* The dead open the eyes of the living.

his writing. The exception is prostitutes or kept women. He was familiar with them and wrote about them sympathetically, describing them with the full range of human feelings rather than merely as erotic objects, while also commenting on the hypocrisy or casual disregard shown by their clients. His first biographer, Herbert Faulkner West, who had spent many hours of conversation with Robert, went so far as to suggest that Robert was probably as well acquainted with courtesans as he was with horses. In his South American writings he refers frequently and fondly to the china girls, waiting in their shanties at river crossings or by up-country stores, or to the more sophisticated women to be found, for example, at the up-market brothel at Cerrito 123 in Buenos Aires.

In *Gaucho Laird* my mother recounts that old admiral Katon, Robert's step-grandfather, had taken him to court on the Isle of Wight when he, Katon, was sitting as a magistrate and Robert was a boy. The case concerned a woman charged with prostitution. The admiral, who clearly felt this would be an instructive experience for young Robert, referred to her as 'the poor whore' and explained to Robert that he had let her off lightly because 'after all, it took two people to commit the fault.' An early influence, suggests my mother. A more compelling influence, were she to have spent those missing years between the ages of 19 and 21 as some have suggested, would have been Gabriela herself. Several of Robert's later stories feature *demi-mondaines*, notably *Un Monsieur* (Hope, 1910) and *Un Autre Monsieur* (Charity, 1912). The subject of both stories is a courtesan named Elise whom Robert portrays as a well-rounded character, attractive and cultured, sensitive and perceptive, independent-minded and courageous. If Elise is a creature of his imagination, then he must have known someone very like her – Gabriela herself, suggests Anne Taylor. For like Elise, Gabriela frequented museums to teach herself about art, and loved to dress stylishly and extravagantly; and like Gabriela, the nameless *cocotte* in *One Hundred In The Shade* (Redeemed, 1927) is an actress, a poet, a fine horsewoman and a Catholic who reads the same books as Gabriela kept in her library.

If one knew what to look for, perhaps there was more of the 'secret garden' in his writing than Robert cared to admit.

In 1901, Garnett published *A Vanished Arcadia*. The copy I have belonged to Gabriela, for Robert has written in the flyleaf: 'This was inspired by Chid's 'Santa Teresa', & like it, was written at Gartmore.' The brand mark follows, then: 'August 19/1901 This is Chid's copy.' Whether or not there was an element of marital competition here, a history of the Jesuits in Paraguay was, on the face of it, an unpromising subject, and one which drew some criticism of Robert as an apologist for religious colonisation. But along with his knowledge of the history – and his sincere belief that the indigenous Guarani were protected by the Jesuits from a far worse fate at the hands of other Europeans – Robert's experience of the country and his description of its extraordinary, almost primeval landscape of forests, rivers and swamps makes for captivating reading. His observation of and sensitivity to his natural surroundings, not only in this book but in many of his tales and sketches, must surely qualify him in twenty-first century parlance as a nature writer. Along with his skill at capturing the spirit of place – whether Pampa town, desert outpost, jungle ruin, mountain fortress or boggy farmstead – comes the often prophetic warning that man will spoil whatever he touches in the natural world. The magnificent cataracts described in *A Vanished Arcadia*, which the Jesuits must navigate as they lead their Guarani flock to safety from Brazilian slavers, today lie beneath the reservoir created by the world's largest hydroelectric project, the Itaipu dam on the Parana River where it borders Brazil and Paraguay.

Horses and horsemanship were another topic to which Robert naturally turned, and where his expert knowledge and lifelong experience came together in a number of tales and sketches. He also wrote one full-length equestrian book, *Horses of the Conquest* (1930), invoking in the preface his great friend W.H. Hudson, 'who loved it all, the scent of folded sheep, the acrid smell of the Gauchos' fire of bones, cow-chips and thistle stocks, the perfume of the evening primrose, and the hot smell of a corral filled with a herd of half-wild mares.' Robert drew on contemporary accounts of the exploits, and sometimes extraordinary feats of endurance, of the mounted conquistadors and their steeds – creatures which until that time, the early sixteenth century, were unknown on the American continent. He reports the Inca historian, Garcilaso de

Vega, chronicler of the conquest of Peru, saying: 'my country was won *á la gineta'*. Robert translates this as 'by men riding in the fashion of the Moors'. The force of that cultural current, the 'carrying stream' of which the poet and folklorist Hamish Henderson wrote – from North Africa, via Spain, to Peru – had not escaped him. Nor had the fact that those horses from Spain were the progenitors of many he himself had ridden. These included the horse he loved best of all – Pampa, an Argentine mustang he had rescued in Glasgow and later exercised in London's Rotten Row, where heads were daily turned by the sight of the elegant horseman and his glossy black stallion. *Horses of the Conquest* is dedicated thus:

> *To Pampa*
> *My black Argentine – whom I rode for twenty years, without a fall.*
> *May the earth lie on him, as lightly as he once trod upon its face.*
> *Vale . . . or until so long.*

In the copy I have, inscribed as a gift to Robert by his mother's great friend, Blanche Fane, there is a photograph of the Lavery equestrian portrait, now in the Museo Nacionale de Bellas Artes in Buenos Aires, pasted onto the page beneath the inscription. Around it, in his sprawling hand, and accompanied by the ubiquitous brand mark, is written:

> I was 39, when the picture was done in the Lawn Park at Gartmore. Pampa was nine years old. He had the brand of Eduardo Casey, Estancia de Curamalal Provincia de Buenos Aires. I bought him for £25, out of a tramway in Glasgow. Pampa is buried at Weybridge.

It was no coincidence that the second of his early biographers, Aimé Tschiffely, was himself a distinguished horseman who in the late 1920s had ridden from Buenos Aires to New York. Tschiffely's knowledgeable, attentive and admiring company must have delighted the by-then octogenarian Robert, as they shared South American yarns and reminisced about the horses – the bays and roans and piebalds, the buckjumpers and pacers, the kickers and biters – they had known and ridden.

The status of women, the natural world, matters equestrian, the curse of progress, the fleeting and trivial nature of man's presence on earth – a handful of the many themes to recur in Robert's writing. His detestation of imperialism is another. He dubbed Queen Victoria the 'Empress of Famine', Cecil Rhodes the 'Bulayawo Burglar' and Rhodesia 'Fraudesia', but nowhere does he turn his fire more directly on Empire than in the shockingly titled *Niggers* (*The Ipané*). In this short, satirical essay, a vivid and entertaining taxonomy of Creation gradually reveals that it is the English who are God's chosen race and that the Niggers of the title are not merely the dark-skinned races but all human beings of every other race on earth, whom the tweed-clad Englishman, in his ignorance and imperial arrogance, deems his inferiors and worthy only of exploitation. 'Niggers who have no cannons have no rights,' Robert writes with barely suppressed rage.

> Their land is ours, their cattle and their fields, their houses ours; their arms, their poor utensils, and everything they have; their women, too, are ours to use as concubines, to beat, exchange, to barter off for gunpowder or gin, ours to infect with syphilis, leave with child, outrage, torment, and make by contact with the vilest of our vile, more vile than beasts.

Writing this on 28 February 2022, the fifth day of the Russian assault on Ukraine, I can only conclude that in this, as in so much of what he wrote, Robert reveals himself as a penetrating observer not only of the best but of the very worst in human nature.

Nineteen

HENDAYE

Two losses

In 1912, Robert published a sketch entitled *A Braw Day*. Twelve years earlier, on a fine, frosty winter's morning, he and Gabriela had left Gartmore for the last time, following the sale of the house and estate to Sir Charles Cayzer, head of the Clan Shipping line, for £126,000. 'It has been a great wrench,' Robert wrote to his old friend, George Mansel, 'but it was sad to see everything in ruins and nothing to repair it with.' The misery of their leaving, captured in the sketch, is the closest Robert ever came to writing directly about his feelings.

Never before, in the long years that he had passed in the old place, had it appeared so much a part of his whole being, as on the day on which he signed the deed of sale. Times had been bad for years, and a great load of debt had made the fight a foregone ending from the first. Still he felt like a murderer, as judges well may feel when they pronounce death sentences.

The house was decrepit, the grounds overgrown.

A desolating smell of straw was everywhere . . . even to the food which an old servant cooked in the great, ungarnished kitchen, just as a tramp might cook his victuals at the corner of a road. The estate land had succumbed to the thrilling beauty of decay. The fences were unmended and slagging wires in places had been dragged by cattle into the middle of the fields; most of the gates were off their hinges, and weeds had covered up the gravel of the walks.

On their last night, Robert and Gabriela sat around a log fire 'talking were-wolves, fairies, and superstitions of another land, with their old Spanish friend and servant . . .' Come morning, as they took their leave, they met an old retainer, billhook in hand, waiting for orders as he had done every day for twenty years. 'Now he held out his hand, opened his mouth, but said nothing, and then, looking up with the air of one well learned in weather lore, said, "Laird, it looks like a braw day".'

Over the previous year, Robert's hopes had been raised by the prospect of a concession to develop a large tract of land south of the Atlas Mountains, from Cape Juby on the coast to the Rio de Oro (the River of Gold – that word again) in the south. But while waiting for the blessing of the Spanish government which now claimed control of the territory, events had overtaken him and the family debts, not to mention the upkeep of Gartmore, had at last proved insurmountable; the toll on him such that Robert had been driven to confide suicidal thoughts to his friend John Lavery. Now twenty years of struggle had ended in guilt, regret and a profound sense of loss and failure.

The family rallied despite the fact that the decision Robert alone had taken would deprive his brother, and later my grandfather, his nephew Angus, from succeeding to the estate. Charlie, who for some time now had suffered from a heart condition, held the position of Deputy Chief Inspector of Lifeboats. On leaving the navy some years earlier, his old friend from naval cadet days, Prince Louis of Battenberg, had secured him a post with the Royal National Lifeboat Institution. Charlie's royal connections would soon lead to him becoming groom-in-waiting to the new king, Edward VII, who, as Prince of Wales, had been a regular visitor to their London house, an admirer of his wife Barbara, and godfather to young Angus – all of which caused Charlie much ribbing from his mother and older brother, both of whom had long held a dim view of Queen Victoria and her offspring.

With characteristic generosity, Charlie professed relief for Robert over the sale, knowing how much anxiety the situation had

caused him. Missy praised him for finding the determination to
complete *A Vanished Arcadia* in the midst of it all; though perhaps
the writing of it had offered him a surrogate for the kind of journey which in the past had proved a panacea for his troubles. 'I often
think that the spirit of some ancestor of the Raleigh period, or
perhaps a Spaniard who volunteered to go with Columbus, or was
a friend of Cervantes, must have entered your body for you are so
unlike a 19th or 20th century man,' Missy wrote. To Gabriela,
more briskly, she wrote that she hoped her health was not suffering, but told her that 'you must try to cheer up. I'm quite sure you
are very sad but it really is for the best now the plunge has been
taken.' Later, Gabriela was to be blamed for throwing away three
hundred years of family heritage, though it was her determination
to sell off the Gartmore feus that had largely rid them of the inherited debt, leaving them free to dispose of most of the proceeds of
the sale as they chose. Her ambivalent feelings about the place are
plain in the letter she wrote to her mother-in-law on 4 December
1900, their last day at Gartmore.

> My dear Mrs Bontine . . . We leave tomorrow. Who would ever
> imagine that we should be sorry and distressed to leave the sour,
> dour faces of these people. It is because they are familiar and one
> has got accustomed to their strange ways. Even their rudeness
> had ceased to grate on one. I had begun to think they did not
> mean it and take it as the fashion of the country.

But as she goes on her tone hardens and she speaks of the neighbouring community of Gartmore as 'that hated and hateful village'
whose malign influence even the incoming Sir Cayser (sic) will not
escape.

Taking Pampa with them – now the only survivor from the early
years, since Jack, the fox terrier they had adopted in Texas, had died
long ago and Talla, Gabriela's adored Icelandic pony, had been put
down two years earlier – they moved to London and a flat in
Margaret Street, near Oxford Circus. Free of debt for the first time
in their lives, they resumed the pattern of travel and writing that
had occupied them for the best part of a decade. It was a pattern

that continued to take them apart from one another, often for long periods. This suited Robert, who had confided in Conrad that he was generally happy when off alone on his travels, but wretched when he found himself alone at Gartmore, as his bargain with Gabriela had dictated. In London, he was able to spend more time with his mother, now in her mid-seventies, who delighted in his company at galleries, concerts and the theatre, and fretted when he was away. The year after leaving Gartmore, 1902, Robert went to Morocco and vanished for two months when a falling horse crushed his foot badly and he was laid up in the hottest weather he had ever known. Or so he told his mother. He may, in fact, have been negotiating the new Moroccan concession, which at that point seemed close to conclusion. But the Spanish government fell before the papers could be signed and by 1904, two years later, the concession had evaporated like a Saharan mirage.

One of the backers for the Moroccan project was Martin Hume, a businessman and writer of historical biographies. Hume had met Gabriela on the boat on her first solo trip to Spain and they had remained in touch. As a successful and popular writer, he was frustrated by what he saw as the flaws in Robert's writing, the obstacles to him gaining wider readership, and felt their friendship sufficiently robust for him to tell Robert so. On reading *A Vanished Arcadia*, he wrote to Robert that for all its excellence he found the book too discursive,

> marred by irritating digressions ... O how I panted for a blue pencil, or power to black out passages like a Russian censor. Why Why Why the devil will you handicap yourself so. There *ought* to be a fortune in your writing and I want to see you get that fortune.

Robert, typically, ignored this advice and continued to expound whenever and wherever the mood took him. His less forthright admirers, Edward Garnett and Joseph Conrad chief among them, encouraged and supported him as his Jesuit history was followed swiftly by another collection of tales and sketches, *Success* (1902), the conquistador biography, *Hernando de Soto* (1903), and more stories and sketches in *Progress and other sketches* (1905) and *His People*

(1906) – a pattern of publication that would continue for the next twenty years, his subjects as diverse and wide-ranging as ever.

Gabriela took less pleasure from their new existence. She was now forty-three, living largely alone at Margaret Street apart from a house-keeper, Miss Ward, with whom she became friends, and visits from a younger woman known only as Grace, but who it seems very likely was Grace Horsfall, her younger sister (or possibly daughter). When not in London, and with her *magnum opus* behind her, she wandered aimlessly and irritably through Europe, travelling now for travel's sake, and finding that she missed Robert wherever she was. 'My dearest old Lob, do take care,' she had written to him as he set out for Taroudant, 'and come back safely, and in future we will go about together as I have felt lately in Spain how lonely one is without the other.'

Loneliness was not Gabriela's only affliction. Her health was deteriorating rapidly, the underlying conditions exacerbated by her continued heavy smoking. Peregrina was no longer always with her when she travelled and her increasingly frequent bouts of illness, often in the remotest of places, became desperate and frightening. 'I suffered so much I thought of shooting myself,' she wrote of one such episode. There were other causes of suffering. In 1900 she had been invited by the actor-manager, Martin Harvey, to translate a popular Spanish play, Don Juan Tenorio, which he intended to put on in London. This she duly did, but on the opening night of *Don Juan's Last Wager*, as it was now called, lavish stage effects failed, the theatre was plunged into darkness, and booing erupted in the gallery. Gabriela's translation received savage reviews. Following this wounding experience she attempted one more piece of work, Genara, a gothic novel which never made it into print. Genara is a Spanish servant girl who falls for Evan, a three-quarter Scottish, one-quarter Spanish aristocrat. Gartmore and Vigo are clearly recognisable in the tale, in which Evan's mother and her friends trick the pair into separating and Evan, on uncovering the decep-tion, goes mad. 'I rather tremble at the thought of a study of madness,' Missy wrote to Edward Garnett on hearing of it.

The truth was that Gabriela was dying and she and Robert both knew it. Robert received the news in the summer of 1903 while staying at the Lake of Menteith Hotel. He had written cheerfully to her of the awful 'improvements' being wrought by Sir Charles Cayzer, including electric light and a 'beastly' motorboat on the Lake of Menteith, along with wholesale rebuilding of the house. 'Oh Chid,' was all he could reply.

Now they had to await the end together, for the disease – diabetes, compounded by heavy smoking and frequent bouts of pleurisy which had ravaged her lungs – was cruelly slow. Earlier that year, Gabriela had written from Naples: 'I have caught a fearful cold on the lungs & am spitting blood.' Perhaps by way of distraction, perhaps since Robert was pining for Scotland – 'I want the North *now*', he had written to Edward Garnett – they set about buying back Ardoch. Gabriela conducted the negotiations. Ill though she was, her commercial instinct remained sharp. 'I shall get it for £2,500 . . . I generally get what I want if I stick at it . . .' she wrote to Robert in February 1904. And again in March: 'We shall get the cottage [as the house was described], but if we display undue anxiety we shall be fleeced.' The purchase completed, they moved in in July 1904, bringing with them the remaining Gartmore furniture which had been stored in the family mausoleum at Port of Menteith. Gabriela set about refurbishing the house while Robert continued to write. Both Robert and his mother confided to friends that Gabriela was looking very ill, but in June 1906 she appeared to rally and set off with Peregrina for Avila. The trip was planned to take three weeks, but it was not until the end of August that Gabriela left the train at Hendaye, just across the border into France, a place she knew well from her many journeys south, and collapsed. Robert was summoned by telegram and wrote to Edward Garnett from the hotel in Hendaye on 1 September, saying that the end was nigh and asking him to write to his mother 'since I cannot'. On 9 September he wrote again to say that Gabriela had died the previous day. 'Mi querido amigo, my poor wife died yesterday. It was a long agony, but I'm glad to say not with much pain. RIP.' Missy who was in Italy, staying at Lake Maggiore, wrote to Garnett offering to go to Hendaye at once, but he persuaded her to stay put. 'Poor, poor soul,' she wrote. 'I truly grieve for her.'

In the summer of 2022 I drove through Hendaye on the way to Spain. A punctuation mark at the western tip of the Pyrenees, it remains today the pleasant small beach resort that it has been since the mid-nineteenth century. At its shoulder the Pyrenean foothills rise sharply, and across the large lagoon which separates the two countries one can clearly see the sight that would have greeted Gabriela on her many journeys south in pursuit of Saint Teresa – the twin spires of the distinctively Spanish church that dominate the opposite border town of Hondarribia.

Robert wrote to Mary Horsfall, Gabriela's younger sister, in Glasgow, a few days later, apologising for not having written previously and explaining that he had asked their brother, William, who had also dashed to Hendaye and later conducted the funeral in Scotland, to do so.

> Your sister was ill for long of diabetes and suffered much. She was in Spain with old Peregrina, her attached maid, and in France. There she caught dysentery and wired for me to come to Hendaye. I was there for nine days but there was no hope from the first. She died brave, resigned, and peaceful and conscious to within an hour of the end. It has been a dreadful blow to me after 25 years of married life and affection. She is to be buried next Wednesday in the chancel of the ruined priory of Inchmahome on the island in the Lake of Menteith. Many of my people lie there. With kind regards and in great grief.

Mary did not receive this letter well. She wrote to another member of the family regretting that Gabriela had not been able to see her brother before she died – he had arrived too late at Hendaye. 'I shall watch the [news]papers,' she went on, 'for I am certain in spite of all the story will come out but we need not mind him [Robert] what I want to find out is what name he registered her death in for then if other than Papa's or Mama's he can be charged with perjury.' The suggestion was that they had not been legally married, either because Gabriela had been underage at the time, or because one or other of them – and it could only have been Robert – was already married at the time. As Mary both suspected and feared, the name on the death certificate was not Caroline Horsfall but Gabrielle Marie Cunninghame Graham. However, nothing more was then heard from the Horsfalls, or anyone else, until my mother uncovered the truth eighty years later.

A fortnight after Gabriela's death Robert wrote again to Edward Garnett.

> No, the funeral was not the worst. Now is the worst. I ordered her coffin alone. I saw to all the details in Hendaye and in London and with the old Highland gravedigger rolled off the stone from the grave, it weighed 800 pounds, and helped him at the grave. He rowed the coffin over just as if he had been rowing out fishing, now talking of crops, now running his hand over his eyes and saying 'she was a bonnie leddie'. It is good for a man to do and see all those things but it is not good for him to sit as I am sitting alone tonight. Yes the people were very fond of us. Thanks for what you say.

In *Gaucho Laird*, my mother had Robert smoke a final cigarette in Gabriela's honour as he sat at the graveside. She was also fond of recounting how once, on a visit to Inchmahome and the small island empty of other visitors, she had found a smouldering cigarette end on Gabriela's grave.

★

On the ruined priory wall, above her grave, Robert placed a bronze plaque which reads:

In Memory Of
Gabriela C Cunninghame Graham
Of Gartmore
Died at Hendaye France
8 September 1906 Aged 45
Los Muertos Abren Los Ojos
A Los Que Viven

'Cunninghame Graham'. The deception maintained until the last, even down to the age – given as forty-five, when she was in fact forty-eight – on both her death certificate and the memorial plaque. And a Spanish proverb, 'The dead open the eyes of the living'. Did

Robert mean that Gabriela had something to impart? And if so, what was one to learn from – or indeed about – her?

There was much about Gabriela that invited questions from the curious. The *Queen* ran an obituary, remarking on the almost unnatural ease with which a Spanish speaker should have taken to English pronunciation. Not only that, but Gabriela had enjoyed success as an English writer and was well-informed and intellectually sophisticated in a way that Spanish women of the time, limited in their education, hardly ever were. A journalist from the *Stirling Advertiser* recalled remarking on her apparent mastery of all things Spanish when she first arrived at Gartmore, at a time when her French character was still very much to the fore. He was surprised at the extent of her knowledge of Scotland and Scottish customs, and astonished at her grasp of the Scottish system of conveyancing. And why was she not laid to rest in the family mausoleum at Port of Menteith? the mourners had enquired. Because of her special affection for Inchmahome Priory as a relic of her faith, and her frequent visits there, the journalist answered tactfully.

What of the wider world, the glittering circles in which Robert and Gabriela came to move? How were they able to maintain their deception there? The obsessively moralistic W.T. Stead, for example, as Clare Clark suggests in *Beautiful Lies*, would have given his eye teeth to run an exposé in his *Pall Mall Gazette*. Is it realistic to suppose that their friends, those prominent late Victorian and Edwardian writers, artists and politicians, simply swallowed the story whole? What of Wilde, Shaw, Conrad, Galsworthy, Chesterton, Wells, Hudson, Morris? These were perceptive, cosmopolitan people. Did they go along with the story out of respect for the deception, or simply out of amusement? Was this perhaps an era in which a certain fluidity of identity was more acceptable? Yet Friedrich Engels referred to Gabriela as 'La Española'. W.B. Yeats, who shared her appetite for mysticism, knew her as 'the little bright American'. Robert's close friend, the artist Will Rothenstein, recalled: 'I shall always think of her as I saw her the first time, in a white monk's habit, & her black hair over her shoulders, & that fire burning deep in her eyes.'

Robert, of course, was complicit in the deception and therein undoubtedly lay a bond between them, a bond strengthened by a number of subsequent events – illness, prolonged separations, financial anxiety, a turbulent political career, family difficulties – which might otherwise have divided them, including the probability of Robert's infidelity. Anne Taylor refers to the 'dashing figure whose amatory pursuits had been the talk of the London clubs and whose conquests had caused Gabrielle once to bitterly end a letter, "After all the others." ' But given the open nature of their marriage, Robert may not have been the only one to stray. Gabriela's close friend, the Spanish writer Emilia Pardo Bazán, was known to be a lesbian, and during Robert's absences his wife may well have sought something more than emotional solace from other close female companions.

Unconventional as it was for the times, however, their relationship survived against all the odds. Their correspondence throughout their frequent separations, as they travelled in pursuit of their respective interests, reveals the depth of their affection for one another; indeed, in a couple for whom intimacy may have been made difficult by early experiences, their absences and the fond letters they occasioned may even have been a sustaining factor in their relationship. In any event, they had much in common. Both had experienced traumatic events in adolescence which had led to a fierce independence of spirit. Both were physically courageous, both handsome and charismatic, and knew it. Both were natural performers. Both loved travel and the arts. Both had a strong sense of social justice. Like Robert, Gabriela embodied many paradoxes. She was, perhaps with good reason, a hypochondriac who subjected herself to the most arduous journeys imaginable; a shrewd business-woman and frugal housekeeper who was given to bouts of wild extravagance, thinking nothing of travelling to Paris to shop for clothes; a socialist who wrote and spoke publicly about women's suffrage and the plight of factory workers, while embracing the more esoteric realms of Catholicism; a free spirit who loved to travel independently yet increasingly pined for Robert when she was left behind.

Furthermore, they were childless. Whether this was by design or not, we do not know. There were certainly factors which might have mitigated against their starting a family: Gabriela's experiences of adolescence in an authoritarian household, the possibility of a teenage pregnancy, along with everything that followed in the three lost years of which nothing is known; Robert's adolescent experience of his father's insanity and the fear that this might be something that could be transmitted. These were shared early traumas which may well have strengthened the bond between them. In any event, the absence of children allowed them both a freedom to nourish the independent sides of their characters, and neither ever expressed any regret about it.

It is easy today, with the perspective afforded by my mother's revelation, alongside those details of their family history shared by the Horsfalls, to see Gabriela as being defined by her secret, one that dominated her and her relationships throughout her life. The reality, I imagine, is that people simply became used to her; she grew into the name and the story – as far as she needed to repeat it; her curious accent probably softened; and people came to accept her as they found her – as a delicately good-looking, chain-smoking, charismatic if somewhat eccentric social campaigner and writer, with a good head for business and a penchant for medieval mysticism.

I like her. I like the fact that she, like Robert, was a storyteller. Not only a storyteller but a performer, as he also was. And perhaps her story was simply the biggest and best performance of their lives. James Robertson, who has written the foreword to this book, said in his novel *And The Land Lay Still*: 'The past is not fixed, it's fluid, every time we revisit it it's different. And the past influences the present and the future, and the present influences the past.' Is that the message Robert wanted to send when he placed the Spanish proverb on Gabriela's memorial on the wall of Inchmahome Priory?

Twenty

CARTAGENA

War horses

In the weeks immediately following Gabriela's death, Robert shut himself up at Ardoch and consoled himself by poring over her papers and letters. Missy fretted. 'Robert thinks of Gabrielle all the time as she appeared in his imagination, not as she really was,' she wrote to Edward Garnett, shortly after the funeral. Perceptive though she was, Missy and her son held widely differing views on how his wife really was – a fact which Missy let slip in a second letter to Garnett, full of premature expectation, a month or two later: 'I seem to see the real Robert emerging from his temporary eclipse. Though I do not think I ought to say this for the tender loyal nature shown in deep grief for poor unsatisfactory Gabrielle is the real Robert too.' For a woman of Missy's era, class and outlook, to deem a person 'unsatisfactory' was the most damning judgement possible; and it ensured that for all her maternal instincts her sympathy would always be qualified, as Robert was aware.

Others had a less complicated reaction to his bereavement. It was a short journey from Ardoch to the Lake of Menteith. In the following months Robert frequently rowed across to Inchmahome to sit at the graveside. He also paid visits to his former Gartmore tenants. 'I often think of poor Mr Graham,' wrote one, Jemima McLean, to Gabriela's housekeeper, Miss Ward. 'He is left so lonely and he is so kind.' Another wrote, 'He is so lonely and his hair has gone quite white.' His many friends offered condolences, Keir Hardie among them: 'We have been through so much together, and in the days gone by have been so much to each other, that a feeling of kinship has grown up in my mind, which almost makes your grief mine also.'

Robert was now fifty-four and struggling to come to terms with the double loss of Gartmore and Gabriela. Within a few months of her death he went down with a bad case of diphtheria. Recovery was slow. Lacking the energy or the will to write or travel, he set about pulling together Gabriela's work for publication. *Santa Teresa* came first, republished in 1907 with a foreword by Robert. The following year saw publication of *The Christ of Toro*, a collection of essays and tales including her account of their journey through Texas and Mexico, *The Waggon Train*. Robert also had privately printed Gabriela's adaption of John of the Cross's *The Dark Night of the Soul*, in which she set out 'a new theory of mystic philosophy'; and a collection of thirty-nine of her poems entitled *Rhymes From a World Unknown*. Wistful, other-worldly and some-times haunting, they found admirers among Robert's friends, in particular Edward Garnett and W.H. Hudson who regretted that Gabriela 'did not cultivate her genius for poetry more.' The collec-tion included a poem which seemed a presentiment of her death, and which may have offered Robert some comfort after the event, *The Promise*:

Love when I am dead, I shall not be very far,
I will peep in at your window, a faint white star;
Or when the wind arises – see the cedar tips –
They'll be my ghost-like fingers seeking for your lips.
I'll wrest the coffin lid and speed me from my lair,
You'll feel the aura of my presence steal softly through your hair.
Forgotten, unforgetting – for you I cannot die,
Nor you for me – We've drunk too deep Love's Immortality

The following year, 1907, a further blow fell with the death, in his fifties, of Robert's oldest and greatest friend, the loyal but irascible George Mansel, who had long since retired from adventuring to manage his family estate in Dorset. Six years later, in the title story of *A Hatchment* (1913), Robert would mourn his friend, imagining him climbing a nearby hill and there drinking in the view that he most loved. 'The wide expanse of down, nothing but grass and sky, like the south Pampa, stretches out to Portland Bill.'

In time Robert's muse returned and he published three more collections of stories and sketches in quick succession: *Faith* (1909), *Hope* (1910) and *Charity* (1912). In the preface to *Faith*, doubtless with the pain of Gabriela's death still sharp in his heart, Robert writes of the sorrow of being a writer since, no matter how pleasant the subject,

> to record, even to record emotions, is to store up a fund of sadness, and that is why all writing is a form of ice-house of the mind in which that which once was a warm and living action, a feeling, scene, experience, joy, or sorrow, is now preserved as it were, frozen, stiff, deprived of actuality, and a mere chopping block on which fools exercise their wits.

For all this, the stories, featuring the same eclectic mix of characters, events and locations – South America, North Africa and Scotland – are rich in colour and energy, the work of a writer in his full creative flow.

Robert had now closed up the flat at Margaret Street and moved to one in Basil Street, close to his mother at Chester Square, dividing his time between Ardoch, where he wrote, and London, where he resumed his friendships and began once more to engage with the worlds of politics and the arts. A frequent and knowledgeable visitor to the Rothenstein's house in Hampstead, he struck up new friendships with artists, among them Augustus John and Walter Sickert. Robert was already an admirer of the Impressionists, and now he was one of the very few to speak up for the Post-Impressionists – Cézanne, Van Gogh, Gauguin and Matisse – when they were first brought to London in the ground-breaking exhibition of 1910 which his friend, the poet Wilfrid Blunt, dismissed as 'works of idleness and impotent stupidity, a pornographic show.'

For all their differences over art, Robert and Blunt had much in common. Like Robert, Blunt loved horses and with his wife Anne, grand-daughter of Lord Byron, had created one of the finest Arab studs in the world. When Robert's beloved black Argentine, Pampa, died in 1911 at the age of thirty-one, it was Blunt to whom Robert turned for consolation. Like Robert, Blunt had been imprisoned, for speaking at a banned anti-eviction meeting in Galway. Like Robert, he was fiercely anti-imperialist and keenly interested in the Arab world, having spent much time in contact with Islamic and nationalist movements in Egypt and Turkey. Now, with the Ottoman Empire on the brink of collapse, both men urged the British government to respect the beliefs and practices of Islam, which they believed should play a central role in the creation of any new nation.

Robert's fascination with the Arab world continued – as special correspondent for the *Daily News* he had reported from the Algeciras conference on the future of Morocco, in 1906 – and later he would gather together three generations of Arabists when he brought T.E. Lawrence, with whom he had been corresponding for several years, to meet Blunt in Sussex.

If international affairs were never far from Robert's mind, national affairs were closer still. During his years in Westminster, his single overriding ambition had been that working men should gain representation in Parliament. In January 1906, a few months before Gabriela's death, a Liberal landslide had ended eleven years of Tory rule. At the same time, members of the Labour Representation Committee, an umbrella organisation composed largely of trades unionists and led by Keir Hardie, won twenty-nine parliamentary seats. A few days later, at their first meeting, they adopted the name 'The Labour Party'. Over the next four years Robert saw bills put forward on several of the issues he had fought for so strenuously in the past: an old age pension for every worker; school meals; and, closest to his heart, an eight-hour day for miners. But when it came to the detail, Robert found his natural scepticism vindicated. School meals were at the discretion of local authorities. Universal old-age pensions started at 70, not 60, and were restrictive and miserly. Support for those out of work was inadequate and selective. Provision for an eight-hour day was diluted with endless concessions to employers.

Robert's contempt for the Liberal party remained as fierce as ever. Replying to a request from the journalist and politician E.D.

Morel for support in denouncing Belgian atrocities in the Congo, Robert wrote ' . . . the party which contains all the great Liberal sweaters is now in power. They have always sold everyone who has put their trust in them and will sell you if they get the chance.' It seemed now that his socialist principles also were being abandoned by all and sundry. His old comrade-in-arms, John Burns, was now a Liberal cabinet minister. Even Hardie, he felt, did not stand up to the government firmly enough. 'They are a hopeless lot,' he told Wilfrid Blunt, referring to the new Labour MPs. 'When they get into Parliament they are no longer to be working men but states-men and try to behave as such. I tell them they would do more good if they came to the House in a body, drunk and tumbling about on the floor.'

He was more approving of what was happening beyond Parliament, where workers' movements were starting to advocate direct action as a way of defending their rights and privileges. Syndicalism, which had originated in France, was now gaining hold in Britain under the leadership of the dockers, Tom Mann and Ben Tillett, whom Robert had known during the dock strike of 1889. With their encouragement, elements of the transport industry came together into one body for purposes of agitation, which soon spread to the railways and mines. After attending three huge meet-ings of strikers in Glasgow, Robert wrote to Edward Garnett of the solidarity he had witnessed there: 'It gave me hope for the future, there has been nothing like it since the Commune of 1870.'

Yet now he faced a dilemma. Socialism, and the syndicalism that went with it, was a pure doctrine that demanded total allegiance and transcended national boundaries. How could he therefore call for socialism, rooted in international solidarity, while also demand-ing government in Ireland by the Irish, or in Scotland by the Scots? Robert had to choose, and at this point in his life he chose socialism. The choice was given sharp focus by his response to events in Ireland. In 1913, the newly fledged Irish Transport Workers' Union, led by James Connolly and James Larkin, who would later play a major role in the Easter Rising, was employing syndicalist tactics to bring Dublin to a standstill. Their activities were condemned by leaders of the Irish Home Rule movement, the successors to those men including Parnell and Davitt whom Robert had so strenuously supported twenty years previously. Now he turned on them. The very men who oppressed the women and children of Dublin were mainly nationalists, he said in the *Glasgow Herald* in December 1913. While it was reasonable to wish for nationhood, he went on, man must have a little bread as well as sunbursts and green flags.

War was now on the horizon and yet again Robert found his loyalties challenged. On the hustings in 1885 he had declared that he would only fight for his country if it was in danger. All his early experience of revolution in South America, and especially the aftermath of the crippling War of the Triple Alliance in Paraguay, had left him opposed to militarism; a view which had hardened as he had witnessed the manoeuverings of the Great Powers in the intervening years. In 1906 he had signed a letter to the *Times* calling for understanding between Germany and Britain. Fellow signatories included Thomas Hardy, John Lavery, Jayne Morris, William Rosetti, William Rothenstein, William Strang, Walter Crane, Edward Elgar and Georgina Burne-Jones.

As war loomed closer, those opposed to it clung to the belief that international socialism would save the day with workers throughout the world rallying swiftly to put a stop to it. They were soon overtaken by events. A mass rally of trades unionists was held in Trafalgar Square in early August 1914. Robert was among those who spoke in protest, calling on workers to unite against a declaration of war. 'Do not,' he implored, 'let us do this crime, or be parties to the misery of millions who have never done us harm.' But by then the British fleet was already on a war footing, the Channel was closed to German ships, and it was far too late.

Now, aged sixty-two, Robert volunteered. Shortly after, he wrote that 'we, perhaps by accident, have been forced into the right course, and that all smaller nationalities as Montenegro, Ireland, Poland and the rest, would disappear on our defeat.' This was a war Britain had been forced into, a war against tyranny, and one for which he could honourably enlist. Three months later, with the honorary rank of lieutenant-colonel, Robert was bound for Uruguay, in charge of a small party charged with buying horses for the British Expeditionary Force in France. His qualifications for this mission were unique: a fluent Spanish speaker and expert horseman who knew the country like the back of his hand. Yet here was another of the many paradoxes that characterised him. Alert to the suffering of any creature, he had only the previous year joined John Galsworthy in launching a campaign against cruelty to performing animals. He held horses in higher regard than he held the majority of humans, and yet he knew well what awaited them in France: they would carry the cavalry into battle, haul guns and ammunition, pull field ambulances and food wagons. The life expectancy of a horse at this early stage of the conflict, amid the mud, gas and shells of the front, was three weeks. Yet despite having opposed the war, he now believed that all measures should be taken to bring it to an end as quickly as possible, and horses had their part to play. Knowing what would become of them, he reasoned, he could at least ensure that they were transported under the best conditions.

Fit, healthy, and back in the arena of his youthful adventures, Robert was enjoying himself. *It is not given to all men after a break of years to come back to the scenes of youth, and still find in them the same zest as of old*, he wrote in *Bopicua* (*Brought Forward*, 1917). He set up his headquarters at Fray Bentos on the River Uruguay, where the Leibig Meat Company had a deep water landing and a launch he could borrow. In February 1915, a couple of months after arriving, he wrote to Charlie:

> Thirty-five years seem to have vanished as, after a long day on Pone [as he referred to horses], I sit in the deserted plaza and watch a swarm of locusts and some yellow dogs and two negro children. Everything is as I left it except there are more houses and a few motors. Pone stands nodding in the sun . . . and the great yellow river with its countless islands flows past the high bluff and Gualeguaychú is only two hours away on the other side.

For several months he spent long days in the saddle, visiting owners, breeders and dealers and arranging for horses to be brought in for inspection. 'I'm really always on horseback,' he wrote to Will Rothenstein, 'from daylight to dusk and nearly always wet through . . . This alternates with days on the train, in motors, in diligences and steamboats. Sometimes I sleep in native huts and again in the Plaza Hotel in Buenos Aires (a kind of Ritz). As it has been the wettest season on record – we are nearly always caked in mud, as the corrals we work are sometimes knee deep in mud.' In *Bopicua*, he describes a huge inspection corral, with animals grazing, smoke rising from campfires where gauchos sit on buffalo skulls, the river gleaming in the distance.

> The horses smelt the water at the bottom of the hill and the whole five hundred broke into a gallop, manes flying, tails raised high and we, feeling somehow the gallop was the last, raced madly by their side until a hundred yards or so of the great lake. They rushed into the water and all drank greedily, the setting sun falling on their many-coloured backs and giving the whole herd the look of a vast tulip field.

He reserved his thoughts about what awaited them for a letter to Missy. 'It was a wonderful sight,' he wrote, 'but sad to think it was their last happy day on Earth. The Kaiser has much to answer for.'

Here in the New World, Robert's thoughts turned again to the conquistadors. When not in the saddle he somehow found time to write a life of Bernal Díaz, a lieutenant of Cortés who had left what is widely held to be the best contemporary account of the conquest of Mexico. Robert liked the old soldier, who had written down his recollections when well into his eighties, for his simplicity and evident truthfulness, but especially because he recorded the history and even the names of the horses Cortés had brought with him from Spain. *Bernal Diaz del Castillo: being some account of him* was published in 1915.

Robert returned to England in May of that year. Steaming up the English Channel, the ship was torpedoed when in sight of land. The captain, with great presence of mind, ran the vessel onto a sandy beach where all the passengers and horses were safely landed. The war was going badly. The Germans were dug in across Northern France and Belgium, and the immense scale of death was starting to be revealed in daily telegrams and columns of names in the newspapers.

In August 1915 Keir Hardie died. Robert described his Glasgow funeral in *With The North-East Wind*, a counterpoint to his lament for William Morris, *With The North-West Wind*. The mood of the piece is sombre, reflecting both that of the country and his own. Hardie he sees as someone 'who was simple and yet with something of the prophet in his air, and something of the seer.' Effective yet ineffectual. In suggesting that Hardie, his old friend, had failed in his main task – to persuade working men to take their destiny in their own hands – was Robert really levelling the same accusation at himself?

Now in his mid-sixties, Robert was not yet ready to retire from public service. By late 1916, German U-boat attacks on merchant shipping had begun to result in food shortages. In January 1917, he accepted a commission from the Board of Trade to explore the possibility of importing cattle from Colombia.

On a cold January morning I found myself aboard the *SS Covina* going down channel in a storm of snow. All lights were out for fear of submarines and other German wonders of the deep. Few passengers on board, for none but those obliged to travel travelled in those days; an ice-cold ship; and the prospect of the danger-zone in front of us – did not exactly make for high spirits or for mirth . . . Day followed day and freezing nights succeeded one another . . . So piercing was the cold and so monotonous the days, the snowstorm so continuous, that it seemed we had embarked upon an Arctic expedition.

So Robert described his departure. He arrived in Cartagena in early February and set off up country to the cattle lands in the Department of Bolívar, around the River Sinú. Here in the north-east of the country forests had been cleared and feed grass planted. Travel was either on horseback or by slow-moving riverboat through country that was remote, flat, sparsely populated and as hot as anything Robert had experienced in Paraguay. His subsequent report noted that since capital was largely in the hands of American businessmen who were charging prohibitive rates for loans, progress in developing a cattle industry was slow and costly. He was asked to urge the British government to set up the lending bank that would help to advance things.

After sending his report Robert travelled into the Andes to Bogotá, which he disliked because of its altitude and climate. Half a century later I also found myself in Bogotá, nearing the end of the South American leg of our journey. Unlike Robert, we had already been in the Andes for several weeks by that time and were acclimatised to the altitude. I remember finding the city nondescript – which may have been as much to do with travel fatigue as anything, though the collection of pre-hispanic gold artefacts in the Museo del Oro was breathtaking, as was the extraordinary Salt Cathedral of Zipaquirá, built within the tunnels of a salt mine, carved out of the inside of a mountain close to the capital.

The purpose of Robert's journey was to report back to the Foreign Secretary, Sir Edward Grey, an old school friend, on the sentiment of Colombia and neighbouring countries towards the United States, which would shortly enter the war as Britain's ally. The support of these countries would counter the threat of German intervention in South America which would become relatively easy once a railway had been built through Morocco, thereby facilitating a short voyage from West Africa to Brazil. Robert duly reported back that an influential minority of Colombians had an abiding hatred of the United States because of the annexation of the Panama Canal in 1903, and the way the Americans had behaved towards them ever since. Despite this, he was ordered to choose a port from which the cattle could be shipped, but the mission was called off when it became apparent that most of Colombia's shipping was German owned.

Yet again his journey produced a book, *Cartagena and the Banks of the Sinú*, this time a part-history, part-travelogue. 'Of all the towns of the department of Bolívar,' wrote Robert,

Cartagena is the most picturesque. Not only is it the most old-world town of the department, but of the whole Republic and perhaps of the whole continent of South America . . . [it] was once the place of meeting of the great Plate fleet, that took the silver gathered together from all the mines of the New World, across the seas to Spain. Many a time the British and French corsairs hung off and on, just out of sight of land, to attack it with varying degrees of success.

Cartagena was also our final stop in South America in 1973, and the departure point for Costa Rica, via the Colombian island of San Andrés, from where we continued our journey through Central America. My journal entry for 11 May 1973 reads:

Cartagena is one of the most interesting towns we have seen in South America. It was founded in 1533 as the Spaniards' main stepping-off point for Peru and the South, and also as a storage place for much of the treasure acquired during the conquest. Consequently its whole history was virtually one long siege, by pirates and the English Navy and seagoing gentlemen in general – and it was fortified accordingly.

I had not read Robert at that time but I had read the *South American Handbook*, an increasingly tattered copy of which I kept in my shoulder bag, and from which that journal entry seems likely to have come, more or less verbatim. Half a century apart, both Robert and I had been captivated by this ancient town with its fortress, narrow streets and massive sea walls, perched at the extremity of the South American continent and lapped by an azure Caribbean.

I have two copies of *Cartagena and the Banks of the Sinú*. One is inscribed to his nephew, Angus, my grandfather, who clearly never read it since some of the pages remain uncut. The other is inscribed to 'Toppie'. This was Elizabeth 'Toppie' Dummett, a widow who was to become his dear friend and companion. Toppie – the name derived from the top hat she wore when out riding – was sixteen years younger than Robert and had lost her husband in the Boer War. Her father came from a wealthy French family, the Miévilles, and her mother was Scots. According to Aimé Tschiffely they had met in Hyde Park when her horse had taken fright and bolted towards the traffic at Marble Arch, whereupon Robert had pursued her and brought her mount under control. That story again. My mother says simply that they were introduced by Missy. By all accounts Toppie was well-off, a good horsewoman and a bright conversationalist. She maintained a keen interest in the arts and hosted a salon at her house in Walton Street attended by writers such as Axel Munthe, A.J. Cronin and Compton Mackenzie. Other guests included Conrad, H.G. Wells, John Lavery and the aristocratic Spanish musician, Segovia. She and Robert travelled widely together, usually chaperoned either by her sister, Louisa Miéville, or occasionally by Robert's niece, my great-aunt Olave, who by then had married Admiral Sir Basil Brooke.

Robert returned to Cartagena to learn that his brother Charlie had died suddenly of an aneurism, aged only sixty-three. 'It seems impossible to be alone in the world without Charles,' he wrote to his mother,

> he was indeed my Pylades. So different to me and much better, yet we understood each other so well. I have no one to speak to but a Spanish bullfighter, perfectly ignorant and yet so kind. I opened the telegram before him and he said '*Le accompagno en su dolor*' and offered to go out and take a walk with me on the walls; it was at night and the heat great. I went and walked on the walls and thought of all our life from Dr Bickmore's [headmaster of Hill House, their preparatory school] and before and Mr Gulliver [the tutor] and all kind of things. Poor dear Lee Cat, to think of his lying dead in Warwick Square and me so far off. This morning all the company of bullfighters met me in the street and took their hats off and 'accompanied me in my grief'.

The two brothers had always enjoyed a close and affectionate relationship. They shared adventures as boys and young men, and continued to correspond regularly throughout their adult lives, no matter where they happened to be. Charlie always responded generously to the decisions his elder brother had taken, not all of which had been to his advantage. During the final months of his life, as heart disease rendered him weaker and wearier by the day, Robert was in South America and was spared the sight of his brother's decline. Charlie's last letter, in February 1917, had reached Robert in Jamaica, on his way to Colombia. Robert dedicated his new collection, *Brought Forward*, to his brother.

Missy now had only Robert. She was ninety-two and although distraught at the loss of her second son and his affable and attentive presence, she maintained her lifelong resolve and attention to the world around her, continuing to hold court at the house in Chester Square. Robert now moved from Knightsbridge to Belgravia and a house at Elizabeth Street, a stone's throw from his mother. Self-pity remained unknown to her. When neighbouring houses were hit in a German air raid in September 1917, she wrote to Robert that 'the servants behaved very well and stayed in the kitchen and were not hysterical.' The tendency of Charlie's widow, her daughter-in-law Barbara, to fuss over her, she found irritating despite having welcomed her so warmly into the family at first. But it was Gabriela whose good fortune on the stock exchange had provided her with the coupé, a small carriage, in which she and her friend Blanche Fane could sally forth to indulge in what they called 'dowagering'. In her final years, Gabriela appears to have done her best to achieve some closeness to her mother-in-law. As well as the carriage, she had taken to buying books for her. And it was Gabriela who was responsible for having restored Ardoch to the family. There Robert now retreated to write, often in the company of his elderly mother. On the foreshore he would ride his third and final horse, Chajá, whom he had brought back from Uruguay in 1915, while Missy gazed across the Clyde to the opposite bank and Finlaystone, where her married life had begun. 'How strange it was that at the very end of my life I should have such happy days and all owing to you,' Missy wrote to Robert, 'so many of the places were associated in my memory with sad things, some of which I thought I had forgotten. Now I shall remember them as connected with you.' Chajá, named after a large and vocal turkey-like bird of Argentina, was to outlive Robert. There is a photograph of my mother aged ten, riding him on the beach at Ardoch in 1938 just as her great-uncle had done.

By the time the war ended, Robert was in his late sixties. He was free of debt. He had an attractive and manageable family seat in

Scotland and a flat in London, not far from Toppie, the woman who had now become his companion. He had a vast network of friends and no shortage of money. He was able to travel which he did frequently, seeking winter sun in Ceylon, the Canaries, and Venezuela where he stayed with the Vestey family of beef barons. His stock was high in those circles where it mattered and he had all the energy necessary now to re-enter the public arena. The only clouds in an otherwise clear sky were the recurring bouts of rheumatism and neuritis, the result of many nights spent sleeping on cold damp ground as a young man in Argentina.

Robert wasted no time. Three days after the Armistice, Lloyd George called a general election. Robert stood as one of three candidates for Stirling West, his home turf. But from the outset, he seemed determined to throw away the opportunity for a return to parliament, just as he had done at Camlachie in 1892. Despite his by now well-known views on the Liberal party, he was selected as the candidate to support the war-winning Liberal-Tory coalition, then turned immediately on his opponents and sponsors alike, and so angered older members of the local Liberal Association that they refused to share a platform with him. Robert promptly resigned in protest, then reappeared a few days later as a non-coalition Liberal.

The *Stirling Observer*, at least, relished his return to the stump: 'If only for his wit and humour, Mr Cunninghame Graham deserves to be returned to the top of the poll, he is so different from his prosaic opponents.' Robert did not disappoint. The coalition candidate he declared was 'raddled like a Highland sheep in a fank.' The trade unions had been 'nobbled by long-haired men and short-haired women whose sexual temperament had developed in excess of their brains.' Conscientious objectors were to be awarded 'a petticoat at the national expense'. The House of Lords? 'He did not think he would have entrusted the operation to which he had submitted that morning to an hereditary dentist. He preferred a skilled operator.'

Chiming with the popular mood, he declared that Germany should make reparation 'to the uttermost farthing', then returned to his old war cries of nationalisation of mines, shipping and eventually of all the means of production. He was especially scornful of his Independent Labour Party opponent, Thomas Johnston, a conscientious objector. Yet the younger man had held the same socialist views as Robert, and had campaigned on Robert's behalf when he had stood for the rectorship of Glasgow University. In 1906 Johnston, who would go on to become one of the great twentieth century Scottish Secretaries of State, had founded a weekly paper, *Forward*, which became the Glasgow mouthpiece of the Independent Labour party. Its contributors included councillors, trade unionists and activists who met regularly at Kate Cranston's tea rooms, recently decorated by the rising young architect, Charles Rennie Mackintosh. As the war progressed, this group became the leaders of the striking Clydeside factory workers whose distaste for the war, coupled with their demands for better working and living conditions, were widely seen to be treasonable. To Robert, the man of action, the sabotaging of the war effort seemed just that, an act of treason, and Johnston, his pacifist ILP opponent, was one of those who had facilitated it.

In the wake of the October 1917 Russian Revolution, it was easy for people who were ignorant of the reality of life in Clydeside to brand the strikers Bolsheviks. Robert was asked if he would recognise the new regime in Russia. As the *Stirling Observer* gleefully reported, Robert replied that the only way he would recognise the 'miserable blood-stained wretches, Lenin and Trotsky, would be at the end of a piece of hard rope on the gallows.' He had previously enjoyed close contact with anti-Tsarist activists and befriended Russians exiled to Britain, partly thanks to the influence of his Russophile editor, Edward Garnett. But when the October Revolution threatened to derail the Allied war effort, yet again, as with the Irish nationalists, he turned against the very people he had previously campaigned for. This was not a war of capitalists, he said in a speech in 1918, it was the working men of Germany who sang the hymn of hate, tortured prisoners, and cheered on the army so long as they were winning.

When the election results were delivered, on 11 December 2018, the coalition candidate, Sir Harry Hope came in with nearly seven thousand votes. Thomas Johnston came second with four thousand. Robert came in last with two thousand five hundred having written to the writer Neil Munro on the eve of the poll that he was sick of 'this infernal folly of elections.'

A few weeks later, the Red Clydesiders called out eighty thousand men in support of a shorter working week. Rumours swiftly spread of a Bolshevik uprising, and after violence between police and demonstrators including several baton charges by the former, the alarmed Sheriff of Lanarkshire requested 'military aid to the civil power'. This came in the form of troops and six tanks which, however, were not deployed as the trouble had largely died down before their arrival.

Robert was now approaching seventy. His temper was growing shorter, it seemed, and his tolerance waning. He had much to feel disillusioned about, much to regret – not least his recent treatment of his young opponent, Johnston, who would later recall Robert's behaviour in the 1918 election with generosity and good humour. He was having to accept that he had failed to bring about the social change for which he had fought so long and so hard. Now he had to stand by and see his ideals turned into a reality he did not like by people he liked even less. His vision of the workers and the poor themselves bringing about their own enlightened emancipation was foundering in bureaucracy and managerialism, as the Labour Party became no more than 'a third party struggling for place, for office, and for the fruit of government, all their high ideals lost, and all their aspirations locked away in some dark corner of their souls.'

Writing to a friend, the playwright Henry Arthur Jones, a year after the election, he said:

I had hoped in Socialism to find a gradual demise of selfishness and the gradual establishment of a better feeling between man and man. You may remember that then (twenty-eight years or more ago) the sweater was excessively aggressive, hours were long, and there was a brutal spirit of materialism about . . . You will admit, I think, that my ambition was not a low ambition. That I was deceived, and that all the golden dreams of Morris have vanished in the nine bestial and inarticulate years of the reign of King Edward, the War, and the increasing inartisticness of everything, the prostitution of the stage and literature, and now in the ever-increasing selfishness and lack of patriotism of the working classes, have not been my fault.

Yet in tribute to Morris and his vision Robert concluded on an optimistic note:

> Often with sea-boots on or wet and miserable in a railway truck with the horses in the Argentine, or sweltering Colombia, or with the skipper on the bridge looking out for torpedoes I have thought – where are the dreams of Morris? But on arriving at port or at the camp, they have come back; they always do. Let us, I say, cherish them . . . *vale*.

Twenty-one

BANNOCKBURN

Independence

Ford Madox Ford recounts how once on a car journey from Edinburgh he heard a 'politically minded lady' remark to Robert:

'You ought, Mr Graham, to be the first president of a British republic.'

'I ought, madam, if I had my rights, to be the king of this country,' Robert replied. 'And what a three weeks that would be.'

Scottish Home Rule was the cause to which Robert would increasingly devote his political energy in the years between 1918 and his death in 1936. As a descendant of the Kings of Scotland, he may have been predisposed to believe in the restoration of Scotland's independence. As a politician he had long held that it offered the only means to ameliorate Scotland's social ills – poverty, disease, poor housing, the effects of clearance and exploitative working practices. Speaking in Coatbridge shortly after his election to Parliament in 1886 he had said: 'We must never forget that the idea of Home Rule originated with the Irish, and we should never lose sight of it till we see a Parliament legislating purely for Scottish matters in Edinburgh or Linlithgow.' The same year he had co-founded the Scottish Home Rule Association (SHRA) with Keir Hardie, and when the Scottish Labour Party was formed two years later, with Robert as president and Hardie as secretary, he had seen Home Rule become embedded in early Labour policy. Later he had witnessed several attempts to legislate on the matter; most recently in 1913 when the House of Commons had passed a second reading of the

Government of Scotland Bill, only for its passage to be interrupted by the outbreak of the First World War.

In all of this, it is clear, Robert came to nationalism neither from any sense of territorial or ethnic integrity, nor of historic grievance, but from the radical left where socialist principles underpinned the desire for change. Home Rule, he believed, offered the means to alter the balance of society, to promote social justice and achieve real democracy by placing control of their destiny in the hands of ordinary people rather than of the privileged and powerful few. As far back as 1889 he had said that Home Rule in Scotland

> comes in my opinion from no sentimental grounds whatever, but from the extreme misery of a certain section of the Scottish population, and their wish to have their own Members under their own hands, in order to extort legislation from them suitable to relieve their misery.

He was also firm in his belief that Home Rule had consequences that transcended borders. 'Nationalism is the first step to the International goal which every thinking man and woman must place before their eyes. But without Nationalism we cannot have true Internationalism.' He was, in modern parlance, a civic nationalist.

Yet there were aspects of nationalism that alarmed him. The emergence of the Red Clydesiders and their determination to bring about social change in Scotland had caused consternation in the years after 1915, when they were seen to draw too strongly on the ideals of socialist *confrères* in other countries, notably Russia where the revolution was only three years off. Their demonstrations and the subsequent return to parliament of their leaders, including William Gallagher and Emanuel Shinwell, served to equate nationalism with a kind of ruffianism in the public mind. Meanwhile, the cheerful, flag-waving nationalism of pre-war Ireland had given way to the lethal commitment of men like Roger Casement and James Connolly, instigators of the Easter uprising of 1916. These were men whom Robert knew, yet whose beliefs he found as dangerous as those of the men who had led the brutal civil wars he had witnessed as a young man in Argentina, Uruguay and Paraguay.

In November 1920, the IRA murdered nineteen young men believed to be British agents in reprisal for the British killing of several Republican volunteers. Despite the fact that the incident had been discussed at a meeting of the SHRA, and the reprisals by both sides condemned, Robert wrote a furious letter of resignation to the secretary, Ronald Muirhead. After excusing the British forces for acting under orders – as he had excused the police following Trafalgar Square – he declared himself a convinced supporter of Home Rule with foreign affairs and defence reserved to Westminster. 'I have no objection to Dominion Home Rule so long as the British Empire is master in its own house and controls the ports and armed services of the Crown,' he wrote. 'As a Scotchman I detest assassination and despise those who resort to it, and I believe no nation was ever freed by recourse to such dastardly methods. Such were not the ways employed by Wallace and by Bruce.'

The letter then continued with an ill-judged opinion. 'These murders are instigated chiefly and certainly paid for by the band of international Jews grouped around their fellow Jew, Mr 'de' Valera in New York.' He went on, 'I have no thought of impugning Jews as a race, only those who 'run' 'de' Valera in New York.' But it was too late. The apology was ignored and the suggestion lingered that he might have fascist and anti-Semitic leanings – despite the fact that his close friends numbered many prominent English Jews, Will Rothenstein chief amongst them; and that he alone among MPs had fought to save Israel Lipski from the gallows, pitting himself against the Home Secretary to the lasting detriment of his parliamentary reputation in the process. As so often in the past, he had spoken impulsively and come to regret it.

Following the Anglo-Irish truce of July 1921, Robert's social connections once again drew him to the heart of great events when his friend John Lavery, the artist, by now famous, wealthy and influential, offered his own large studio at 5 Cromwell Place as a neutral meeting place for the parties to the Anglo-Irish Treaty. Both Lavery and his wife were of Irish origins, he from Belfast, she from County Galway. A notable beauty, Hazel Lavery's skill as a hostess did much to relieve tensions between their distinguished guests: Lloyd George, Winston Churchill and Lord Birkenhead for the British; Eamonn de

Valera, Arthur Griffiths, Erskine Childers and Michael Collins for the Irish. As Lavery's friend, Robert was afforded a ringside seat at the negotiations. But when Michael Collins was subsequently shot and later, when Kevin O'Higgins, Ireland's new leader whom Robert had come to know well, was murdered, his resolve that similar events should never unfold in Scotland was strengthened.

In time Robert made up with the SHRA. At the urging of Muirhead, who recognised his value and was still, perhaps, a little in awe of him, he continued to write and speak for them. But his energy for the nationalist cause was muted throughout the 1920s as Home Rule appeared to slip from the parliamentary agenda. With the Liberals sidelined and Labour now in the ascendancy, the SHRA did what it could to ensure the party maintained its commitment to Scotland. But in 1924 an attempt to put Home Rule on the statute book failed, largely because of Ramsay MacDonald's indifference. In 1927 the Labour party formally renounced Home Rule as a policy.

Momentum for the cause of independence was not wholly lost. By the late 1920s there were two main players, the Scottish Home Rule Association and the Scots National League (SNL). The latter, founded in 1920 and led by Sir William Gillies and Ruaraidh Erskine of Marr, uncompromisingly chose independence, or separate statehood, rather than Home Rule as its stated goal. There was a religious aspect, along with romantic notions of Celticism, to Erskine's nationalism that did not endear him to Robert. Nevertheless, the Scots National League boasted a thousand members and fifteen branches as well as its own newspaper, the *Scots Independent.*

A third body was the Glasgow University Student Nationalist Association (GUSNA), founded in 1927 and led by two young students, John McCormick and James Valentine. It was McCormick who, after being turned down by J.M. Barrie, convinced Robert to run for the rectorship of Glasgow University in late 1928. McCormick had taken a copy of Hope from Glasgow's Mitchell Library.

As I read I became fascinated both by the man and his writing. Here was really a great Scotsman and, although his name was unfamiliar to my own generation, I was sure we could soon remedy that. But what were his politics? I knew that in his young days he had been a Radical and had later taken part with Keir Hardie in the formation of the Labour Party. But, for many years, he had been missing from the political scene altogether and seemed to have spent most of his time in South America.

Aged seventy-six, Robert took to the rectorship challenge with gusto and in the end was narrowly defeated by the incumbent prime minister, Stanley Baldwin. 'The ladies voted against me,' Robert wrote to Edward Garnett, 'because Mr Baldwin has given them the franchise.' Although he had won a clear majority of the men's vote in this contest, his own long-standing support of votes for women was by now long forgotten. Yet it was a result which still surprised and delighted Robert and brought the nationalist cause to nation-wide attention.

A few weeks previously, in late October 1928, the three bodies, SHRA, SNL and GUSNA, had put aside whatever differences they had and merged to become the National Party of Scotland. Robert was elected president. In his first speech, before a crowd of three thousand in Glasgow's St Andrew's Hall, he made the case for the new party by asking, among others things, why unemployment in Scotland was far higher than in England; why Scotland's housing was a scandal and disgrace to Empire; and why four million acres of the Highlands should be 'delivered over to American millionaires to exhibit their fat white knees and debauch the population with their dollars'. He went on: 'A Scottish party alone can take these matters into consideration and solve them, if it is in the power of man to do so.'

The new party was attracting distinguished supporters, novelists such as Eric Linklater, Neil Munro and Compton Mackenzie – who would avenge Robert's defeat by being elected rector of Glasgow University in 1931, and the poet Hugh MacDiarmid (Christopher Grieve). The presence of these powerful literary voices did much to ensure that there was a cultural dimension to the movement, although they did not all sing to the same tune. On the right wing stood MacDiarmid who called for a small elite to direct activities in a 'powerfully, spiritually dynamic way ... aristocratic standards must be re-erected. We in Scotland have for too long been grotesquely over-democratic. What is wanted now is a species of Scottish fascism.' Beliefs such as these, his admiration for 'big men' like Mussolini and his founding in 1930 of Clann Albain, a paramilitary organisation not dissimilar to Mosley's Blackshirts, resulted in his expulsion from the party. As president, it was hard for Robert to distance himself entirely from these views, however much he deplored them; though he left the management of the new party to others, knowing that he was temperamentally unsuited to the task, and believing anyway that he could do more good in the world beyond as a public figure and speaker. Declining an invitation to stand as a candidate for Paisley at the 1928 general election, he wrote to Muirhead: '. . . the dunghill of active politics is a young man's game . . . It is a dunghill I know for I have been on (or in) the hill.'

On 23 June 1928, the anniversary of the Battle of Bannockburn, Robert spoke at the first annual meeting of the National Party of Scotland, demanding that the Scottish parliament should be restored with full control over all Scottish affairs.

If there is an individual nationality in Europe it is our own. We have our own laws, our own customs, our own habits. In the Highlands our own speech – even in the Lowlands we preserve the oldest form of the Saxon language. And it seems to me that when Ireland, the Dominions, and other portions of the Empire have their separate legislatures that it is a very simple thing for Scotland – Scotland that has done so much towards the formation of the British Empire – to ask for that restoration of its ancient Parliament . . . Then against that assumed inferiority complex that we are told about, it has been assumed, friends, that Scotland owes its prosperity today to the Act of Union. Nothing more false. When our ancient Parliament was filched away from us by fraud and bribery the dominant partner took good care that we should remain in an inferior position. Take, for example, the position of the Scottish peers. Any sweater, any profiteer, any newspaper shark, anyone in England, who has got enough money to pay into the party fund, is made a lord and sits by virtue of his money a hereditary legislator in England . . . Besides, with a population such as ours, free, active, well-educated and laborious, it was inevitable that Scotland should become prosperous. Union had nothing more to do with it than Stirling Castle or than *Stuc a Chroin* . . . Scotland lies today under the heels of England and every measure for the alleviation of Scottish grievances is legislated for, debated on, and decided by men who know no more about Scotland than I do about the Emperor of Korea. We must change that. We must do something to wipe away the National disgrace under which we lie in regard to matters such as these. We want a National Scottish Parliament in Edinburgh in order to deal with Scottish measures under the eye and pressure of a Scottish electorate.

A year later, in 1929, he gave an interview to *Reynolds Illustrated News* in which he again made the link between socialism and nationalism. 'It stands to reason that the affairs of any country can be better managed from their national centre than from a Parliament constituted 400 miles away.' He went on to cite unemployment, slum housing and foreign ownership of the Highlands as matters in pressing need of attention, noting that less than twelve hours had been devoted to Scottish business during the previous year in Westminster.

In 1930, at a gathering of the National Party of Scotland at King's Park, Stirling, again on the anniversary of Bannockburn, he gave what is arguably his most well-known speech on independence. Scotland was a distinct nation, as different from England as it was from Germany, France, Russia or any other nation, he said. Nationality was 'the atmosphere of the world' – within the last decade no less than twenty nationalities had come into being, Ireland, Finland, Poland, Latvia, Estonia among them. Why should Scotland lag behind? Was it not an injustice and a sin against political science that one nationality should be subservient, a mere appendage of the predominant partner? It was in vain for Scots to look for help in their struggle for autonomy from any of the existing parties. Yet unlike the Irish, the Scots had no need to shed their blood. All they needed was to vote. A parliament in Edinburgh would encourage a renaissance, a re-birth of literature, art and sentiment, he went on, citing the cultural flowering that had taken place of late in the south of Ireland. That same national sentiment would reveal the slums of Glasgow as a scandal, the empty Highlands as the playground of the rich. He concluded with a call to all Scots 'never to cease agitating until we get this autonomy for Scotland which alone can revive our ancient spirit and make real Scotsmen of us.'

In the general election of 1931 the National Party of Scotland fielded five candidates. Robert enjoyed himself, touring the hustings and speaking, so long as he could memorise his speeches, whenever the opportunity arose. 'Quite your party leader,' he wrote to Garnett. 'Back to the soapbox again. It is amusing.' Now frail, and mindful of the weakening power of his voice, he still stood erect in his double-breasted suit, his aquiline features crowned by a shock of white hair, and he could still rouse the crowd, not least with his customarily sardonic humour. Of the Union, he regretted

as a Scotsman, because we always had a good name for business, that those Judases who sold our country, got so little for them-selves. £26,000 was all they received for their assent to the Bill of Union. £26,000! Why, their patron saint, Judas, got almost as much, taking into consideration the greater purchasing power of money when he did his deal.

Of Home Rule, he wished 'for the blessing of a national parlia-ment, with the pleasure of knowing that the taxes were wasted in Edinburgh instead of in London.'

In the event only three of the five National Party of Scotland candidates secured their deposits, despite their president's strenu-ous campaigning on their behalf, despite the large turnouts at gath-erings and rectorial elections. When it came to the ballot box, nationalism and perhaps a party led by writers and poets had failed to capture the public mood. Nevertheless, Robert continued to appear whenever the party demanded it, fist raised and microphone in hand, roaring on Glasgow Green as he had in earlier days. In old age, the cause of independence was providing him with a political home, something to fight for, and perhaps, in its still-embryonic state, an antidote to the disillusionment he felt with Westminster and the machinations of its parties of all stripes.

Furthermore, his view of independence was hardening. At the 1932 'Scotland's Day' rally at the Wallace birthplace monument at Elderslie, he declared that he would repeal the Union and make a solemn declaration of Scottish sovereignty, followed by a treaty between Scotland and England. Scotland would have its own army, its own coinage, postage stamps, and power to send ambassadors overseas. It would also have the power to institute its own fiscal system. The king, he asserted, was King of Scotland, and should be crowned in Edinburgh. There had been too little bitterness in Scottish politics, he said. More bitterness was needed to draw the people together.

Some months later he wrote an article entitled *The Awakening of a Nation* for the *Scots Independent*, in which he spoke of 'race consciousness'. But this was no assertion of blood-and-soil nationalism. Rather than suggesting that the Scots were in any way superior, in particular to their neighbours, the English, this was a call to Scots to remind themselves of who they were; that they had their own distinct identity which had become overlooked as for too long they had been junior partners to a union which no longer served them. 'At last our eyes have opened and by degrees we are beginning to observe ourselves without the aid of English spectacles,' he wrote.

In 1934, at the instigation of John McCormick, secretary of the National Party of Scotland, a merger took place with the Scottish Party to form the Scottish National Party. Robert was appointed honorary president and his Graham kinsman, the Duke of Montrose, president. Montrose had been the figurehead of the Scottish Party, a breakaway unionist group which favoured dominion Home Rule and an Imperial parliament, as opposed to the full-blooded independence supported by the NPS. For this reason, chiefly, he would quit the party for the Liberals within the year.

But the timing of the merger was not favourable. Hitler had come to power as German Chancellor in 1933 and ideas of nationalism of any kind swiftly lost their appeal with the electorate. In a climate in which some of his literary acquaintances now turned their pens to the support of fascism, the octogenarian Robert redoubled his commitment to parliamentary democracy, believing a Scottish parliament to be the only way to solve Scotland's chronic economic and social problems. He had already warned against the evils of xenophobia in an article in the Scots Independent in 1931:

> The enemies of Scotland are not the English, for they were ever a great and generous folk, quick to respond when justice calls. Our real enemies are amongst us born without imagination, bound in the fetters of their own conceit, impervious to progress, and who fail to see that what was right and just last year, to-day may have become through altering conditions rank injustice.

It was injustice that had driven Robert throughout his entire political career, his sense of it a visceral and energising force that often led him to action where other more cautious, and as events sometimes proved, wiser, men would have hesitated. It was the injustice of the plight of Scotland's working classes, along with the injustice of a union that denied them the opportunity for change, which drove him to the forefront of a movement where, despite his old age, he was still able by virtue of his passion to win hearts and minds for the cause and carve himself an enduring niche in the pantheon of champions for Scottish independence.

Robert's final political gesture, a year before he died, was to send a message to those attending the 1935 Bannockburn Day celebrations, saying that he believed they were moving towards victory. Yet five months later, at the General Election, the newly fledged Scottish National Party registered a tiny 1.3 per cent of the Scottish vote. Knowing full well that a long road lay ahead, Robert was consoling himself for the fact that he would not live long enough to see around the first bend, let alone to journey's end.

Twenty-two

INCHMAHOME

Final stories

Robert's mother, the redoubtable Anne Elizabeth, had died aged ninety-six in March 1925. Despite the tensions of earlier years over his inheritance and his marriage to Gabriela, they had remained close. In later life their relationship had settled into one of regular and affectionate companionship. Now that she was gone, along with his wife and both brothers, the octogenarian Robert had only Toppie Dummett at his side. He continued to spend most of his time between London and Scotland, enjoying the company and perhaps the admiration of those mostly younger than himself who visited Toppie's London house or attended nationalist gatherings. These were sociable moments which stood in marked contrast to the solitude he sought while writing at Ardoch or St Anne's Lodge, the house he had inherited from a cousin on the Isle of Bute. Although his creative energy was slowing he pushed himself to keep writing, determined that his voice should still be heard despite his advancing years. Between the publication in 1917 of *Brought Forward* – the last of the regular collections of sketches and not one of his best, according to Frank Harris – and his death in 1936, he would publish a further fourteen books; although the next collection of short pieces, *Redeemed and Other Sketches*, dedicated to Elizabeth Dummett, would not appear until 1927.

Of late, Robert had been spending time each year in Spain. In a departure from his customary settings of South America, Morocco and Scotland, this now furnished the backdrop to a number of the sketches in *Redeemed* and subsequent collections. His retreat was an isolated farmhouse, la Dehisa de Encinar, in the shadow of the Sierra de Guadarrama, a short distance north of Madrid. The place had been the last refuge of his great friend Dino, Duke of Frías, the wildly improvident Spanish aristocrat who had died in 1909. Now Robert was welcomed by Dino's widow, Maria de Frías, who gladly offered him the opportunity to enjoy the wilderness once more. As he recalls in *Fin de Race* (*Writ in Sand*, 1932):

> ... the track ran through more wood, and crossed another stream ... and finally ended quite suddenly in a little clearing, in which stood the house, a long, low one-storey building, such as a child draws on a slate. In daylight the house stood stark, surrounded by a few old oaks, without garden, planted shrubs or anything to soften the hardness of the Castilian landscape ... A stream whose high banks were fringed with willows, ran close to the house. Taking advantage of the cover in winter, wolves made their way down from the mountains in their nocturnal raids. A fence of strong wire-netting, twelve feet at least in height, kept them off from the house. In winter, especially when snow was on the ground, they came and howled outside the barrier, and were answered by the dogs, either from terror or by affinity of race. Even in summer they were heard occasionally. Their melancholy, long drawn-out howl once heard, never to be forgotten, that seems to chill the marrow of the bones, especially when heard alone, far off from houses, with your horse trembling underneath you, was quite in keeping with the wildness of the place.

There is a melancholy and a sense of resignation to many of the sketches in *Redeemed*, while reminiscence and a fondness for things past is a recurrent theme in *Writ in Sand* and the final collection, *Mirages* (1936). The titles of all three collections are suggestive of Robert's growing preoccupation with his own mortality and the transient nature of the human experience; though he still finds the energy to rail, with customary irony, against his two principal *bêtes noires*: modernity and Empire. Elsewhere, the familiar miscellany of incidents, anecdotes and character sketches recalled from three continents sits alongside obituaries of Wilfrid Blunt and Joseph

Conrad, and candid portraits of his friends and former companions in adventure: Dino Frías, wealthy, gifted and feckless, who attracted women 'as valerian attracts cats'; Bibi Carleton, the Catholic-raised, 'sub-cutaneous Moslem', adored by everyone from the Sultan to the loafers on the beach; Joseph Crawhall, the artist, whose unkempt appearance and monosyllabic delivery gave rise to the nickname 'Creeps'; and Walter Harris of the pigtail and yellow-footed grey-hounds, whose eccentric and extravagant personality was mirrored by his once-splendid Moroccan villa, Dar el Jinoun.

For all Robert's passion and generosity, his close observation of the human condition and his many personal experiences in adoles-cence, in South America, at Westminster and elsewhere, left him with a world-weary, even cynical cast of mind. He struggled to believe in an intrinsic human goodness and found people generally corruptible – by the mere fact of their life circumstances, if nothing else. His absence of belief in a higher purpose lent a realism to many of his stories and sketches, enabling him to describe events simply as they took place, without the need for any moral theme or undertone – though not without empathy for his subjects. Where such a sub-text does exist, the commentary is invariably wry. In *The Gold Fish* (*Thirteen Stories*, 1900), a sheikh entrusts seven goldfish in a fine crystal bowl to his fastest runner and commands him to take it, a gift, to a distant neighbour.

> Set upon the road, his shoes pulled up, his waistband tightened, in his hand a staff, a palm-leaf wallet at his back, and in it bread, some hemp, a match or two (known to him as el spiritus), and a letter to take anywhere, crossing the plains, fording the streams, struggling along the mountain-paths, sleeping fitfully, a burning rope steeped in saltpetre fastened to his foot, he trotted day and night – untiring as a camel, faithful as a dog.

The runner crosses the mountains and the desert, spilling not a drop, until eventually he loses his way, succumbs to exhaustion, lies down and dies. The water and fish spill into the sand, leaving only the unbroken crystal bowl which still 'glistened beautiful as gold, in the fierce rays of the Sahara sun.' An impossible journey ends in failure, a pointless death and the survival only of a now-useless object.

During this time, from his mid-sixties onwards, Robert had also written nine other books, all but one of them drawing on the accumulated knowledge of his South American years. Perhaps the most interesting of these, for the strangeness of the tale it tells, is *A Brazilian Mystic* (1920). This concerns the life of one Antonio Maciel, later known as *el Consulheiro*, the Councillor, born of poor farmers in the Brazilian hinterland of the Sertão. Following an altercation with another man involving his, Maciel's, wife, he was jailed but escaped and disappeared for ten years, only to reappear as a wild-eyed prophet and healer whose ability to attract followers to the small churches he was rebuilding in remote settlements in the Sertão so alarmed the authorities that they had him arrested on a charge of murdering his mother. Maciel, however, demonstrated his mother still to be alive and was duly released. He returned, a martyr, to the Sertão where shortly, in the vacuum left by the abdication of Brazil's Emperor Don Pedro, he found himself the *de facto* governor of the region. The central government, where Republican voices held sway, now sent troops to remove Maciel, whose own deeply conservative, monarchist followers had anointed him the earthly representative of the 'hidden king'. This was a reference to the myth that Sebastien, King of Portugal in the sixteenth century, who had fallen in battle against the Moors, would one day return in a moment of crisis. For three years, Maciel and his growing body of followers held out in an isolated farm in a mountainous valley, until eventually government forces armed with field guns bombarded the settlement prior to entering it and killing everyone present.

> Dressed in his long blue tunic . . . his hands crossed . . . clasping a crucifix against his breast he lay, waiting for the coming of the king, that Dom Sebastian who he believed should come to rule the world in glory, blot out injustice, cast down the mighty and exalt the poor in spirit . . . his body lay on a ragged piece of matting and both his eyes were full of sand.

Robert tells the story with obvious enjoyment and an intimate familiarity with his subject. He knew the ways of life in the Brazilian hinterland, if not Sertão itself. He knew Portugal well through visits from nearby Vigo. He had written of the 'hidden king' in his sketch *A Sebastianist* (*Hope*, 1910), describing an old man's dream of the final battle, which happened to have taken place at Bibi Carleton's town in Morocco, Alcazar el Bebir, which he also knew. And he had encouragement from friends to pursue this subject. One of those was Theodore Roosevelt whom he had met several times in Rome while staying at the Hotel Beau Site, which they both favoured. When President of the United States, Roosevelt had written to Robert encouraging him to write about the Brazilian frontiersmen as he had done their Argentine counterparts, a letter which Robert reproduced in his preface to the book.

Robert placed Maciel 'just on that borderland where dwell saints and visionaries,' suggesting that he was neither mad nor entirely sane – a description which might, in his more impulsive moments, have been applied to Robert himself. Taking as his primary source Os Sertões, an account by the Brazilian historian Euclides da Cunha, which he had bought in Rio de Janeiro – and which certain Brazilian scholars accused him of plagiarising – Robert concludes with a characteristic dismissal of morality and religion:

> when faith, works, philosophy, logic and the rest of the panaceas preached during the last 2000 years fail, all that is left to reasonable men is to pay the boot-maker's and tailor's bills with regularity, give alms to the deserving and to the undeserving poor, and then live humbly under the sun, taking example by other animals.

Robert's next two books were histories of the Spanish conquest: *New Granada* (corresponding to modern-day Colombia, Ecuador, Venezuela and Panama) and *The River Plate* (Argentina and Uruguay), published respectively in 1922 and 1924. Then in 1925 came *Doughty Deeds*, the previously mentioned biography of his tough and industrious eighteenth century ancestor, the first Robert Cunninghame Graham. Although there was much in Doughty Deeds' life that found echoes in Robert's own, the family papers yielded little of real interest about him and Robert places Gartmore at the centre of the book – a place about which he still remembered every detail, a quarter of a century after its sale.

The following year Robert published *Pedro de Valdivia: conqueror of Chile*, another history of the Conquest. This met with the stern disapproval of at least one reviewer, D.H. Lawrence, who wrote: 'Mr Graham has shown us, not Valdivia, but himself. He lifts a swashbuckling fountain pen, and off he goes. The result is a shoddy, scrappy and not very sincere piece of work. The *Conquistadores* were damned by insensitiveness to life, what we call lack of imagination. And they let a new damnation into the America they conquered. Yet at least they never felt themselves too good for their job, as some of the inky conquerors did even then, and do still.' He accuses Robert not just of shoddy workmanship, but of condoning the brutality meted out by the Spaniards to the Indians; though this was no more than to be expected, he goes on, from men of action who were usually failures in the long run. 'Their precious energy makes them uproot the tree of life and leave it to wither, and their stupidity makes them proud of it.'

In *José Antonio Páez*, his 1929 biography of the Venezuelan leader who fought with Bolívar in the Venezuelan War of Independence, Robert revives a family connection: his maternal grandfather, Admiral Charles Elphinstone Fleming, had on occasion mediated between Páez and Bolívar, and had dined with Páez in Caracas in 1829. Here was an underdog whose extrovert character and resilience as he struggled to free his country from the Spanish yoke appealed to Robert. This was followed in 1930 by the equestrian study, Horses of the Conquest.

His final book, *Portrait of A Dictator*, a biography of the Paraguayan Francisco Solano López came out in 1933, the year Hitler took power as Chancellor of Germany. He wrote the book as a warning, although it was now sixty years since the events he was describing, and its subject had by then become a national hero, the ambush by Brazilian troops at Cerro Corá known throughout South America as symbolic of the plucky small nation pitted against its larger neighbour. Robert was especially fascinated by López's mistress, an intelligent, beautiful and altogether formidable Irish woman by name of

Eliza Lynch. Madame Lynch, as she was known, was by her husband's side at Cerro Corá, where both he and their teenage son were killed, having refused to surrender. She is said to have buried their bodies with her bare hands, before submitting herself to capture by the Brazilian army. Later, banished from Paraguay for having allegedly encouraged her husband in his bellicose ambitions, she made her way to Paris, where she bought a fine house in the Rue du Rivoli. Robert wrote:

> I saw her several times in London in 1873 or 1874, getting into her carriage. She was then apparently about 40 years of age. Of middle height, well made, beginning to put on a little flesh, with her abundant hair just flecked with grey. In her well-made Parisian clothes she looked more French than English and had no touch of that untidiness that so often marks the Irishwoman.

Nor did she in the least resemble someone who had faced death, lived at times as a fugitive, and buried both her lover and son with her own hands.

With twenty-seven books and an impressive body of newspaper and magazine articles to his name, as well as numerous prefaces to other people's books, Robert was a substantial literary figure and one who for many reasons offered interesting potential as the subject of a biography. Although he had always said that if one wanted to know him one should read his work, he was not averse to the attention of someone such as the young American literature student, Herbert Faulkner West, who had recently arrived in England and was looking for a subject. Having approached and been turned down by Henry Williamson, West turned to Robert who, with his characteristic kindness towards those younger than himself, entertained him to lunch at Martinez Spanish restaurant in Regent Street. Upright and alert, with a thin, aquiline face and wavy hair, Robert appeared to the young writer 'like an eagle'.

In the summer of 1929, West – 'Don Heriberto' as Robert now called him – was duly invited to stay at Ardoch where he proposed a biography. West then returned to Dartmouth College at Hanover,

New Hampshire, an East Coast Ivy League institution with an exceptionally fine library. From here he sent in questions which Robert considered carefully, then answered. Thus Robert controlled precisely what was recounted and what was not.

For instance, West proposed to say that Willy Bontine had been injured in 1880. Robert replied with the by-now familiar trope that he had suffered a horse fall. 'You might say during his service with the Scots Greys in Galway his horse fell, or stepped on his head, or something of the kind.' West duly obliged, thus sidestepping the story of Willy's long illness and incarceration. This was the biography also in which the notion was put forward that Robert been brought up by his grandmother and her family in Cadiz. It also had the first account of his purported meeting with Gabriela in Paris and the winter they are supposed to have spent at Gartmore after their marriage. But these details are proved wrong both by family papers and by the public records of the Court of Session in Edinburgh.

Robert's nephew, Angus, my grandfather, quizzed West on the Spanish upbringing story. Where had it come from? he asked. As far as he knew, Catalina had been on the Isle of Wight with her second husband during Robert's boyhood, which he had spent at Finlaystone, then Gartmore, and later London. There had been no visits to Spain that Angus knew of, and Catalina had few relatives there, Aunt Jimenez being the only one Robert knew.

West's book, *A Modern Conquistador: Robert Cunninghame Graham: His Life and Works* (1932) was a disappointment. Though Robert was pleased to be back in the limelight he found it dull, while younger readers were dismissive of both the book and its subject. T.E. Lawrence wrote to the publishers, C.J. Greenwood in 1932,

> the Cunninghame Graham duly arrived. It is a disappointing book. Anything about the old don should've been written with a swagger. He is an artist as you see if only he takes off his hat to a lady in the street. His pen swaggers too; and he cannot therefore sustain a book; though he writes the best five or six pages imaginable . . . A wonderful old man . . . Not much brain you know, but a great heart and hat and what a head of hair!

Two years later, in 1934, both the hat and the head of hair were to feature in his final portrait, painted by the Scottish artist James McBey, who later recounted that during the sitting Robert constantly chatted about his travels in South America. To Robert's delight the picture was hung a year later in the Royal Academy. 'My dear McBey,' he wrote, 'THE picture looked splendid in the Academy this afternoon and was admired. Being hung rather high shows it off.'

While West was an academic, Robert's second biographer was the opposite, a man of action whose literary success derived from his account of the remarkable fifteen thousand mile ride he had undertaken with his two horses, Mancha and Gato, from Buenos Aires to New York between 1925 and 1928. The author of the best-selling *Tschiffely's Ride*, Aimé Tschiffely was a young Swiss who knew the Pampas, had ridden with gauchos, and had faced great physical danger. The two became fast friends at once and Robert began to feed him reminiscences. With his wife Violeta, Tschiffely became a regular visitor to Ardoch. Much later, at the widowed Violeta's request, my mother became literary executor of the Tschiffely estate. The biography, *Don Roberto: being the account of the life and works of RB Cunninghame Graham*, was published in 1937, the year after Robert's death. Again, the younger man had fallen under the older one's spell and this book was even more admiring and less critical of its subject than West's. Nevertheless, it was well-received by a public eager for a good yarn. This one delivered 'the adventure of being Cunninghame Graham', as G.K. Chesterton had put it, at full tilt. 'The kind of man every boy wants to be', 'Don Roberto the human dynamo', 'Man of swagger' ran the headlines. But not everyone swallowed the story whole. The *Times* warned that the book was really an autobiography, edited by Tschiffely. V.S. Pritchett wrote: 'they were, those who knew him, inclined to soft-pedal the Spanish grandmother; at the gaucho they raise their eyebrows a little.' And there were omissions. Tschiffely, like West, had failed to tell the full story. The meeting with Gabriela in Paris was faithfully reproduced, as was her purported ancestry, and no further questions were asked. The business-cum-information-gathering enterprises in Morocco were absent. So too was the Scottish nationalism.

This was the carefully branded Don Roberto that the world had come to know: the aristocratic, quixotic adventurer, tilting at the twin windmills of injustice and idiocy wherever he found them.

'When I asked him why he wasted his time on me,' wrote Tschiffely later, 'he told me that since his friend W.H. Hudson had died, until he had met me there had been no one with whom he could talk about gauchos and the Pampa which were his spiritual home.' Once, on a visit to Tschiffely's lodgings in a rundown part of Notting Hill, Robert left his car and chauffeur and walked Tschiffely to 40 St Luke's Road, where Hudson had lived, describing his neighbourhood as 'a desert of macadam, mud and fog'. They talked together of Hudson, before Robert walked up the steps and gently, respectfully touched the doorknob.

It was Hudson who drew Robert back to South America for his final and, as it transpired, fatal visit. Hudson, born in Argentina, had come to England only at the age of twenty-five where he lived in great poverty, a virtual recluse because of his anxiety about poor health. His novels made him famous but it was his deep knowledge of the Pampas and their natural history that really drew Robert to him. They began to correspond in 1890 and Robert did whatever he could to promote Hudson through reviews and introductions to friends like Conrad and Violet Hunt. Hudson rewarded these kindnesses with a dedication to his story El Ombú. Robert cherished his friend's words: 'to my friend RB Cunninghame Graham, *singularismo escritor Inglés*'.

In 1923 Robert had been invited to chair the committee in charge of commissioning a memorial sculpture to Hudson. It was to stand in the bird sanctuary in Hyde Park. Jacob Epstein, a young modernist American sculptor and a protégé of Robert's, was chosen and duly came up with Rima, Hudson's earth goddess, attended by four birds. Unveiled by the Prime Minister, Stanley Baldwin, the sculpture was greeted with horror. The ampleness of Rima's bosom caused the Prime Minister, on pulling the unveiling cord, to flinch. 'Take this horror out of the park', cried the press. But the *Times*, whose art critic praised it as one of the most beautiful memorials in the country, published a petition to keep it, signed by Robert,

Ramsay McDonald, John Lavery, Sybil Thorndyke and Ben Tillett. It is there to this day.

A decade later Robert was contacted by a young Argentine, a Dr Pozzo, to say that he had located the house where Hudson had been born. Would Robert, as chairman of the memorial committee, make a ceremonial visit and help with the Spanish translation of Hudson's work? Now aged eighty-three, Robert agreed. With Toppie Dummett and her ever-attendant sister, Louisa Miéville, he left Liverpool in January 1936, arriving in Buenos Aires on 19 February. He had not been in Buenos Aires since 1915 and was amazed at how it had become a thriving modern city. Dr Pozzo met them off the boat and a whirl of receptions began. Robert was interviewed for press and radio and hailed as the 'great spirit of the past', a writer whose love of Argentina had endeared him to her people. Yet he seems to have harboured a presentiment of what was shortly to come. Explaining to a reporter that he was currently writing a preface to Hudson's work, he was asked what he would write next. 'Just the preface to my death,' he replied with a shrug.

In the following days he made the planned pilgrimage to Hudson's wooden-roofed ranch house at Quilmes, ten miles outside the city, noting that the open plain with which he had been so familiar was now 'cut with fences.' There, in the dilapidated house, he sat at a small table and wrote to Hudson's old friend and biographer, Morley Roberts. The photograph of him, sitting at the table, pen in hand, is one of the last that was taken of him. Gaunt, lined and tired, the hooded eyes half closed, he still has his fine shock of hair and is dressed in a linen jacket and jaunty bow tie.

He had made pilgrimage to many places, he wrote to Morley, but none had impressed him more than

the humble *rancho* with its wooden roof, brick floors, primitive doors and air of aloofness from everything modern (*gracias á Dios*). It can have altered little since our great and beloved friend passed his boyhood here. The same tall thistles grow in the plain that flows all about the house, just as the sea flows about an atoll in the Pacific, almost as if it were lapping at the foundations of the house. The same flocks of birds . . . still haunt the trees which have grown up in the deserted *chacra* [smallholding] . . . The same stream, the same rivulet of which he writes in *El Ombú* still runs between the house and the Monastery of Santo Domingo. Little I think has altered. Nature of course is resuming her sway; but three remain of the twenty five *ombus*. All the plants Hudson loved, fennel, evening primrose and the rest are here to mourn him.

The only discordant note was the presence of 'a chestnut horse, unfortunately a *mestizo* [crossbreed], tied to a post in front of the house.'

In early March Robert wrote to Edward Garnett that he was 'in bed with a slight touch of bronchitis.' The letter, dictated though with a postscript added in his own stumbling hand, was the last of a correspondence lasting forty years. He was cheered by the arrival of an advance copy of *Mirages*, in whose preface he had written: 'although they tell us that death is the wages of the sinner, as far as I can see, it seems to be not very different for the saint.' Shortly after this he wrote describing Hudson's birthplace to Herbert Faulkner West: 'Mi querido Heriberto . . . it is a small rancho near a wood and the great plains surround it like a sea. Someday I hope to send you my account of it . . . We are going through a heatwave that is rather trying and the sun has inflamed my eyes which makes my writing worse than ever. However it is nothing much and is passing off.'

But it did not. Pneumonia set in and on 20 March 1936 he died peacefully in his Buenos Aires hotel room. His body lay in state at the Casa Del Teatro (formerly the Cervantes Theatre – a final quixotic echo), crowds gathered and the President of the Argentine Republic paid his respects along with the Minister of the Interior and the President of the Argentine Academy of Letters. Sir Nevile Henderson, the British Ambassador, paid tribute:

The world is poorer for the death of Cunninghame Graham, the lover of freedom, the friend of the common people, the champion of reform, at times when reform was not always popular, the defender of the cause of small nations and of backward peoples.

A large procession followed the coffin to the docks, led by Tschiffely's horses, Mancha and Gato, for whom Robert had brought with him from London a bag of oats. The *Almeda Star*, on which he had reserved his passage home, departed on schedule on 26 March. Back in Scotland by late April, the coffin arrived at Port of Menteith, accompanied, according to one report, by a riderless horse in whose stirrups Robert's empty boots were reversed. He could scarcely have managed it better: the final pilgrimage to Argentina, which he loved almost as much as Scotland, there to pay his respects at the birthplace of the one person more than any who had understood his attachment to the country; followed by a journey across the water to Scotland and a final resting place beside his ancestors on his beloved island of Inchmahome.

On a blustery April day of sunshine and snow flurries, the service was held in the Port of Menteith church. Mourners, including my grandparents and great-aunt, represented every stratum of society, from the Duke of Montrose to John Fergusson, the Gartmore village blacksmith. Afterwards, pipers accompanied the coffin to the jetty and a small motor launch carried it across the water to Inchmahome. There, in the chancel of the ruined priory, Robert was buried beside Gabriela. On his stone, in place of a cross, was carved his brand mark.

Epilogue

ARDOCH

Moving on

18 September 2014 dawned grey and dull. I drove to Glasgow for a meeting, looking out for saltires in windows, on flagpoles, flying from cars. There were disappointingly few. On the streets of Glasgow people were going about their business as normal. After all the weeks of campaigning it felt strangely flat. The world – the Scottish world at any rate – did not seem to be holding its breath. Yet this was the day on which, as Jim Sillars, former Deputy Leader of the Scottish National Party, had said, 'between the hours of seven a.m. and ten p.m., absolute sovereign power will lie in the hands of the Scottish people.' Later that evening, as observers at the local count in the Bells Sports Centre in Perth, my wife Sarah and I rode the emotional rollercoaster as the results came in: our own area, Perth & Kinross, a disappointing majority for NO, Glasgow and Dundee both YES by large majorities, the rest of the country a mixed bag. But by 3.00 a.m. the final result was clear. We drove home tearful and exhausted.

Was Robert on my mind that day? I can't in all honesty recall. But that it had come as close as it did, with forty-five percent of the Scottish electorate voting for independence, would surely have amazed and delighted him as much as it would have disappointed him. His belief that it was only proper for Scotland to govern herself was not, as my mother maintained, mere posturing, an older man looking to hold onto his place in the limelight. One has only to read his many speeches to hear the fire and feel the indignation at his country's subordination to the rule of Westminster.

Robert believed in Scotland's independence as he believed in many other things through his life – the right of working men to decent working conditions, the right of women to the vote, the right of the disadvantaged of all races not to be exploited or oppressed, the right of animals to be treated with kindness and respect – with a passion.

I understood it now. In my life to date I had felt passion for certain people, for my work as a writer, for the music I made, for opportunities to travel, but never before for a cause. In my sixties, the cause of Scotland's right to self-determination had come unbidden to lodge in my head, heart and guts. There was reasoning there, but there was a storm of emotions, too: anger, indignation, frustration, longing, all the things to which Robert was referring when, speaking at the launch of the National Party of Scotland in 1928, he said: 'You may say, friends, that what I have been touching on are mere sentimental questions. But sentiment is the strongest force to move mankind.'

Sentiment drove Robert. He was a man of powerful convictions and enormous energy, which is doubtless why he reverberates in my life three generations later, my mother the lightning rod. Robert was essentially compassionate, a crusader stirred by the injustices he first witnessed in South America as a young man, later by the plight of the Victorian working man, later still by the disregard in which Scotland and her people were held by those in power at Westminster. Yet in proportion to his crusading passion came susceptibility to disappointment, which is why, I believe, he guarded his private feelings fiercely, for fear of having them trampled on as they had been through the whole wounding era of his father's insanity and the *curator's* reign; why also he determined that no one would ever again have control over his life. And why in public life, in his politics and his writing, he cultivated that note of cynicism which is so often present when he speaks of human behaviour and the human condition. He had been let down, or seen others being let down, too many times.

That he could be both passionate and world-weary was one of the many paradoxes in his character that challenge and fascinate all who come to study him – and he has exercised many more scholarly minds than mine. He could hold apparently contrary positions without discomfort: the aristocratic socialist, the Scottish laird with the manners of a Spanish *hidalgo*, the hard-riding dandy, the romantic realist, the cosmopolitan nationalist, the progressive who deplored the effects of progress, the visionary antiquarian, the anti-imperialist, anti-racist admirer of the Spanish Conquest, the moderniser with one foot in the past, the disdainful writer of literary prefaces who chatted easily in Scots with the Gartmore tenants, the lover of horses who corralled them for certain slaughter.

It is as if all his life he hosted a running dialogue between twin voices, opposing yet often complimentary; and it is this that has made him so difficult to place in either the cultural or political landscape. Born six months after the opening of the Great Exhibition of 1851 – a celebration of modern industrial technology and design – Robert grew up in an era of fascination with the future and all the wonders of the modern world; yet his childhood was steeped in the stories of an ancestral past, and throughout his life he evinced a longing for an earlier, nobler age of courtesy, respect and simple wisdom. To him the least acceptable face of modernity was the wealthy industrialist, the rapacious (as he saw it) Liberal 'sweater', who extorted labour from those least able to resist, while professing to stand for progress; yet those very industrialists supported the party which offered Robert the platform he needed to argue for a different kind of progress: social justice and relief for the poor whose indebtedness he understood only too well from his own personal experience. Money was difficult for Robert, raised in the belief that it was plentiful, only to discover in adolescence that the opposite was true, yet not being someone who by nature could tolerate a life of poverty; politically empowered, nevertheless, by his relative wealth yet undermined in his socialist principles by his moneyed appearance. Highly educated and widely read, Robert longed for the working man to claim his right to education and the place in the corridors of power that would surely follow; and despaired to discover that that was not always to be the case. No diplomat, indeed someone who actively relished causing shock and outrage, Robert would not hesitate to give offence where he felt it was deserved, yet he could also be charming and affable; and whatever his mood, he always had at his disposal the orator's gift, whether speaking from the benches of the House, or entertaining friends with a tale, summoning the skills of raconteur and mimic which in another life might have seen him step out on the stage. He could be swift to pick things up and let them go again, or to follow one passion with another; yet he also possessed a doggedness which would see him clinging to an idea or belief long after others would have relinquished it. His energy, particularly during the six years in Westminster, could be furious, as if he was in the grip of some driving force which allowed him no respite – and perhaps even resulted in him becoming a person he did not greatly like – which would go some way to explaining his effective self-sabotage in the election of 1892. Following such episodes he could become ill and depressed, although I do not believe the suggestion that he might have suffered from bi-polar disorder: the highs and lows were not sufficiently regular, nor was there anything about them to suggest mania – they were simply that, highs and lows. Reserved as he was, reluctant to expose his interior world, he could also appear indifferent to others; yet he enjoyed an enormous circle of friends and was capable of great generosity to those whom he felt deserving of his support. He cared deeply about injustice and had the imagination to be empathetic. It is impossible to read what he wrote about working men and women, indigenous peoples, and animals without concluding that he was a humanitarian and that at his core lay a deep reservoir of kindness.

All these traits, often contradictory, were part of his magnetism as were his many other gifts: the good looks; the abundant hair and deep brown eyes; the lean, athletic physique; the courage – both physical and moral; the swordsmanship and horsemanship. That these gifts could be counterpointed by vanity, impulsiveness, arrogance, haste, dismissiveness, recklessness, lack of attention, a dogged refusal to back down, moments of poor judgement and an inability to hear others, renders him mercifully human. And to answer the charge of dilettantism – my father's dismissal of him as an 'old fraud', for example – one need only turn to his legacy: militant trade unionism, a party of Labour, free education, the eight-hour working day, decent living standards for working people, Irish Home Rule, a Parliament restored to Edinburgh, the formation of the Scottish National Party and a vigorous Scottish independence movement, the vote for women, recognition of the rights of animals, the foundation of National Parks – all bear his fingerprints.

In the conclusion to his recent book, *RB Cunninghame Graham and Scotland: Party, Prose, and Political Aesthetic*, Lachlan Munro argues that Robert held 'an ambition for Scotland, mankind and the natural world that was prophetic, relevant and inspirational . . . his was a much-needed voice of opposition to conformity and complacency; an heroic voice of courage and independence which, in its time, excelled all others.' Yet on Robert's centenary, in 1952, Hamish Henderson, the poet and folklorist, had asked: Who remembers Cunninghame Graham?

Why does he remain so overlooked at a time when what he valued has never had greater resonance? Robert stood for kindness, decency, self-respect, tolerance, equality, social justice, internationalism. With the early twenty-first century rise of the right, the new era of populism, of authoritarian leaders and ethnic nationalism, these are values that offer a vital counterweight, a necessary note of sanity. Reviewing Lachlan Munro's book in the *National*, Alan Riach quotes the Irish historian, Owen Dudley Edwards: 'The choice in Scotland is now between UK nationalism clutching destruction, and Scottish nationalism working to save people and planet at home and around the world.' 'It's as stark as that,' concludes Alan Riach. 'Cunninghame Graham is one of the best guides to the present moment.'

Yet Robert is not widely hailed as the progressive that he surely was. Labour have largely written him out of their history, partly because of one of the greatest contradictions of all – his aristocratic antecedents, partly because of his subsequent support for Scottish independence which the modern Scottish Labour Party, doctrinaire to the last, to this day cannot tolerate. The Scottish National Party respectfully acknowledges him as one of the founding fathers but treats him as an eccentric uncle and something of an anachronism, while perhaps tacitly acknowledging that he would have detested the machinery and management of modern party politics. Wider Scotland, meanwhile, with small pockets of exception in political, literary and academic circles, has simply failed to adopt him as the inspirational national figure that he should and so easily could be.

Is it that the contradictions in his character have made him too hard to place for twentieth and twenty-first century audiences increasingly used to narrow definitions of people and lives? Had he not died so soon before the outbreak of the Second World War, might he have found an easier niche in the Scottish national consciousness? Or is it that Scots of the 'I kent his faither' mentality found someone quite so gifted too hard to swallow? It is certainly true that Robert could at times be the victim of his many gifts. A lot of things came very easily to him and as a result he could be casual, even slapdash. But in a Scotland where national self-esteem was at an especially low point after the war, there may simply have been no place for the memory of so flamboyant, so multi-faceted, so quixotic, so charismatic a character.

Coming to know these diverse aspects of his character, to see him in the round, is part of what has been so important in writing this book. I am, after all, one quarter Cunninghame Graham and can never entirely escape the adventure of being such. But Robert had become, for me, a mythical figure in great need of demythologising. Writing about him has allowed me to regard him as merely one of a number people in my family history who may have had some bearing on the person I am today, rather than as the towering figure of my childhood. Being raised in the awareness of belonging to an 'old', and by implication illustrious, family (though all families are old; some just know more about their past than others) has been, on balance, more of a burden than a blessing. In middle age I had to work hard to break the spell, the bounds of convention within which I had been raised. I have also experienced bruising difficulties over inheritance, although nothing in comparison to the burden that Robert had to bear. Coming to know him seems like the final chapter in that process of shrugging off, not only because he validates my feelings about Scottish independence – which run counter to most of what I was brought up to believe – but because recasting him as a normal, flawed human being removes an eclipsing colossus from the landscape of my past and allows me to connect with some of those all-too-human aspects of his character in which I see mirrored my own: among them a tendency to be led by the heart rather than the head, occasional impulsiveness, and a certain dogged reluctance to let go of things or listen to opposing views.

Robert and Gabriela have been watching over me during much of the writing of this book. Their two large portraits hang one on either side of a set of French doors. I rescued them from a family attic shortly before the start of the pandemic. Both are badly damaged. My cousin Robin reminds me that they were once stored in the stables at Ardoch because they were not deemed good enough to hang in the house. There they were used for darts practice by the children. Both were painted in 1884, six years into the marriage, when Robert was thirty-two and Gabriela twenty-six. I love the thoughtfulness and vulnerability in the portrait of Robert (see the cover). I am less keen on Gabriela, who has been beautified with a cupid's bow mouth and soulful eyes. She is wearing a rosary and holding what could be a bible. She looks suspiciously like a copy of the well-known portrait by Percy Jacomb Hood, though very little like the young woman who presents a determined face to the world in early photographs. But I have liked the pair of them looking on as I write.

For my mother, Robert modelled much of what she most valued, courage, generosity and a curiosity about the world chief among them. This description of him from *Should Auld Acquaintance*, the autobiography of William Power, the Glasgow journalist and leader of the Scottish National Party from 1940 to 1942, highlights many of the traits which would have drawn my mother to her great-uncle:

> He was the natural pride of a fine race, superb manhood, and mental independence. Those who imagined that he had the less pleasant kind of pride should have seen him, at a private literary function, going round the room talking delightfully with

everyone he thought was in the slightest danger of being over-looked. It was all the finer since he had, in mixed company, the shyness of a man of action who is also something of a literary recluse. He was too big a man to be afraid of appearing 'faintly absurd' in the eyes of conventional snobs, he espoused struggling causes that appealed to his chivalrous and patriotic instincts, and lent them the aegis of his own prestige.

Robert also furnished her with the project that dominated the second half of her life, and perhaps secured her independence in a second marriage in which she might easily have been subsumed by her husband's career – her executorship of Robert's literary estate, and the research and writing of *Gaucho Laird*. Like Robert, my mother was an enormously energetic person who lived a good part of her life in the public arena. She had an abundance of warmth and charm, and an ability to put people instantly at ease. But there was a reflective side to her nature and in that interior world I believe she lived a great deal of the time through the life of her great-uncle Robert.

My own first point of connection with Robert was South America, in my early twenties, although it was not until several decades later that I came to understand through his writing that we had had very similar reactions to the liberating vastness of the Pampa with their almost hauntingly isolated settlements, the sub-tropical charm of rural Paraguay with its clouds of butterflies and slow-moving, jungle-fringed rivers. In a little over six months, South America worked its way so far under my skin that I still think about it regu-larly, half a century later. My younger brother, Simon, was not immune either. He went out to Venezuela and lived there for nearly a decade, from the late nineteen-seventies until the late nineteen-eighties, following, it could be said, our three-greats grandfather, Admiral Elphinstone Fleeming, who had been present in 1823 at the Battle of Maracaibo, the final act in the Spanish American Wars of Independence. Simon worked in Caracas briefly as an English teacher before turning to photography and making a successful career in advertising. Like Robert, he needed to get away from the constraints of life in the UK to discover his *métier*. There is a photograph of him at his wedding, in his mid-twenties, slim and bearded. The resemblance with Robert is striking.

Now that I know Robert's writing, I find almost everything he wrote about South America transporting. Although I was there a century after him, the atmosphere, the mood he conveys takes me back at once. This is partly to do with shared experience, but it is also to do with the quality of his writing, his ability to capture with a few pen strokes the spirit of a place, the mood of a moment, the timbre of a conversation – and with them the strong sense of something now lost forever. The writer Robert MacFarlane, in his 2019 book *Underland*, speaks of solastalgia – the unhappiness felt by people whose landscape is being transformed around them. A kind of vicarious solastalgia is present in much of what Robert wrote, not only about South America but Scotland and North Africa also.

My journal of my South American trip reflects my own attempts to capture the spirit of the place, although I was in my early twenties at the time and I knew then, partly because Robert by his own example had granted me the requisite dispensation, that I would not start to write seriously until later in my life. In the event, I was forty when my first novel was published. Robert was forty-three when his first book appeared.

I believe that for his South American sketches alone, Robert deserves much wider recognition as a writer. And to cement his position as a Scottish writer, serious attention should also be given to his Scottish sketches. Yet again, his portraits of people, places and events – many of them infused with an arresting melancholy – have a ring to them that can only have come from long personal experience and deep affection, combined with a mostly unsentimental and sharply observant eye. That he should not be the subject of serious study as a late-nineteenth, early-twentieth century Scottish writer seems to me a glaring omission. Robert may have been educated in England, he may have written about Texas and Paraguay, Morocco, Iceland and Spain, but he lived more than half his life in Scotland and when he wrote about it he did so as a proud Scot, fully cognisant of all the weaknesses and foibles that that entailed.

In a postscript to their forthcoming collection of Robert's Scottish sketches, *A Careless Enchantment*, Lachlan Munro and Robin

Cunninghame Graham suggest that in writing about Scotland, what he was chiefly doing was documenting a lost past, compelled by his own humanity to preserve for the record the lives, and ways of life, of people whose stories would otherwise be obliterated by the passage of time. In this, I would add, he was echoing what he had sought to achieve in his writing about South America and North Africa. These worlds he had experienced were vanishing or vanished arcadias, all.

It is clear from his writing that Robert grasped only too well that which eludes so many politicians: how the cultural and political identities of a nation are deeply intertwined. This understanding was to dawn on me with some force on my return to Scotland after twenty years in London. I had left in the early Seventies. Now it was the early Nineties and I found myself reappraising much I had taken for granted in childhood and adolescence. There seemed to be a new energy in Scotland, the sense that a cultural renaissance was taking place, and with it an awakening national confidence. Scots were at last starting to tell themselves a different story. New, distinctively Scottish literary voices – those of James Kelman and Irvine Welsh to name but two – were making themselves heard. And the music . . . I had left to the strains of strict tempo country dance bands led by figures such as Jimmy Shand and Bobby MacLeod, the music I had been raised on and had played as a teenager. I returned to find Scotland's musical tradition in the hands of new custodians: boundary-breaking musicians such as Martyn Bennett, genre-defying bands such as Shooglenifty. Change was in the air and a parliament was soon to be restored to Edinburgh.

Not long after my return, war broke out in the former Yugoslavia. Horrified that we could be hearing of atrocities such as the Srebrenica massacre in Europe in the dying years of the twentieth century, I decided to write an admonitory story about civil war in a future Scotland. As mentioned previously, I was living at the time in a Highland glen and was becoming increasingly aware of the vexed issue of land ownership and the need for reform. When I chose this as the *casus belli* in my story, *The Witness*, I had no idea that land reform and crofters' rights had been central to Robert's early political thinking. As my grasp of what was happening in millennial Scotland strengthened, as my political awareness grew, it seems in retrospect as if Robert was there at every step, his sentiment validating my own on issues such as social justice, the monarchy, land reform, abolition of the House of Lords, internationalism and eventually independence. On almost all of these issues I was also fortunate to enjoy the particular view afforded to me by a seat on the board of the Edinburgh International Book Festival, the world's largest celebration of the written word. To paraphrase one review of the festival from the early 2000s: if you really want to know what's going on in Scotland and the wider world, don't go to Holyrood, come to Charlotte Square. I believe that remained the case throughout my fourteen years on the board. And it was at the Edinburgh International Book Festival, in August 2018, that to my amazement 200 people turned out to hear me talk about Robert on a Tuesday lunchtime. From that event, a number of subsequent conversations led me to starting work on this book

A decade earlier, I had completed the third in a series of young adult novels when I learned that my publishing contract would not be renewed. In reaction, I started to write a weekly blog which I called *A Few Kind Words*. This was something I could publish myself and over which I had control. At first I wrote about language at work and the need for organisations to be kinder, more humane in the way they spoke, which was also the theme of the writing courses I was running. I fairly soon broadened the scope to encompass anything that had struck me during the preceding week – incidents, conversations, things I had read or seen or heard, and so on – while maintaining the underlying theme of kindness, in its original sense of kinship, as a metaphor for human connection. Over the following nine years I published more than 350 short pieces. Looking back on them now, I believe that the very best of them, a handful perhaps, had something of the quality of Robert's sketches. This short form worked for us both: in Robert's case because it suited his natural pace and energy, his gift for the thumbnail portrait, and allowed him to say what he wanted without having to go too deep; in my case because it was a welcome antidote to the labour of fiction, and because it compelled me weekly to marshal my thoughts on a wide range of subjects; and for both of us, above all, because it satisfied the deep urge to tell stories, real, imaginary or somewhere in between, and in doing so to investigate the wellspring of connection, human kindness.

Finally, in spring 2021, in the run-up to the general election, I made a series of short weekly videos on the subject of Scottish independence. The first was a howl of frustration, indignation and anger at the high-handed way the Tories in Westminster were treating not only Scotland, but the whole of the UK. When it unexpectedly gained a substantial audience, I kept going for another seven weeks. This was by far the most exposing thing I had ever done and I had to armour myself against the inevitable criticism – relatively easy to bear from people I did not know, less so from friends or acquaintances. Again, with the benefit of hindsight, I believe Robert was at my shoulder as I made those short recordings. Without his example I might not have found the courage to make them at all.

Within the next year or so Scotland faces the prospect of a second independence referendum. I will then be approaching my mid-seventies, a couple of years short of the age at which Robert presided over the founding of the National Party of Scotland. Although in these pages I have completed my exploration of his life, he will not be gone from mine, and I am sure that when the time comes I will invoke his spirit again – and that I will not be alone in doing so.

For now, though, it is time to move on. I take my leave of him in the bookroom at Ardoch, writing by lamplight – he never had electricity installed. The house is quiet, the only sound the scratching of his pen, the occasional whistle and rattle of a train passing along the darkened embankment at the foot of the lawn. Perhaps his head is full of South America. Perhaps he imagines Bunny – 'cabalo mexito bein' – solid, patient beneath him. Perhaps he is recalling Facón Grande, Facón Chico, Pancho Pajaro, as he puts down the last lines of the last story in his last collection, *Mirages*, published the year of his death:

Most of them have been in Indian skirmishes and heard the pampa Indians yelling, striking their hands upon their mouths as they came on like a storm cloud, brandishing their spears.

Where they ride now is a matter of conjecture; no one remembers them but I who write these lines that I have written in memoriam, hoping that someday they will allow an old companion to ride with them, no matter where they ride.

ACKNOWLEDGMENTS

Many people have written about my great-great-uncle before me and each has presented his extraordinary story through a different lens. I am grateful to them all for helping to keep his memory alive. They include Herbert Faulkner West, Aimé Tschiffely, Alicia Jurado, Cedric Watts and Laurence Davies, Alexander Maitland, Anne Taylor, my mother Jean Polwarth (née Cunninghame Graham) and, most recently, Lachie Munro. I am especially grateful to Anne Taylor, whose meticulously researched *The People's Laird* offered valuable insights into hitherto unexplored aspects of Robert's and Gabriela's lives. Lachie Munro, who completed his *RB Cunninghame Graham and Scotland* a year before I finished this book, was most generous in sharing his research with me. My first cousin, Robin Cunninghame Graham, fielded my endless questions with good humour and painstakingly fact-checked the manuscript for me. I am indebted to my friend, James Robertson, for his support and for writing the foreword to this book. Billy Kay and Carl MacDougall were good enough to lend their names to my application for Creative Scotland funding. Laurence Davies, elder statesman of the Cunninghame Graham cognoscenti, kindly encouraged my early efforts at telling Robert's story. Joe Farrell, Gerry McGarvey, Rob Gibson and members of the Cunninghame Graham Society gave me a platform to try out those early efforts. Barbara Constantine helped shed light on Gabriela's story by sharing Horsfall family material with me. The Birnam Writers' Group, along with friends and neighbours in Birnam, responded enthusiastically to early readings and talks. My brother Simon took photographs and helped with the reproduction of the images. Willow Findlay took the most imprecise of briefs and responded with three beautiful maps. Jenny Brown, my agent, waited patiently for more than twenty years for me to come to the book – it would never have seen the light of day without her; neither without Donald Smith, director at the Scottish Storytelling Centre, who first encouraged me to give the talk which became the book; nor without Jean Fraser, publisher at Scotland Street Press, who has known and admired Don Roberto's story since childhood. Also at Scotland Street Press, Catie Gladstone wielded a sympathetic editorial pen, for all our two forebears' political differences. Despite everything, my mother planted the seed, but did not live long enough to see it bear fruit. And Sarah, as always, gave me the most valuable support of all: her love.

I gratefully acknowledge support from Creative Scotland towards the writing of this book.

FURTHER READING

Clark, Clare *Beautiful Lies* (Harvill Secker, 2012)

Cunninghame Graham, Jean *Gaucho Laird* (The Long Riders' Guild Press, 2005)

Dolan, Chris *Everything Passes Everything Remains* (Saraband, 2020)

Faulkner West, Herbert *A Modern Conquistador: RB Cunninghame Graham, His Life and Works* (Cranley & Day, 1932)

Fraser, Ian M. *RB Cunninghame Graham, Fighter for Justice: An Appreciation of his Social and Religious Outlook* (Ian M Fraser, 2002)

Jurado, Alicia *El Escocés Errante* (Emecé, 1978)

MacGillivray, Alan & McIntyre, John C. (Eds.) *The Cunninghame Graham Collection,* 5 Volumes (Kennedy & Boyd, 2011, 2012)

Maitland, Alexander *Robert and Gabriela Cunninghame Graham* (William Blackwood, 1983)

Munro, Lachlan *RB Cunninghame Graham and Scotland: Party, Prose, and Political Aesthetic* (Edinburgh University Press, 2022)

Munro, Lachlan, (Ed.) *An Eagle In A Henhouse, Selected Political Speeches & Writings of RB Cunninghame Graham* (Ayton Publishing, 2017)

Sassi, Carla & Silke Stroh (Eds.) *Empires and Revolutions: Cunninghame Graham and his Contemporaries* (Association for Scottish Literary Studies, 2017)

Taylor, Anne *The People's Laird* (The Tobias Press, 2005)

Tschiffely, Aimé *Don Roberto: The Life of RB Cunninghame Graham* (William Heinemann, 1937)

Watts, Cedric (Ed.) *Joseph Conrad's Letters to Cunninghame Graham* (Cambridge University Press, 1969)

Watts, Cedric & Laurence Davies *Cunninghame Graham: A Critical Biography* (Cambridge University Press, 1979)

BIBLIOGRAPHY OF ROBERT BONTINE CUNNINGHAME GRAHAM'S WORKS

Notes on the District of Menteith: for Tourists and Others (Mackay, Stirling, 1895)

Father Archangel of Scotland and Other Essays (with Gabriela Cunninghame Graham, A&C Black, 1896)

Mogreb-el-Acksa: A Journey in Morocco (Wm Heinemann, 1898)

The Ipané (T Fisher Unwin, 1899)

Thirteen Stories (Wm Heinemann, 1900)

A Vanished Arcadia: Being Some Account of the Jesuits in Paraguay, 1607 to 1767 (Wm Heinemann, 1901)

Success (Duckworth, 1902)

Hernando de Soto; Together with an Account of one of his Captains, Gonçalo Silvestre (Wm Heinemann, 1903)

Progress (Duckworth, 1905)

His People (Duckworth, 1906)

Faith (Duckworth, 1909)

Hope (Duckworth, 1910)

Charity (Duckworth, 1912)

A Hatchment (Duckworth, 1913)

Scottish Stories (Duckworth, 1914)

Bernal Diaz del Castillo: Being Some Account of Him (Eveleigh Nash, 1915)

Brought Forward (Duckworth, 1916)

A Brazilian mystic: Being the Life and Miracles of Antonio Conselheiro
(Wm Heinemann, 1920)

Cartagena and the Banks of the Sinú (Wm Heinemann, 1920)

*The Conquest of New Granada: Being the Life of Gonzalo Jimenez de
Quesada* (Wm Heinemann, 1922)

The Dream of the Magi (Wm Heinemann, 1923)

The Conquest of the River Plate (Wm Heinemann, 1924)

Doughty Deeds: An Account of the Life of Robert Graham of Gartmore
(Wm Heinemann, 1925)

Pedro de Valdivia, Conqueror of Chile (Wm Heinemann, 1926)

Redeemed: And Other Sketches (Wm Heinemann, 1927)

José Antonio Páez (Wm Heinemann, 1929)

Thirty Tales & Sketches (collected by Edward Garnett, Duckworth,
1929)

Horses of the Conquest (Wm Heinemann, 1930)

Writ In Sand (Wm Heinemann, 1932)

Portrait of a Dictator: Francisco Solano Lopez (Wm Heinemann, 1933)

Mirages (Wm Heinemann, 1936)

Rodeo: A Collection of the Tales and Sketches (selected by A.F. Tschiffely,
Wm Heinemann, 1936)

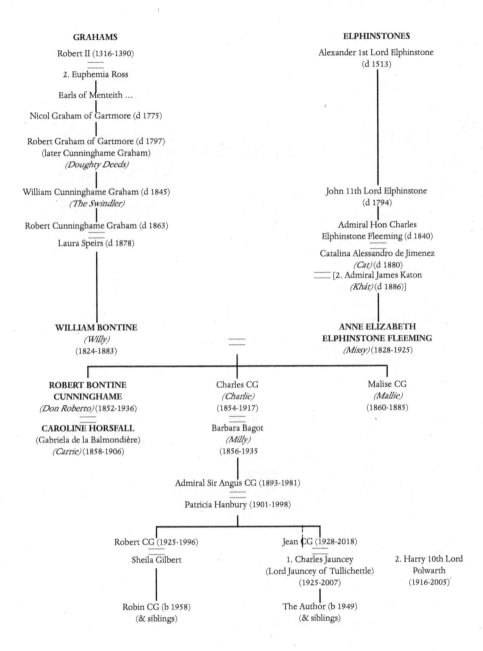

GRAHAMS

Robert II (1316-1390)

2. Euphemia Ross

Earls of Menteith …

Nicol Graham of Gartmore (d 1775)

Robert Graham of Gartmore (d 1797)
(later Cunninghame Graham)
(Doughty Deeds)

William Cunninghame Graham (d 1845)
(The Swindler)

Robert Cunninghame Graham (d 1863)

Laura Speirs (d 1878)

ELPHINSTONES

Alexander 1st Lord Elphinstone
(d 1513)

John 11th Lord Elphinstone
(d 1794)

Admiral Hon Charles
Elphinstone Fleeming (d 1840)

Catalina Alessandro de Jimenez
(Cat) (d 1880)
[2. Admiral James Katon
(Khát) (d 1886)]

WILLIAM BONTINE
(Willy)
(1824-1883)

**ANNE ELIZABETH
ELPHINSTONE FLEEMING**
(Missy) (1828-1925)

**ROBERT BONTINE
CUNNINGHAME**
(Don Roberto) (1852-1936)

CAROLINE HORSFALL
(Gabriela de la Balmondière)
(Carrie) (1858-1906)

Charles CG
(Charlie)
(1854-1917)

Barbara Bagot
(Milly)
(1856-1935

Malise CG
(Mallie)
(1860-1885)

Admiral Sir Angus CG (1893-1981)

Patricia Hanbury (1901-1998)

Robert CG (1925-1996)

Sheila Gilbert

Jean CG (1928-2018)

1. Charles Jauncey
(Lord Jauncey of Tullichettle)
(1925-2007)

2. Harry 10th Lord
Polwarth
(1916-2005)

Robin CG (b 1958)
(& siblings)

The Author (b 1949)
(& siblings)

Robert Graham of Gartmore added the name Cunninghame by inheritance from his first cousin, 15th Earl of Glencairn. Similarly, Hon Charles Elphinstone added the name Fleeming by inheritance from his grandmother, daughter of 6th Earl of Wigtoun.

TIMELINE

1852	Robert born
	Family moves to Finlaystone
1854	Charles born
1860	Malise born
1861	Finlaystone sold, back to London
	Robert to Hill House
1864	Willy restrained
1865	Robert to Harrow
1866	Family moves to Gartmore
	Willy removed to Dumfriess-shire
1867	Robert removed from Harrow
	To tutor in Middlesex
	Charles to HMS Britannia
1868	Robert to tutor in Brussels
1870	Sails for Montevideo
1872	Returns to England
	Visits Charles in Halifax, NS
	Sails again for Montevideo
1873	In Paraguay
1874	Returns to England
	Visits Iceland
1875	Visits Charles in Gibraltar
	To West Africa with Mansel
1876	Back to Argentina
1877	Returns to England

1878	To Spain with Charles
	Marries Gabriela
1879/80	Spain, Texas, Mexico
1881	Living in Vigo
1883	Returns to England
	Willy dies
1884	Moves to Gartmore
	Malise ordained
1885	Malise dies
	Stands for NW Lanarkshire
	Defeated
1886	Stands again, elected MP
	for NW Lanarkshire
1887	Ardoch sold
	Bloody Sunday
1888	Trial and Pentonville
	Hardie stands, is defeated
	'I never withdraw'
	Scottish Labour Party formed
1890	Journalism: *Daily Graphic*
1891	Visits Morocco
	Deported from France
1892	Stands for Camlachie
	Defeated
	Hardie elected
1893	Discharges *curator bonis*
1894	Gabriela publishes *St Theresa*
	Gold mine expedition
1895	*Notes on the District of Menteith*
1896	Writes for *Saturday Review*
	Father Archangel of Scotland
1897	To Tarudant
1898	*Mogreb el Acksa*
1899	*The Ipané*
1900	Gartmore sold; to Margaret St
1902	Travelling in Morocco
1903	Gabriela's health

	Buys back Ardoch
1904	Moves into Ardoch
1906	Gabriela dies at Hendaye
1907–14	Books and journalism
1914	Uruguay to buy horses for War Dept
1916	Charles dies
1917–36	14 further books published
1917	Colombia to arrange beef imports for UK Govt
1919	Stands for Stirling West
	Defeated
1925	Mother dies
1927	*Redeemed & Other Sketches*
1928	President National Party of Scotland
1929	Herbert Faulkner West visits
	30 Sketches & Tales re-published
1931	Campaigning for Scottish Home Rule
1932	Faulkner West's biography:
	Cunninghame Graham: his life & works
1934	Meets Aimé Tschiffely
	President Scottish National Party
1936	*Mirages* published
	Visits Hudson's birthplace
	Dies in Buenos Aires
	Buried on Inchmahome
1937	Tschiffely's biography: *Don Roberto*

INDEX